HARVARD ECONOMIC STUDIES

· Volume CXXI ·

Awarded the David A. Wells Prize for the year 1961–62 and published from the income of the David A. Wells Fund.

The studies in this series are published by the Department of Economics of Harvard University. The Department does not assume responsibility for the views expressed.

THE THEORY OF
TRADE AND PROTECTION

. . . .

William Penfield Travis

HARVARD UNIVERSITY PRESS

Cambridge, Massachusetts

· 1 9 6 4 ·

Distributed in Great Britain by Oxford University Press, London

Library of Congress Catalog Card Number: 64-16070

Printed in the United States of America

TO MY PARENTS

PREFACE

The subject of trade and protection is one of the oldest in economic science. When I wondered, first, how much protection actually distorts the allocation of resources and lessens economic efficiency and, second, what the effects of its alleviation would be, I somewhat naively thought that theoretical and empirical methods of answering the question would be ready at hand. I found instead too many models and methods and that they could give, according to their selection, whatever answer one might want to find. The whole controversy was, after all, bound up in opinion and prejudice that a welter of alternative assumptions and mixed approaches had made possible.

The number of theories and methods in international trade that have survived over the past two hundred years is excessive, if one believes in a natural mechanism that eliminates inferior members of a species. What special climate has permitted them to persist? I believe that a passage in John R. Hicks's *Value and Capital*, bearing witness to an attitude prevalent in modern economics, reveals the answer:

This is a book on Theoretical Economics, considered as the logical analysis of an economic system of private enterprise, without any inclusion of reference to institutional controls. I shall interpret this limitation pretty severely. For I consider the pure logical analysis of capitalism to be a task in itself, while the survey of economic institutions is best carried on by other methods, such as those of the economic historian (even when the institutions are contemporary institutions). It is only when both these tasks are accomplished that economics begins to near the end of its journey. But there is a good line for division of labor between them, and it is a line we do well to observe [p. 7].

This methodological Manichaeism is indeed common today, though it was absent from the work of the first masters of economics, notably Adam Smith. There is no such thing as an abstract system of capitalism separate from the control of institutions which distort or improve markets. All economic studies, moreover, must use pure logical analysis. It will always be necessary to make assumptions, of course, and perhaps more so in some fields than in others. But these should be regarded as strategic retreats that one makes before brute Nature rather than as characterizations of a dream world.

The conventional treatment of the Heckscher–Ohlin trade theory is an example of the unnecessary damage which the methodological split can do. That theory, which forms the analytical basis of this book, uses the clear, distinct, and reasonable idea that trade is a vent for surplus, the same idea that classical trade theory employed. It is more nearly complete and powerful than classical theory, however, for it goes beyond commodities to apply the idea to relative surpluses and deficits of factors that produce commodities. Commodities are only one intermediary through which countries can trade the services of their factors. Despite its greater reasonableness even on purely classical grounds, the Heckscher–Ohlin theory has failed to displace its forerunner because it does not seem to explain actual trade flows.

The apparent failure of the theory must lie somewhere in its assumptions, or rather in the assumptions which people attribute to it. Those concerning competition, tastes, factor mobility, production functions, and factors are clearly strategic—because there is no reason to suppose that their failure to apply exactly will alter the conclusions more in one direction than in another. It is thus only possible, but not likely, that they can falsify the theory in a particular situation. To assume that trade restrictions do not systematically alter the results is, on the other hand, a serious mistake. Protection is applied expressly to counteract or even to nullify economic forces. It is a determinant of trade structure which is potentially as powerful as any objective one. Any theory of trade must accordingly build in methods for analyzing and separating out its influence. This realization is the secret to the first part of my question about distortion in the allocation of resources. For including protection in a trade theory provides the method for analyzing its effects upon a country's production and trade structure.

The factor-price equalization theorem, a logical deduction of the Heckscher–Ohlin theory, helps to describe production and trade under free trade and thus to answer the second part of the question about the lifting of protection. The validity of many of its other assumptions depends, moreover, upon the freedom of trade, as Chapter One shows. One question remains, however, and that is whether or not the actual factor endowments of nations diverge too much for commodity trade alone to balance them under free trade. Chapters One and Two devise a method for answering this.

Chapter Three demonstrates that relative factor endowments alone cannot explain actual trade flows, while Chapter Four shows that factor endowments and protection combined can do so. Chapter Five, in the spirit of my criticism of Hicks's statement, is an historical study of the commercial policies of several important industrial countries, and it is designed to show the close correspondence between historical reality and the logical analysis of the preceding chapters. Chapter Six discusses the effects of commercial policy upon the allocation of resources within an economy, as opposed to its effects upon primary factor returns.

Many people have told me, and I am disposed to believe them, that this book is hard going. Despite my efforts to minimize their number, many graphs and equations remain. The treatment is not highly mathematical, however, and the barest notions of partial derivatives and simple matrix manipulations will carry the reader through. Appendix I contains a dictionary of symbols for his convenience.

I greatly regret that there is not space enough to express my appreciation to all those persons and organizations whose knowledge, advice, and encouragement have contributed to the contents of this book. I must, however, give credit to those without whose active support it would have been impossible for me to conceive and present what is to be found in the following pages.

Professor Charles P. Kindleberger provided encouragement at an early and crucial stage, helped me to fix on the important problems to be solved, and read the manuscript with care and helpful comment. The Sloan Research Fund at the School of Industrial Management, Massachusetts Institute of Technology, granted generous financial assistance for travel, purchase of documents, and preparation of the manuscript. I am exceedingly grateful to Jean-Marcel Jeanneney and to the Service d'Etudes de l'Activité Economique, its directress, Madeleine Le Clerc, and its excellent staff for providing me with an office and stimulating assistance during the summer of 1959. I shall never be able adequately to express my gratitude to Jean-Claude Casanova, formerly of the French Ministry of Industry, for his friendship, interest, and encouragement both in this country and in France. Without his assistance, I could not have obtained much of the essential material for this study.

Only someone who saw this work at the stage in which Professor Wassily Leontief first saw it could possibly measure the great improvement that his aid and inspiration made possible.

I completed the book as part of my work for the Harvard Economic Research Project, which Professor Leontief directs, and have profited greatly from the facilities of the Project and from the assistance of Elizabeth Gilboy, Alan Strout, Phoebus J. Dhrymes, and the other staff members. The reader will be able to see how much the book owes to the input-output studies which Professor Leontief and the Harvard Economic Research Project have done so much to develop.

Only I am responsible for the demonstrations and opinions to follow, but several men have gently urged me to abandon some that undoubtedly would have haunted me. Professors Abram Bergson, Paul H. Cootner, Gottfried Haberler, Harry Johnson, Thomas C. Schelling, and Bernt Stigum were particularly helpful in that role and made suggestions that enabled me to improve greatly what I have written. Bettina C. Sechrest suggested many stylistic improvements and patiently and efficiently typed and retyped the entire manuscript many times. I am greatly indebted to Stephen Friedlaender, who drew all the diagrams.

My greatest thanks go to my wife, Cynthia Morss Travis. Wives will ever bear the most oppressive burdens of the lonely and absorbing tasks of scholarship. Cynthia not only assumed those burdens, but followed every detail of the book's arguments and strengthened and refined them by judicious exclusion as well as by apt addition. She artfully rewrote parts and edited the whole manuscript. There is not a single page of this book which her intelligence and labor have not greatly improved.

Boston, Mass.   W. P. T.
October 1963

CONTENTS

APPENDICES

TABLES

THE THEORY OF
TRADE AND PROTECTION

THE EQUALIZATION REGION

THE Heckscher–Ohlin theory is the only complete and general explanation of international and interregional trade. The classical theorists explained comparative advantage by assuming that production functions differ internationally. Since they recognized only one factor of production, this assumption provided the only possible basis for trade. It was not, therefore, founded on general observation. As a result, the classical theory advanced no more than a particular statement of comparative advantage. Other accounts rely on equally gratuitous assumptions, including national differences in markets, mechanical, inventive, and technological ability, adaptability, stage of development, and the like. The disadvantages inherent in all such explanations are obvious; aside from their limited scope, the assumptions arbitrarily fix many of the variables which should be the objects of policy. Furthermore, it is altogether too easy to find special causes for trade, and these cannot all be woven into a coherent account. Only a general theory can prevent the unconscious shifting of alternative assumptions and emphasis which nullifies so much analysis.

The Heckscher–Ohlin theory escapes this criticism. By admitting any number of distinct productive factors, it appeals both to direct observation and to common sense. Its main assumptions are that factors of production are comparable internationally, that production functions are technical relationships which, like cooking recipes, are everywhere the same though not necessarily everywhere known, and that commodities use factors in different proportions. The theory concludes that under free trade countries will export goods which use their abundant factors. Herein lies the basis of comparative advantage. From this, the theory predicts that free trade among countries will tend to equalize their factor returns.

Protection systematically opposes the forces which, according to the theory, cause countries to trade. By distorting and reducing trade flows, it prevents countries from producing and trading according to their comparative advantage. As a result, they are unable to balance one another's surpluses of labor, capital, and land, and this in turn perpetuates existing differences in factor earnings and living standards among countries. In addition, protection accounts for other observable characteristics which appear puzzling in view of the theory's predictions, including the failure of many countries to specialize, despite the great differences in their relative factor prices, and the preponderance of raw materials and the dearth of finished manufactures in international trade. Protection, then, causes deviations in trading patterns from those which the Heckscher–Ohlin theory predicts given free trade among nations.

The most sensitive assumption of the Heckscher–Ohlin theory is that commodities differ in their use of the various primary factors. If, for example, all commodities used factors in the same proportion, differences in relative factor endowments would be no basis for trade. In addition, if the relative factor intensities of commodities can vary with changes in relative factor prices, the identification of comparative advantage in any particular instance becomes difficult. While common observation eliminates the first possibility, the second requires a special technique to handle all situations systematically and to show their relative importance.

The concept of the equalization region, which I develop in this chapter and apply throughout the book, provides the necessary technique. It not only permits a systematic analysis of the various problems encountered in ranking commodities according to their factor intensities, but also provides a full statement of the necessary and sufficient conditions for the optimal solution to world production and trade, within stated limits of unequal relative factor endowments. Thus it clarifies the assumptions and conclusions of the Heckscher–Ohlin theory and, at the same time, extends their applicability to all free-trade situations.

FACTORS OF PRODUCTION AND THEIR MEASUREMENT

The question of the identifiability and measurability of factors of production has been raised by many critics of the Heckscher–

Ohlin theory, perhaps most insistently by Romney Robinson.[1] He denies the usefulness of the theory on the grounds that, since both capital goods and raw materials move in trade, there is no operational significance to the notion of relative factor supplies. The least developed country, he claims, could produce the most capital-intensive goods simply by importing some capital goods with which to make them. But Robinson is making a mistake in this assertion. Once capital goods are installed in a country, its capital endowment rises by an amount exactly equal to the value of those capital goods in the only sense relevant to the theory of comparative advantage. Whether nationals of the particular country or others own the capital goods does not matter. If the country's citizens own the capital goods, the country could not have been capital-poor in the first place.[2]

Robinson's claim that the ability of raw materials to move internationally renders meaningless the concept of relative scarcity of factors of production is also incorrect, though not for the same reasons. The production of raw materials is not in itself raw-material-intensive, even if the products using them are. The error here consists in confusing goods with processes. It is, however, a natural error, considering the almost universal tendency

[1] Romney Robinson, "Factor Proportions and Comparative Advantage: Part I," *Quarterly Journal of Economics*, 70:169–192 (May 1956).

[2] The above assertions equate the factor capital with a stock of such items as machines which are necessary or useful in production. This general definition of capital implies that capital cannot be an allocable factor of production. Some components of the physical stock which constitutes capital can, of course, be moved from one occupation into certain others. This is true, for example, of many factory buildings and of many types of machines. Only a fraction of the total capital stock can be directly reallocated in this fashion, however. The other ways of doing so depend upon the diversion into new uses of two current *flows*, stemming from depreciation allowances, on the one hand, and savings, on the other. They depend for their effectiveness within any given time period, therefore, upon the size of these flows relative to the value of the capital stock. Under dynamic conditions, because of this somewhat anomalous nature of capital, it is entirely possible for, say, a capital-rich country to fail to develop certain capital-intensive exports (or to forestall their importation because they were new goods and its *rate* of capital formation was low, compared to that of other countries). In time, such abnormalities should disappear either as the capital-rich country becomes in fact labor-rich, owing to its low rate of capital formation, or as it has time to shift its capital into the newer activities. It is worth emphasizing that countries with rapidly growing capital stocks can achieve structures of production which represent their comparative advantage more easily than those which grow more slowly.

of trade theory to telescope a series of productive processes into one. This distinction is important and is treated more thoroughly below.

In another place Robinson claims that the attempt to identify the original natural resource as a factor is to make of that term "one of the Alice-in-Wonderland terms which can mean whatever you like it to mean." Before arriving at this point he says: "It can be argued that a country is endowed with fixed supplies of certain natural resources. But natural resources are not factors, if the term factor is taken to mean an agent capable of yielding services in cooperation with other agents. A natural resource becomes a factor only after some measure of preliminary investment, perhaps the investment of a considerable amount of capital."[3] But it is extremely doubtful that Robinson has here set up a criterion that distinguishes natural resources from what is generally understood by "factor of production." The investment of capital necessary to render natural resources capable of cooperating with other agents is itself an example of cooperation.

This is not to deny, however, that there is a problem in defining factors so that they can be measured quantitatively. This problem, arising with respect to all factors, is probably most difficult when quantities or relative endowments of natural resources are to be measured. It is true, for instance, that one unit of labor cannot be carelessly equated with another; labor includes many different types which are not, in every occupation, perfect substitutes for one another. Nonetheless, the structure of the labor force can be studied, and different groups or types of labor defined, in such a way that members of each group are effectively the same factor of production, and these members may then be counted.

But it is hard to compare and to quantify land inputs. Agricultural land is perhaps the easiest to quantify; it does make some sense to say that one man tills twelve acres in the United States and six in France. In this case, the similarity of climate, terrain, and structure of agricultural output gives such a comparison meaning. Yet a similar statement attempting a comparison between Ghana and Greenland would be without interest. This example borders on the case in which land is taken as the source of minerals. Neither the acreage of such deposits nor the total known reserves gives an accurate account of the economic quantity of the resource in question. Two countries may have equal known reserves of coal. The seams, however, may be wide and close to the surface in one country; narrow, steep, subject to flooding, and far below the surface in the other. It cannot be maintained, in such a case, that the two countries have the same amount of natural-resource-producing land.

The ordinary theory of rent provides, conceptually, a way out of this quandary. Assume that the mineral source is just like a piece of agricultural land, with the exception that coal rather than barley or oats is to be farmed. The only difference then between extracting a mineral and extracting a crop is that the former activity can be carried on, at a given rate, for a limited period of time. An equilibrium rent or royalty for the mining site will be determined to measure the amount of natural resource which can be obtained with a given amount of capital and labor.

Unfortunately, this analogy implies that it is impossible unambiguously to measure *relative* natural resource endowments of two countries or regions unless free trade equalizes all factor prices. If factor prices are not equalized, production functions will need to be completely specified, as will the quantities of factors employed and the amount of output produced. In short, one cannot predict the equilibrium structure and level of trade without first knowing these as essential data for making the prediction. This indeed points up a weakness of any theory of comparative advantage based on relative factor supplies. It really reveals not so much the failings of a particular theory as it does the poverty of equilibrium theory in general. Economists observe only equilibrium points in the economic universe. They never see production functions, only their effects. But if they are lucky and clever they can sometimes make limited projections from this knowledge alone. That is, although the underlying data may be severely limited, safe guesses can often be made simply on the basis of a reasonable theory.

A specific example may help to illustrate the point. Suppose

that the United Kingdom and the United States were to form a
customs union involving free trade between the two nations, but
no factor movements. What would be the distribution between
them of coal output? In the United States, 5 percent of the vast
coal reserves consist of measured reserves in beds twenty-eight
or more inches thick and less than a thousand feet below the
surface. These beds produce virtually all the coal now being
mined. The average depth of coal mines in Great Britain is
greater than a thousand feet, and many coal beds are more
steeply pitched than those in the United States.[4] If the United
States and Great Britain formed a union, it seems likely that the
total coal requirements of the two regions would be satisfied
entirely by United States production. (They certainly would
be if there were no transport costs.) Then it is as if, in a world
consisting only of these two countries, all of the natural-resource coal were to be found in the United States and none in
Great Britain. In practice, therefore, measuring relative resource
endowments to determine equilibrium solutions in trade may not
be an entirely hopeless task.

THE ASSUMPTIONS OF THE THEOREM

The most important assumption of the factor-price equalization theorem is that trade is completely free. Does this mean
that under free trade factor prices will in fact be equalized, or at
least very nearly? Or are the other assumptions too strong to
guarantee any such potentially useful result? Will an *a priori*
knowledge of the factor intensities of processes, even though those
intensities are observed only for a given set of primary factor
prices, suffice to indicate what patterns of production are likely
to result from a given set of factor endowments when trade is
liberated? Any answer to these questions requires an examination
of the plausibility and restrictiveness of the various assumptions
of the factor-price equalization theorem.

The theorem states that complete factor-price equalization

[4] These facts were taken from Charles A. Scarlott, "Fossil Fuels: Reserves,
Use, and Prospects," *Natural Resources*, ed. Martin R. Huberty and Warren L.
Flock (New York, 1959), pp. 419–420.

will occur in the general n-goods, r-factors, m-countries case, provided that transportation costs are zero, factors are perfectly mobile intranationally, trade is free of all restrictions, production functions are homogeneous of degree one and unaffected by nationality, all countries produce some of each commodity, n, exceeds r, and the ranking of commodities by intensity of factor use is invariant with respect to relative factor prices. The theorem is true, moreover, regardless of demand conditions.[5]

The assumption of zero transport costs is obviously false, and it must accordingly be admitted that some disparity of factor prices will always exist because of these expenses. The only question concerns their relative importance, and the only safe answer, of course, is that it depends. It depends on the possibility of offsetting the regional surpluses and deficiencies of factors through the trade of goods that are inexpensive to transport. The seriousness of transport costs, therefore, will be less, the less restrictive the other assumptions prove to be. There is evidence that transport costs, as a percentage of the value of world trade, are not especially high compared to, say, tariffs. According to an inquiry of the National Industrial Conference Board early in 1957, transport costs were not an important obstacle to foreign producers who contemplated exporting to the United States market. Thirty-nine firms offered information on this subject, and of these fifteen estimated that sending a foreign-made product to the United States added only about 5 percent to the unit cost of production; twelve estimated between 5 and 10 percent; and ten others placed the percentage between 11 and 20.[6]

Transport costs, moreover, depend partly on trade restrictions, which tend mainly to hinder the movement of merchandise whose value per unit of weight is high.[7] Bulky and heavy raw materials

[5] Paul A. Samuelson, "Prices of Factors and Goods in General Equilibrium," *Review of Economic Studies*, 21:1–20 (1953–1954).

[6] Testimony of Martin Gainsborough, *Hearings before the Subcommittee on Foreign Trade Policy of the Ways and Means Committee*, 88th Congress, December 2–13, 1957; reviewed in *Etudes et conjoncture*, 10:963ff (October 1958).

[7] Not only the commercial policies of trading nations, but also the pricing policies of transportation companies have this effect. The principle of the purely revenue tariff, as well as the policy of the typical transportation company, is to charge what the market will bear, and of course high-value merchandise can bear more.

move, in general, unencumbered by artificial restrictions. Consequently, since trade restrictions favor goods with high transport costs, it must be supposed that average transport costs, as a percentage of the value of world trade, are higher than they would be under free trade.

A further assumption which apparently violates reality is that production functions are identical in all countries. While in practice it is extremely difficult to say whether observed differences in productivity stem from different factor proportions, from differences in the quality of supposedly homogeneous factor inputs, or from differences in the functions themselves, it is clear that the last type of difference may exist in certain circumstances. Under perfect competition, however, and with perfect mobility of factors among firms within a given industry, each firm would have to operate with the same production function.[8] This is not necessarily true when factors cannot move freely from country to country, even under free trade. Each production function for one country may differ by the same multiplicative constant from its counterpart in another, and patterns of comparative advantage will remain the same as if that constant had been unity. In such unlikely circumstances, foreign trade would not play the major role in rendering production functions identical. In time, however, this would presumably occur through the play of domestic competition.

The assumption that production functions are homogeneous of degree one is necessary for the proof of the theorem, but obviously does not hold exactly.[9] It should be pointed out, however, that there is some flexibility to this assumption. Many

[8] One way in which production functions for the same product may differ is by a multiplicative constant. If factors are paid their marginal productivity, as they must be under perfect competition, the return to each factor will differ by this same constant if employed in establishments with different production functions. If markets are perfect and factors free to move, the firms with the lower multiplicative constant or constants will be driven out of business as their factors move to the firms offering higher rewards; or else their managers will have to bestir themselves to correct the situation, in effect by re-establishing identity with the more efficient firms. Eventually, therefore, only one type of production function will be possible.

[9] External, as well as internal (to the firm) economies or diseconomies of scale must also be ruled out. Samuelson, p. 2.

production functions may show increasing returns up to a certain critical size but exhibit constant returns to any size that is an integral multiple of that size. If this is so, the homogeneity assumption can be relaxed in favor of the weaker restriction that the size of an industry is large relative to the capacity at which constant costs begin. The assumption can also be stretched somewhat to meet the case of true and continuing increasing-returns-to-scale sectors. Here again the restrictiveness of the assumption will depend on the freedom of trade. Free trade equalizes the effective market size for all countries participating, and thereby helps to ensure that the increasing-returns-to-scale industries will be more or less randomly distributed among countries.[10]

It remains to consider three assumptions which, while seemingly separate, are in fact inextricably connected. These state that all countries must produce at least some of each good, that the number of commodities must equal or exceed the number of factors, and that the ranking of commodities by factor intensity must be invariant with respect to relative factor prices. On the face of it, the first part of this threefold assumption would not seem to cause much concern. After all, most industrial countries produce at least some of each product which the lack of specific resources does not rule out. In fact, countries tend to produce not only the same basic list of commodities, but to do so in quite nearly identical proportions.[11] But, at the same time, it is clear that this state of affairs could be the result of commercial policies designed to let all flowers bloom. Part of the problem is to know whether or not specialization would occur under free trade.

It is also necessary to know how restrictive the requirement is that the number of goods must exceed the number of factors. It would appear not to be restrictive, since distinguishing more industries by vertically disintegrating production processes can

---

[10] Recent work indicates that aggregate production functions are in fact homogeneous of degree one. This affords presumptive evidence that either component production functions are also homogeneous of degree one, or else that the importance of those that are not is small. See M. W. Reder, "Alternative Theories of Labor's Share," *The Allocation of Economic Resources*, ed. Moses Abramovitz and others (Stanford, 1959), pp. 192–200.

[11] See below, Chapter Three and Chapter Six.

make n virtually as large as desired. This identification of sub-industries, of course, involves distinguishing intermediate goods, and these, to qualify as commodities facilitating factor-price equalization, must be able to move in trade. The extent to which these assumptions can be modified when intermediate traded goods are introduced into the analysis is especially important. This alteration of the theorem greatly diminishes the danger that it will fail to hold because the number of factors exceeds the number of commodities. In addition, it is no longer necessary that some of every good be produced in each country and therefore that the number of goods produced in a given country equal or exceed the number of factors in the world. In fact, it is not even necessary, as Ohlin thought,[12] that each factor be found in each country so long as products of each factor can be traded.

Samuelson has shown that consideration of intermediate goods does not alter the statement of the factor-price equalization theorem.[13] But the introduction of intermediate goods, by changing the relationship between the number of commodities and the number of factors, and the relationships among the factor intensities of *activities* (which now become the unit of observation rather than goods), creates situations in which other important formal conditions of factor-price equalization are more likely to hold. Differences in relative factor endowments themselves help to determine the number, variety, and importance of intermediate goods in world trade.

One must be careful, however, as Samuelson warns, that the distinction of goods and factors is not purely arbitrary:

The results seem to depend in a very essential way upon the exact relation of n to r. The thoughtful reader will no doubt be somewhat worried by this result; for after all, the number of commodities or of factors is not always such a definite thing. If we wished, we might call blue-eyed people different

[12] Bertil Ohlin, *International and Interregional Trade* (Cambridge, Mass., 1933), p. 105.

[13] Samuelson, pp. 1, 15–20; see also Chapter Four below. Pearce states flatly that introducing intermediate goods would make no difference because, within any country, all secondary production functions can be stated in primary form. This condition is true, but it amounts to assuming arbitrarily that countries do not trade intermediate goods, and these in fact constitute the bulk of world trade. See I. F. Pearce and S. F. James, "The Factor Price Equalization Myth," *Review of Economic Studies*, 19.2:118 (1951–1952).

factors from brown-eyed ones and simply by reclassification make r go from less than to greater than n. Or we could call all autos with even-number serial listings a different good from those with odd-numbers, and thereby change the relation of n to r. Moreover, it is possible that Nature has already done one of the above things. From a production viewpoint two quite different commodities might turn out to have the same a's or to require the same proportions of inputs. Or two apparently different inputs might turn out to be perfect substitutes for each other in every line.[14]

It is essential, then, to see in what cases increasing n relative to r enables free trade to equalize factor prices when otherwise this would have been impossible, and to see in what cases this is equivalent to making the type of distinction against which Samuelson cautions.

Before pursuing the discussion of the restrictiveness of these final assumptions, however, it will be necessary to acquire some new tools. These tools can best be explained with reference to the two-good, two-factor cases, even though their principal usefulness lies in making it easier to transcend the limitations of those particular assumptions.

THE THEOREM OF CORRESPONDING POINTS

The consequences of introducing intermediate traded goods explicitly into the analysis of the Heckscher–Ohlin theory will be taken up again in Chapter Two. The method of analysis there will depend expressly on what Kelvin Lancaster has called the Theorem of Corresponding Points. Lancaster's theorem, stated for two countries, two factors, and two commodities, may be explained with the aid of Figure I-1.[15] The rectangles X_1CX_2D and $X_1'C'X_2'D'$ represent the box diagrams for two countries, A and B. The point X_1 is the origin for the isoquants of commodity x_1, and X_2' is that for the isoquants of x_2. The production function for each good is the same in both countries. Country A's total endowment of capital is given by the distance X_1C, its endowment of labor by X_1D. Similarly, country B's endowment of labor

---

[14] Samuelson, p. 9.

[15] This diagram and the proof of the theorem are essentially the same as those employed by Kelvin Lancaster. See his "The Heckscher–Ohlin Trade Model: A Geometric Treatment," *Economica*, n.s., 24:25–28, 31–32 (February 1957).

is given by $X_1'D'$ and her endowment of capital by $X_1'C'$. As the figures are placed, total world supplies of capital can be represented by the distance X_1M or NX_2', and of labor by X_1N or MX_2'. In the diagram, A has more capital per unit of labor than does B—that is, it is more capital-rich (labor-poor) than B.

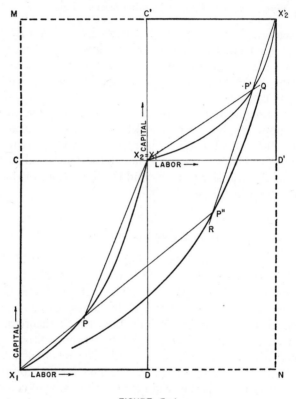

FIGURE I-I

Let P be some point on A's contract curve. In $X_1'C'X_2'D'$ draw $X_1'Q$ so that it is parallel to X_1P. Call the point of intersection of $X_2'R$ and $X_1'Q$, P'. It then follows from the Theorem of Corresponding Points that P and P' form a pair of points so that:

(i) If P is on the contract curve for country A, then P' is on the contract curve of country B.

(ii) The marginal productivities of both factors in both industries are the same at P and P' or, in other words, factor prices in terms of either good are equalized.

(iii) The commodity-price ratio is the same at P and at P'.

(iv) So long as X_1D/X_1C does not equal X_2D'/X_2C', the proportions in which the two goods are produced at P' will differ from those at P, the proportions being such that each country produces relatively more of the good which is more intensive in the use of the factor in which that country is rich. (Both factors are fully employed in each country.)

The proof of the first three parts of this theorem follows in a straightforward manner from the nature of homogeneous production functions and from the properties of rays through their origins. Since the production functions are assumed identical in both countries, the set of x_1 isoquants spreading out from X_1' in $X_1'C'X_2'D'$ is the same as the set spreading out from X_1 in X_1CX_2D. Therefore, since angle $D'X_1'P'$ equals angle DX_1P, those properties which hold along $X_1'P'$ also hold along X_1P. Similarly, those properties relevant to the x_2 isoquants which hold along X_2P also hold along $X_2'P'$. Marginal productivities are constant and uniquely determined along any ray through the origin of a homogeneous production function. Thus the marginal productivities of labor and capital in the production of x_1 are the same along $X_1'P'$ as along X_1P, and the marginal productivities of labor and capital in the production of x_2 are the same along $X_2'P'$ as along X_2P.

Since P and P' lie, respectively, on both X_1P, X_2P and $X_1'P'$, $X_2'P'$, the marginal productivities of labor and capital in the production of both x_1 and x_2 are the same at the points P and P'. If P lies on the contract curve in country A, the ratio between the marginal productivities of labor and capital in country A is the same in the production of x_1 and x_2. But the same equality holds in country B, so that P' must lie on the contract curve for B.

The second part of the theorem, the equality of marginal productivities, follows directly from the properties of rays through the origin. The third part follows directly also. Since the commodity price ratio in A is given by the ratio of the marginal productivity of a factor in one industry to that in the other, and since both of these marginal productivities are the same at P and at P', the commodity price ratios must be the same at these two points.

The fourth part of the theorem — stating that the proportions in which the two goods are produced at P' will differ from those obtaining at P, with each country producing a higher proportion of the good using more of its relatively abundant factor — can be omitted here since it is intuitively obvious, especially with the aid of Figures I-5 through I-7 below, and yet fairly difficult to prove. Moreover, it is probably the most well-known result of the Heckscher–Ohlin trade model, whose important properties the Theorem of Corresponding Points merely summarizes.[16]

It is clear that there is only a certain range along the contract curve of either country in which corresponding points can be found. This is because one of the pair will hit the origin of the Edgeworth box to which it belongs before the other will. In the example depicted in Figure I-1, imagine that P begins to slide toward X_1. Point P' will then slide toward X_1', but when P arrives at X_1, P' will be stranded short of X_1'. Point P' will win the race in the other direction, so it follows that there are points on each contract curve, in the general case represented by non-identical factor proportions, at which corresponding points cannot exist. These points represent the situations in which one country or the other or both is specializing on one or the other of the two goods.

Free-trade equilibrium will ensure that at least one of the two countries specializes on one product, or that production is established in the two countries at corresponding points. If corresponding points can exist (this outcome depends on the relative factor endowments of the countries and on world tastes), competition under free trade will establish them. This is because such a pair of points satisfies the conditions of competitive equilibrium within each country (from part i of the theorem) and implies the same terms of trade between the two commodities within each country (from part iii).

[16] For a full proof, see Lancaster, pp. 26–28.

When production in the two countries under free trade takes place at corresponding points, the two economies can be considered as one.[17] Since there exists in X_1CX_2D a series of x_1 isoquants spreading out from X_1, and in $X_1'C'X_2'D'$ a series of x_2 isoquants spreading out from X_2', the rectangle $X_1MX_2'N$ can be thought of as a box diagram for an economy having factor endowments equal to the sum of the two countries' individual endowments. This is shown in Figure I-1, where the lengths X_1N and X_1M already represent the combined amounts of labor and capital, respectively, in the world consisting of countries A and B.

Let P and P' be corresponding points in X_1CX_2D and $X_1'C'X_2'D'$. Produce X_1P to P'' where it meets $X_2'P'R$. Then P'' has the same properties which are common to P and P' — namely, the same factor and commodity prices as hold at P and P' — and so it must lie on the contract curve of the combined economy. Moreover, since P and P' are corresponding points, X_2P is parallel to $P'P''$, and $X_1'P'$ is parallel to PP''; $PX_1'P'P''$ is therefore a parallelogram such that PP'' is equal to $X_1'P'$, and $P'P''$ is equal to X_2P. The production of x_1 in the world is given by the distance X_1P''. But this is the same as X_1P plus $X_1'P'$, or the amount of x_1 produced in A plus the amount produced in B. Similarly, world production of x_2 is equal to the sum of the amounts of x_2 produced in the two countries separately. Therefore, in all respects over the range of commodity prices for which corresponding points exist in the two countries, these two countries are exactly equivalent to a single country whose factor endowments are equal to the sum of the endowments of the two countries.

This result provides a convenient way of viewing the essence of the world trade problem and of separating it from a number of very tricky problems that can affect its solution only in certain circumstances. These special problems have to do with demand conditions and their attendant problems regarding elasticities, factor-supply functions, and changes in relative factor intensities as functions of relative factor prices.

Suppose now that one had started with a diagram such as Figure I-2, representing a world to be broken up into two separate

[17] Lancaster, pp. 31–32.

countries, rather than one that was created by letting separate countries trade freely. As long as corresponding points exist, it makes no difference whether one thinks of the world or of the countries as prior. Suppose that point P'' represents the output

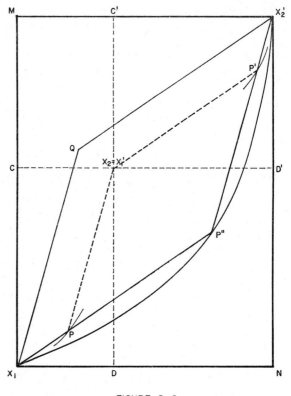

FIGURE I-2

of each good in these circumstances. This point represents the solution to a general-equilibrium, production-demand model, and the solution is in no way affected by the existence of separate countries. Thus the determinants of this solution, the magnitude of world factor supplies (the size of the box), the nature of demand conditions which dictate where along the world contract curve, $X_1P''X_2'$, point P'' would fall, and so on, do not concern the international-trade economist so long as whatever countries he chooses to distinguish have corresponding points.

The solution to the problem of international trade is logically distinct from that to the problem of world production.[18] It arises in consequence of dividing up the world's supply of factors into two or more bundles, whose factor proportions are not necessarily the same as those of the world as a whole, and of determining a joint production and trade solution which will keep all factors in each bundle fully employed.

In the Edgeworth box shown in Figure I-2, world supplies of the two factors, F_1 and F_2, are given by the lengths of the two sides, X_1N and X_1M. The proportion of world endowments of these factors is given by the ratio X_1M/X_1N. The world may be divided into two countries, A and B, represented by the sub-boxes X_1CX_2D and $X_1'C'X_2'D'$. There are an infinite number of ways of doing this: the vertical line DC' may assume any position between the two vertical axes, X_1M and $X_2'N$, of the world box, and the horizontal line CD' may assume any position between the horizontal axes, X_1N and $X_2'M$. In general, F_2^A/F_1^A will not be equal to the ratio of world endowments of these same factors, F_2^W/F_1^W or, in other words, the ratio X_1C/X_1D will not be equal to X_1M/X_1N. In what circumstances will the solution to the world production problem (represented by point P'') remain unaltered?

The division of the world's factor supplies among different countries amounts to a constraint on the solution of the production problem. In some instances, this will mean that the optimum solution to the problem under the constraint will be inferior to the unconstrained solution. But there is a set of situations in which the constrained solution will be just as good as the other. This is the set of situations covered by the factor-price equalization theorem.

The set of possible factor divisions among countries with the above property can be illustrated by Figure I-2. The point $X_2 (X_1')$, illustrating one possible division of factors, can of course assume any position within the *factor space*, equivalent in this

---

[18] The section entitled "General world-wide equilibrium and equalization regions" in this chapter analyzes this distinction.

case to the area of the Edgeworth box, $X_1MX_2'N$. Only points lying in a set which has yet to be determined set up two countries so that free trade will equalize factor prices.

The shape and position of this set of points can be easily determined by reference to the Theorem of Corresponding Points. For each pair of countries chosen so as not to disturb the solution to the world production problem at P'', there must be a pair of corresponding points, P and P', located on lines drawn from the commodity origins, X_1 and X_2', to P''. It is obvious that all corresponding points must lie on the straight lines X_1P'' and $X_2'P''$, since only one straight line is possible between two points. They may, however, lie anywhere along these lines, so long as there is one to each segment, X_1P'' and $X_2'P''$. Consequently, point P may lie anywhere between X_1 and P'', and P' may lie anywhere between X_2' and P''. Since P and P' remain corresponding points despite these shifts, X_2P must remain parallel to $P'P''$, and $X_1'P'$ must remain parallel to PP''. This implies that the point X_2 may lie anywhere within or on the boundaries of the parallelogram $X_1QX_2'P''$, where Q is the point of intersection of a line drawn through X_2' parallel to X_1P'' with a line through X_1 parallel to $X_2'P''$. If X_2 lies on the boundary of the parallelogram $X_1QX_2'P''$, but not at one of the corners, P'' or Q, one country is specializing in one of the two commodities. For example, if X_2 lies between X_1 and Q along X_1Q, country A (X_1CX_2D) will specialize in the production of x_2. If X_2 lies at Q, country A will produce all of the world's x_2 and country B will produce all of the world's x_1. If X_2 lies at P'', A produces all of the x_1 and B all of the x_2. Complete specialization is not necessarily incompatible with factor-price equalization.

The parallelogram $X_1QX_2'P''$ may be called the *equalization region* because, whenever a point such as X_2 lies within that region, factor prices remain as they were before the division, and the solution to the world production problem is consequently unaffected. Notice that the region includes its boundaries, which might be called *specialization boundaries* since specialization occurs in at least one country whenever X_2 coincides with any segment of the boundary to the equalization region.

The area of the parallelogram, $X_1QX_2'P''$, relative to the size of the rectangle, $X_1MX_2'N$, gives one indication of the chance that complete factor-price equalization will occur under free trade. For convenience, the ratio of these areas may be called the *likelihood* of complete equalization.

It is apparent from Figure I-2 that, given the curvature of the contract curve $X_1P''X_2'$, the likelihood of complete equalization depends upon the position of the world consumption point, P'', along that curve. As P'' approaches either origin, X_1 or X_2', the parallelogram gets narrower and narrower until, when P'' coincides with either origin, the parallelogram has degenerated into a straight line, the diagonal X_1X_2' of the box. This is, of course, the familiar case of fewer goods than factors, where factor-price equalization through trade is generally impossible. It is interesting to notice that this is simply a limiting case of a decrease in the demand for one or the other commodity. Likelihood is, therefore, partly a function of world demand conditions. It is also a function of the degree to which the world contract curve bends away from the diagonal of the box. This curvature in turn depends upon world factor endowments and upon the shapes of the two production functions.

The interrelationships of these two determinants may be visualized with the help of the diagram given in Figure I-3. This diagram is designed primarily to demonstrate the derivation of contract curves from the underlying factor availabilities and production functions. Since the latter are considered to be homogeneous of degree one, the production function for any good, such as x_1, can be entirely represented by any one of its isoquants — for instance, the one labeled x_1 in Figure I-3. Similarly, the production function of the other good, x_2, can be entirely depicted by any one of its isoquants — for instance, the one marked x_2 in the figure. It is therefore possible to derive contract curves from these two isoquants alone, without having to draw, as is usually done, many isoquants for each production function in order to find the locus of their points of tangency with isoquants for the other good.

Before doing this, however, it is necessary to superimpose the world box on the same diagram. Since it is intended to show easily what happens to the equalization area (and to the contract curve which, along with the world consumption point, determines that area) as the world factor proportions change, the dimensions of the box are defined to allow maximum flexibility. Because only the relative size of the equalization area counts, let the diagonal

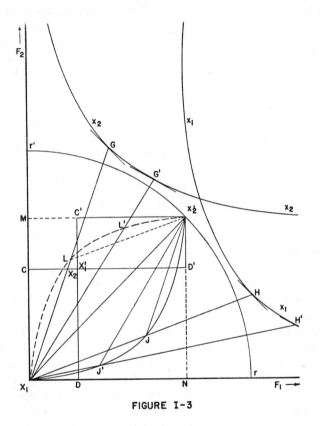

FIGURE I-3

of the box be of constant length, regardless of factor proportions. Thus as the world becomes, say, more F_2-intensive, X_2' will move away from r toward r' along the quarter circle rr', defined by the diagonal of the world box.

The contract curve for this box may be derived in the following manner. Choose a point, such as H, on the isoquant x_1 and draw the tangent to that isoquant at that point. Find the tangent to the isoquant of x_2 parallel to this tangent, and mark the point of tangency, G. Draw X_1H and X_1G. From X_2', somewhere on the segment rr', draw a line parallel to X_1G and let this line intersect X_1H at J. Now rotate the two lines, X_1G and X_1H, in either direction, but in such a way that they always intercept the two isoquants at points where tangents to the isoquants are parallel. A new pair of such points is indicated on the figure by G' and H'. Draw a new line, $X_2'J'$, parallel to X_1G' through X_2. The intersection of this line and $H'X_1$ at J' will always lie on the contract curve between X_1 and X_2'. The contract curve is therefore the locus of such intersections.

The proof of this construction is straightforward. When referred to the isoquants x_1 and x_2, the point X_1 in the diagram is the origin for each; thus it really represents two commodity origins, superimposed for convenience into a single point and utilizing a common set of factor axes, X_1F_1 and X_1F_2. When reference is made to the Edgeworth box, $X_1MX_2'N$, however, these origins and axes are separated. The commodity origin for the x_2 isoquants is now placed at X_2', and the F_1 axis for these isoquants now lies along $X_2'M$. The point G, were it also transposed, would accordingly lie along $X_2'J$ produced, and point G' would lie along $X_2'J'$ produced.

Therefore, an isoquant for x_2 with its origin at X_2' passes through J. But $X_2'J$ was drawn parallel to X_1G, and so angle $MX_2'J$ is equal to angle NX_1G. It follows (from the properties of rays through the origins of homogeneous production functions) that the tangent to this x_2 isoquant through J is parallel to the tangent at G. That tangent in turn, by construction, is parallel to the tangent to the x_1 isoquant at H, and therefore to all tangents to x_1 isoquants at their points of intersection with the ray X_1H. The x_1 isoquant through J must then share a common tangent with the x_2 isoquant through the same point, which therefore must lie on the contract line for these two commodities in the box $X_1MX_2'N$.

Now suppose for a moment that J is also the world consumption point, analogous to the point P'' in Figure I-2. If J is the consumption point, the equalization region for the world depicted by the box $X_1MX_2'N$ is the parallelogram $X_1LX_2'J$, where L is the intersection of the straight line through X_2' parallel to X_1H with X_1G. If the world consists of two countries A and B, represented by the rectangles X_1CX_2D and $X_1'C'X_2'D'$ in Figure I-3, factor prices will be equalized under free trade so long as the point X_2 (X_1') lies within the parallelogram $X_1LX_2'J$.

It is clear that as J moves with the rotation of X_1G and X_1H, the point L does also. Point J traces out the contract curve, X_1JX_2', while L traces out its image, X_1LX_2'. All possible equalization regions, each one corresponding to a consumption point, must lie within the (American) football-shaped area, $X_1LL'X_2'JJ'$, enclosed by these two curves. The greater the area of this football relative to that of the Edgeworth box, the greater the likelihood that trade will be able to equalize factor prices completely. It can readily be seen, for instance, that if the isoquants, x_1 and x_2, were moved closer to one another, so that the point G approached the point H while point X_2' was unchanged, the football would become narrower although the area of the box would not change.

Now imagine that the isoquants are fixed both in shape and in position, but that the point X_2' moves around the quarter-circle rr'. In general, such rotation will alter the relationship between the area of the football and that of the Edgeworth box, and thus change the likelihood of factor-price equalization. This may be illustrated rather dramatically by drawing the isoquants for x_1 and x_2 in such a way that, at some sets of world factor endowments, one good is F_2-intensive and, at others, the relative intensity of the two goods is reversed. Figure I-4 is drawn to illustrate what happens when such crossovers of factor intensities are allowed to occur. It is exactly the same diagram as that of Figure I-3, except that the isoquants are drawn so that they are tangent to one another at point T. (The isoquants in the earlier diagram can, of course, never be tangent.) In addition, two possible world boxes, $X_1MX_2'N$ and $X_1M'X_2''N'$, have been included. The points J and J', belonging to the two boxes respectively, represent points on their contract curves and have been derived in the same manner as point J in Figure I-3. Points Q and Q' have the same role as L in Figure I-3.

Notice that whereas in box $X_1MX_2'N$ point J lies below Q, J'

in box $X_1M'X_2''N'$ lies above Q'. It can be seen that as the world becomes, say, more F_2-intensive, causing the point X_2' to rotate counterclockwise, the football-shaped area $X_1JX_2'Q$ becomes narrower and narrower. This is because the points such as G and H on the isoquants for x_1 and x_2 come closer and closer together.

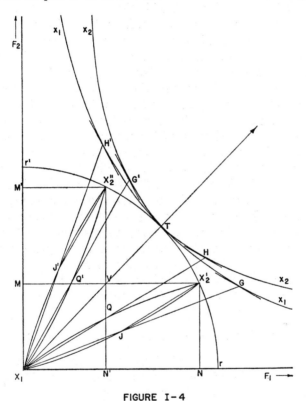

FIGURE I-4

At T they coincide so that the contract curve, X_1JX_2', becomes a straight line, and the football-shaped area degenerates to the same straight line. When this occurs, there is no longer any scope for factor-price equalization under free trade, aside from that afforded by the trivial case in which both countries are given factors in identical proportions and when tastes in both countries are also identical.

As X_1X_2' continues to rotate past point T, the possibility of factor-price equalization reappears and its likelihood increases as x_1 becomes more and more F_2-intensive relative to x_2. In those cases where strong Samuelsonian factor intensity[19] cannot be assumed, but where isoquants are fairly well-behaved otherwise, likelihood is seen to increase with the divergence of the world endowment ratio of the two factors from the critical ratio where the two isoquants exhibit identical factor intensities.

There will be more than one such critical ratio if the isoquants are tangent at more than one place. If so, it will generally be more and more difficult for the ratio of world endowments of the two factors to differ very much from one of these critical ratios. In this case, it is the underlying similarity of the two production functions, not the existence of factor-intensity crossovers, that causes trouble for factor-price equalization. Even with only one critical ratio, as shown in Figure I-4, it is difficult to obtain the fat football appearing in Figure I-3. This is because when isoquants for two different commodities are parallel along some ray from a common origin, their slopes along any other common ray from that origin cannot, in general, diverge as much as in the cases in which crossovers do not occur. The converse of this reasoning indicates that, as a rule, if commodities within a given economy do exhibit quite different factor intensities, the chances are good that factor-intensity reversals do not occur.

GENERAL WORLD-WIDE EQUILIBRIUM AND EQUALIZATION REGIONS

It will be useful, both for placing in a more general context the preceding discussion of equalization regions and for better understanding the next two chapters, to show diagrammatically the

[19] The possibility that the ranking of goods with respect to their capital-labor intensity might not remain the same at all relative factor prices was first pointed out by Abba Lerner, and it was recognized by Samuelson in his first formulation of the factor-price equalization theorem. Both Lerner and Samuelson seem to have regarded factor-intensity crossovers as unlikely, but of course they recognized that they must be assumed away in order to guarantee the theorem's holding. This additional assumption has come to be called the assumption of strong Samuelsonian factor intensity. Some recent writings have attacked it. For an excellent history of this qualification to the factor-price equalization theorem, see Richard E. Caves, *Trade and Economic Structure* (Cambridge, Mass., 1960), pp. 89–92.

relationship among the equalization region, the transformation
curve, and the indifference curves. Figure I-5 illustrates the
manner in which a country's transformation curve may be de-

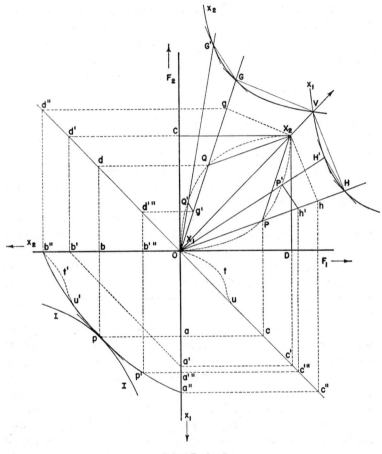

FIGURE I – 5

rived from the box giving its factor endowments. The curves
x_1 and x_2 are isoquants for the goods produced by industries X_1
and X_2; they represent some arbitrary, but constant, output for
each of those industries. The length X_1C gives the amount of

F_2, and X_1D the amount of F_1, which the country possesses. Tangents to the x_2 and x_1 isoquants through points G and H, respectively, are parallel to one another. Point Q, on the ray X_1G, is chosen so that the line X_2Q is always parallel to the ray X_1H; P, in X_1H, is chosen so that X_2P is always parallel to X_1G. As G and H move along their respective isoquants, the point P traces out the contract curve, X_1PX_2, as explained earlier.

Assume for the moment that the two production functions are both homogeneous of degree one. The distance X_1G represents the amount of x_2 corresponding to the output of the x_2 isoquant. The isoquant passing through any point along the ray X_1G, such as X_1Q, bears the same proportion to the output of the x_2 isoquant through G as X_1Q bears to X_1G. The same proportionate relationship holds along X_1H. The point V, which happens to lie at the common intersection of another ray from the origin X_1X_2 and the two isoquants, represents the same output of each commodity as do the points G and H.

Suppose that the country concentrates entirely on the production of x_2. To find the amount produced, when all factors are fully employed, draw X_2g parallel to VG. The country will produce X_1g/X_1G times the number of units of x_2 which the x_2 isoquant represents. Similarly, X_1h measures the amount of x_1 that the country can produce if it produces nothing else. The distances X_1Q and X_1P indicate a possible combination of both commodities. Other possible combinations can be found as follows. Find another pair of points, G' on the x_2 isoquant and H' on the x_1 isoquant, through which tangents to the two isoquants are parallel. Draw the rays X_1G' and X_1H'. Draw a ray through X_2 parallel to X_1G'. This ray, as explained in the previous section, will intersect the ray X_1H' at a point lying on the contract curve, the point labeled P' in Figure I-5. Point Q' is found by allowing the line through X_2 and parallel to X_1H' to intersect X_1G'. Now draw a line through Q' parallel to $G'G$, and one through P' parallel to $H'H$. These lines intersect X_1G and X_1H at the points marked g' and h' in Figure I-5. The production of x_2 at Q' will equal X_1g'/X_1G times the number of units of x_2 which the x_2 isoquant represents, because the production functions are homogeneous of degree one. Production of x_1 at P' will equal X_1h'/X_1H

times the number of units which the x_1 isoquant represents. The distances X_1g' and X_1h', therefore, represent another combination of the output of the two commodities, fully utilizing both factors.

A simple graphical device makes it possible to translate these combinations into the familiar transformation curve. The rays $Oucc'c'''c''$ and $Od'''dd'd''$ in the fourth and second quadrants map distances on the F_2 and F_1 axes into the x_2 and x_1 axes, in that order. Their slopes are equal to one. On the x_2 axis, Ob'' corresponds to the production of an amount of x_2 equal to that at point X_2, where all resources combine to produce that single commodity. The combination of F_1 and F_2, indicated by Q, produces an amount of x_2 represented by Ob. Point P, the coordinates of which are the remaining supplies of F_1 and F_2, corresponds in the same way to Oa on the x_1 axis. These two points, a and b, serve in turn as the coordinates of the point p on the transformation curve, $a''p'pu'b''$, in the third quadrant. The point b''' derives from Q', and the point a''' from p' in the same way, and similarly serve as the coordinates for the point p' on the transformation locus. As the point P on the contract curve slides along, through such points as P', the point p in the third quadrant, connected to P in the manner described, traces out the transformation curve.

The point on the transformation curve at which the country produces depends upon demand conditions. The curve marked I is a market-demand or, under proper assumptions, a community-indifference curve. The coordinates of its point of tangency with the transformation curve at p are the outputs of the two commodities. For a single country, Figure I-5 gives not only the equilibrium output of each commodity, but also, by the inverse of the common slope of the tangents to the two isoquants x_1 and x_2 at G and H, the ratio of factor prices. In addition, by the Cartesian coordinates (not shown) of the points P and Q, it shows the allocation of F_1 and F_2 to the production of each commodity and, by the inverse of the slope of the tangent common to the indifference and transformation curves, the relative prices of the commodities at equilibrium.

Figure I-5 makes it possible easily to visualize the relationship among the shapes and positions of the isoquants, those of the transformation curve, and the factor endowments. For example, if the isoquants were L-shaped, with their corners at G and H, the transformation curve would consist of two straight-line sections with the kink at p, but the two ends at the points b' and a', since gX_2 would be horizontal and hX_2 vertical. The angle between the two sections of the transformation curve would become more and more acute as the points G and H moved farther and farther apart, and would become ninety degrees if one of the two cornered isoquants ever coincided with one, and the other with the other, axis.

Suppose now that isoquants are L-shaped, but that only one of the factors, F_1, is recognized. The classical economists allowed that capital existed but not that it contributed to value; it was necessary rather to employ than to cooperate with labor. Therefore, let the amount of F_2 (capital) required to employ F_1 (workers) in either occupation always be forthcoming. Now, under the assumption of fixed factor proportions, the slopes of the rays X_1G and X_1H give the F_1, or labor requirements, of the two commodities x_2 and x_1, respectively. The maximum amount of x_1 which the country can produce is found by mapping X_1D, its total labor (F_1) endowment, into Oa' with the aid of $Oucc'c'''c''$. The maximum amount of x_2 that the country can produce is found by extending DX_2 until it intersects X_1G, extended to meet it, and by laying out this vertical distance along the x_2 axis. The transformation curve of this classical trade model will be a straight line.

If the rays X_1G and X_1H have the same slope, and if that slope coincides with the diagonal of the Edgeworth box, X_1CX_2D, then the transformation curve will also be a straight line. If the isoquants x_2 and x_1 share a common tangent at X_2, for example, the transformation curve will be that indicated by $a'b'$. This would also be the transformation curve if the isoquants x_1 and x_2 were L-shaped, their corners touched the point X_2, and one of the factors were in unlimited supply.

Figure I-6 is essentially the same as Figure I-5. In the new diagram, however, the Edgeworth box, $X_1MX_2'N$, and the transformation curve derived directly from it, $(a'')p''(b'')$, are those of the world and not of a single country. Two countries, A and B,

are distinguished; their factor-supply boxes are X_1CX_2D and
$X_2C'X_2'D'$. The diagonal, X_1X_2, of country A's box is extended
to meet the x_2 isoquant at Z, the x_1 isoquant at V; X_2g is parallel
to GZ, and X_2h to VH. The point g shows A's maximum output
of x_2 when it is mapped into the point b on the x_2 axis by means of

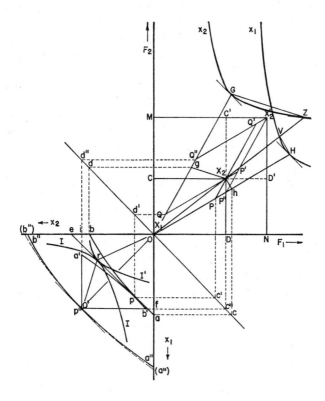

FIGURE I-6

the ray $Od'dd''$. Points h and a similarly show the maximum
possible output of x_1. Points P and Q can be mapped directly into
the coordinates for point p on country A's transformation curve,
apb, just as points P and Q in Figure I-5 were mapped into point
p in that diagram. The transformation curve for country B can
be obtained in the same way by temporarily placing its box,

$X_2C'X_2'D'$, so that X_2 lies at X_1. The origins of the transformation curves of both countries will then lie at O in the third quadrant.

But one transformation curve, say that of country B, can be transplanted so that its origin lies at O' and its two corners at the points a' and b'. If country B's transformation curve, with its origin at O', is allowed to slide along country A's curve, the point O' traces out, as an envelope curve, the world transformation curve, $a''p''b''$. This curve coincides for part, but not all, of its length with the curve, $(a'')p''(b'')$, derived directly from the world box, $X_1MX_2'N$. This occurs because, as O' slides toward, say, the x_1 axis and P'', on the world contract curve, slides toward X_2, X_1H rotates toward, and finally coincides with, X_1X_2V. At that time, country A will specialize completely on x_1. As p'' moves still closer to the x_1 axis, it must follow the curve ending at a'', and not that ending at (a''), for X_2 will lie outside the equalization region. If p'' moves in the other direction, toward the x_2 axis, P'' will move down the world contract curve, $X_1P''X_2'$, until the ray $X_1Q''G$ becomes parallel to, and $X_2'P''$ coincides with, X_2X_2', the diagonal of country B's box, and country B specializes on x_1.

Demand conditions in the two countries determine where along the world transformation curve, $a''p''b''$, world production and consumption will take place. The indifference curves, I, referred to the origin, O, and I', referred to O', are taken from the preference maps of countries A and B, respectively. One can think of $O'iOf$ as an Edgeworth box diagram; its dimensions give the amounts of the two commodities available for distribution to the two countries. Free-trade equilibrium occurs when the line, ep, whose slope is equal to the world terms of trade, is just tangent to one of A's indifference curves, to A's transformation curve, ab, to one of B's indifference curves, and to B's transformation curve, $a'b'$. If demand conditions place p'' on a part of $a''p''b''$ that does not correspond to $(a'')p''(b'')$, ep will not be tangent, of course, to one of the transformation curves, but will touch it in a corner. The slope of the tangent to the world transformation curve at p'' is, by the nature of envelope curves, equal to that of the transformation curve of either country at p, provided that complete specialization does not occur in either country.

This can also be seen by considering that when X_2 lies within the equalization region, the point p on the transformation curve of each country, and p'' on that of the world, both derive from the same pair of rays, X_1G and X_1H. Tiny displacements of the parallelogram, $X_1P''X_2'Q''$, as H and G shift slightly along their respective isoquants, will have nearly identical effects on all three transformation curves. The same reasoning indicates that at points where the transformation curves of the two countries share the same slope, factor prices will be the same in the two countries. If one country does specialize completely, the slope of the world transformation curve at p'' will equal that of the country which does not specialize; p will lie at the corner of the transformation curve of the other country and, unless X_2 lies just on the specialization boundary, the slope at that corner will not be equal to that at p''.

The consumption and production point for the world as a whole is P'', but this does not necessarily imply that production and consumption take place in the same point for each country. Nor must production and consumption necessarily occur along the world consumption-production vector, Op''. In Figure I-6, for example, consumption actually takes place at the point r, where ep, I, and I' are all tangent to one another. At this point, the tastes of the labor-rich country, A, whose origin is at O, are biased toward the capital-intensive good and those of the capital-rich country, B, toward the labor-intensive good. This combination of tastes and factor endowments, it can be seen, favors international trade, for the exports of A are equal to the vertical, and those of B to the horizontal, distance between p and r. Trade, with such preference maps, would occur even if A and B had identical factor endowments; that is, even if X_2 lay along the diagonal of the world box, X_1X_2'. If trade were restricted, the point p on the transformation curves of the two countries would lie closer to b, and the point O' would lie somewhere inside the world transformation curve, $b''p''a''$.

Figure I-6 shows how demand conditions may determine whether a point such as X_2 will lie inside the equalization region, $X_1P''X_2'Q''$. This occurs whenever the point X_2 lies within the football-shaped area formed by the contract curve, and by its image traced out by Q'' (area $X_1LL'X_2'JJ'$ of Figure I-3). If the point dividing world factor endowments among countries A and B lies outside this area, the transformation curve for the two countries together will lie everywhere inside the transformation curve for the undivided world. This is shown in Figure I-7.

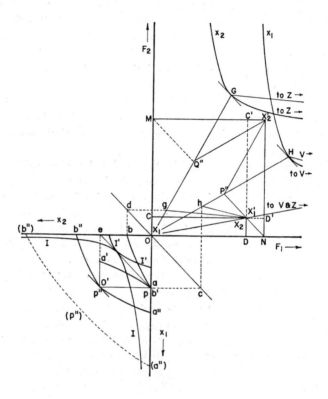

FIGURE I-7

World factor supplies are indicated by the box $X_1NX_2'M$. These are divided among countries A and B at the point X_2. The diagonal X_1X_2 of the box X_1CX_2D, extended, crosses the x_2 isoquant at Z and the x_1 isoquant at V. As before, X_2h is parallel to HV. If country A, whose origin is X_1, concentrates on the production of x_1, its maximum production of that commodity would be X_1h. The ray, Oc, whose slope is one, maps this output onto a, along the vertical axis of the third quadrant. Similarly, X_2g is parallel to GZ, and the output of x_2 corresponding to point g is given by point b on the x_2 axis. Points a and b are thus two points on the transformation curve of country A. Other points can be found exactly as described in connection with Figure I-5. Similarly, the transformation curve for country B can be obtained by simply placing the origin of its box, $X_1'C'X_2'D'$, at X_1, and proceeding as before. The resulting transformation curve, $a'b'$, will have its origin at O, but it can be shifted to O'. Now if the transformation curve, $a'b'$, is allowed to slide along the transformation curve, ab, O' will trace out the combined transformation curve $a''p''b''$ in Figure I-7. The transformation curve, derived as in Figure I-5 or I-6 by treating the world as a single integrated economy, is the dotted line $(a'')(p'')(b'')$.

The point on the transformation curve $a''p''b''$ at which world production and consumption take place is determined by world demand conditions, here represented by the indifference curves, I and I', with origins at O and O'. The transformation and indifference curves illustrated are such as to cause each country to specialize, so that p, b', and a all coincide. But this is not a necessary result, even though X_2 lies outside the equalization region. If world tastes had been sufficiently biased toward, say, x_1, the world consumption point, p'', would lie somewhere along the segment $p''a''$ of the world transformation curve and country B would produce some of both commodities. This can be seen also by imagining that point X_2 moves out along the ray X_1X_2, so that the box $X_1'C'X_2'D'$ becomes thinner than before. As this happens, the transformation curve for country A moves out from O, but retains its shape, while that for country B becomes smaller. Eventually $a'b'$ will disappear and ab will be the world transformation curve, with country A, this time, producing both goods.

The same reasoning can be applied to appreciate the consequences of the division of the world's resources among separate countries. As X_2 moves along the line $Q''M$ toward M (or along $P''N$ toward N), the divergence of relative endowments of F_1 and F_2 in the two countries increases. The transformation curves, including that for the world as a whole, shrink toward their origins and, as they do, the difference in their shapes increases. Figure I-7 indicates that if either factor fails to migrate, the loss of world production can be much more serious than that following upon the restriction of trade when factor endowments lie within the equalization region. Moreover, the potential seriousness of trade restrictions increases apace with the distance of the point dividing world factor supplies from the equalization region. An important question, therefore, is the size of the equalization region, or rather the *likelihood* of factor-price equalization in the actual world. The next chapter is devoted to forming an impression of that likelihood.

The analysis so far has assumed that only two countries exist. This assumption, however, is by no means necessary. Each of the sub-boxes within the world factor space, $X_1 M X_2' N$, of Figure I-6 may be considered not as a single country, but as a region (or customs union) comprising any number of countries. Further, any such region may be subdivided indefinitely into its component countries, in the same way that the world factor space of Figure I-6 was divided among countries A and B. Each region comprising two or more countries will, in turn, have its own equalization region, and the regional transformation curve (apb or $a'pb'$ in Figure I-6) will be the envelope of the individual countries' transformation curves. If the countries' factor endowments lie outside the regional equalization area, the regional transformation curve will have a kink, like that of $a''p''b''$ of Figure I-7. Where many countries are distinguished, their separate transformation curves will form a chain in the third quadrant, and the world transformation curve will be the envelope of all of them. As the number of countries multiplies, it will be increasingly difficult to distinguish pairs which exhibit widely differing factor endowments; as a result, the analysis will not suffer if the countries are aggregated into larger regional blocks. For the analysis of tariffs, however, it is formally necessary to study each country separately (see below, Chapter Four).

The diagram of Figures I-5 through I-7 provides the means to analyze certain consequences of relaxing the assumption of homogeneous production functions, identical in every country, and to show the implications of technical change. The general production function assumed so far has been of the form:

$$x_j = \psi_j(F_{1j}, \ldots, F_{rj}; x_{1j}, \ldots, x_{nj}) \quad (j = 1, \ldots, n) \tag{i}$$

where F_{kj}, for all subscripts k ($k = 1, \ldots, r$), is the amount of factor k, and x_{ij}, for all subscripts i ($i = 1, \ldots, n$), is the amount of commodity i which industry j uses to produce x_j, and where the form ψ_j has been taken as homogeneous of degree one and the same in all countries. The intermediate-good inputs, x_{ij}, and the inputs of primary factors other than F_1 and F_2 have so far been assumed equal to zero in the diagrams. Instead of assuming homogeneity of the whole function ψ_j, it is probably realistic to suppose that many production functions have a homogeneous component; that, for instance, after a certain minimum output has been attained, further increases involve neither increasing nor decreasing returns to scale. Or it may be, as suggested above, that the same minimum costs can be achieved at several discrete outputs. In addition, some forms of technical change undoubtedly enhance the productivity of each factor in roughly the same proportion. The form ψ_j could accordingly be decomposed into a composite function of the type:

$$\begin{aligned} x_j &= \alpha_j\beta_j[\gamma_j(F_{1j}, \ldots, F_{rj}; x_{1j}, \ldots, x_{nj})] \\ &= \psi_j(F_{1j}, \ldots, F_{rj}; x_{1j}, \ldots, x_{nj}) \quad (j = 1, \ldots, n). \end{aligned} \tag{i$'$}$$

In (i)$'$, α_j is an efficiency coefficient, entering as a multiplicative constant. Neutral technological change will change its value, and therefore the slope of the corresponding reflecting line, $oucc'c'''c''$ or $od'''dd'd''$, in Figure I-5, and thus alter the transformation curve $a''p'pub''$. The function β_j of the function γ_j reflects the influence of scale. If ψ_j were everywhere homogeneous of degree k, for example, β_j would give:

$$\begin{aligned} \beta_j[\gamma_j(F_{1j}, \ldots, F_{rj}; x_{1j}, \ldots, x_{nj})] \\ = t^k\gamma_j(F_{1j}, \ldots, F_{rj}; x_{1j}, \ldots, x_{nj})(j = 1, \ldots, n) \end{aligned}$$

where t is the scale factor. The line $Otucc'c'''c''$ in Figure I-5 graphs a β function which causes ψ_j to exhibit first decreasing returns to scale, then increasing returns, and finally, past u, constant returns to scale. The line segment $ucc'c'''c''$ may, moreover, be considered as the envelope of curves similar to *otu*, their points of tangency, like *u*, all lying on it. If that function holds in the diagram, the transformation curve in the third quadrant is $a''p'pu't'b''$ instead of $a''p'pu'b''$. Notice that except for the segment between u' and b'', this homogeneity of varying degree does not affect the transformation curve; nor does it change, under conditions which the diagram depicts, the final equilibrium in any way. Finally, the form

$$\gamma_j(F_{1j}, \ldots, F_{rj}; x_{1j}, \ldots, x_{nj}) \quad (j = 1, \ldots, n),$$

taken as homogeneous of degree one, corresponds to the functions whose isoquants are shown in the first quadrant of the diagrams. If γ_j differs among countries, those isoquants will have different slopes along rays of equal slope from the origin, X_1. Technological changes which affect the relative marginal productivities of inputs accordingly affect γ_j by rotating or otherwise distorting its isoquants. Neutral technological changes, changing only the numbering of isoquants, would not be imputed to the function γ_j but rather to α_j, if they did not cause scale to operate any differently, or to β_j, in addition perhaps to α_j, if they did.

The effects of international differences in the various parts of ψ_j upon factor prices can be examined by considering the relationship between goods and factor prices. Under perfect competition and in the absence of production taxes or subsidies:

$$p_j{}^A = p_{ok}{}^A \Big/ \frac{\partial \psi_j(F_{1j}{}^A, \ldots, F_{rj}{}^A; x_{1j}{}^A, \ldots, x_{nj}{}^A)}{\partial F_{kj}{}^A}, \text{ or}$$

$$\alpha_j{}^A \beta_j{}'^A p_j{}^A = p_{ok}{}^A \Big/ \frac{\partial \gamma_j{}^A(F_{1j}{}^A, \ldots, F_{rj}{}^A; x_{1j}{}^A, \ldots, x_{nj}{}^A)}{\partial F_{kj}{}^A}$$

$$(j = 1, \ldots, n), (k = 1, \ldots, r) \quad \text{(ii)}'$$

where the symbol p_o refers to the prices of primary factors, $p_{ok}{}^A$ being that of factor k in country A, and where $\beta_j{}'$ is the first derivative of the function β_j or, in other words, its slope. It can be seen that the composite coefficient, $\alpha_j \beta_j{}'$, if it differs in value from unity, effects factor prices through the homogeneous-of-degree-one function γ_j exactly as changes in relative commodity prices would affect them through the function ψ_j, if it were considered homogeneous of degree one. It would therefore affect relative factor prices in the same way as tariffs would, say, if factors are paid their marginal-value products.

Chapter Four analyzes the effects of changes in relative goods prices on relative factor prices. One can also examine them for the two-commodity and two-factor cases, as shown in Figures I-5 through I-7. In the two-by-two examples, however, differences among countries in the coefficient $\alpha_j\beta_j'$ will always be factor-biased if the functions γ_j differ among countries. If there are many goods, there is no reason to suppose the efficiency coefficients, α_j, to be factor-biased and differences in efficiency to alter anything but absolute factor returns as among countries. Even if the β functions depend somehow on factor intensity, perhaps because fixed capital tends to be lumpy, their existence will not necessarily distort relative factor prices. This is because the value of β_j' will typically be less than one, greater than one, and equal to one according to the size of output and will therefore sometimes discriminate in favor of, sometimes against, a particular factor.

If efficiency coefficients differ among countries and there are only two factors and commodities, there will be no equalization region. There will still be a region as between any two countries, however, within which neither of the two trading partners completely specializes. The delineation of its boundary will be more difficult than that of the equalization region, since factor movements within it will alter the pattern of world production. Fortunately, while international differences in efficiency coefficients may exist in the short run, Darwinian competition would eliminate them in time, particularly under free trade. So they cannot be the ultimate reason why relative factor prices diverge so much among nations.

The more serious possibility that returns to scale are constant or nearly so only after a certain output is attained modifies the equalization region only trivially, and does so only by reducing its size to an extent which depends upon the outputs at which all economies of scale can be realized. Suppose that the output of x_1, which the point u' on the transformation curve $a''p'pu't'b''$ of Figure I-5 gives, corresponds to the point P on the contract curve $X_1PP''P'X_2'$ of Figure I-2. If a country employs more labor and capital, along the ray X_1PP'', than that which the coordinates of P indicate, it has achieved minimum costs. The other country will be able to achieve minimum costs as well, so long as the country whose origin lies at X_1 produces no more x_1 than the amount corresponding to the length PP'' of X_1PP''. Mark off, therefore, a point on that ray just as far from P'' as P is from X_1. Through P and this new point (not shown on the diagram) draw two lines, both parallel to X_1Q, intersecting $X_2'Q$. The area which these lines and the relevant segments of the former specialization boundaries enclose is the new equalization region. If the other industry also exhibits the same scale characteristics, two similar parallel lines must be drawn intersecting X_1Q and $X_2'P$ at a common distance from their end points to represent the scale at which returns become constant. The equalization region will then be a similar but smaller parallelogram to the original equalization region. The boundaries of the smaller region will not indicate complete specialization, but rather the smallest output of the relevant industry consistent with its full realization of scale economies. Notice, however, that the segments of the original specialization boundaries, corresponding to the outputs of each commodity at which each country realizes full economies of scale, will still be relevant. Since the percentage of the total world demand of almost any commodity that one plant or firm of minimum optimal size can fill is very small, the new equalization region is practically tantamount, under this new assumption about production functions, to the one that prevails under the ordinary assumption. Moreover, possible large economies of scale of some industries relative to the sizes of their markets is only an argument for their location in one or a few countries, and in this case they will not disturb the likelihood of factor-price equalization.

· II ·

FREE TRADE AND SPECIALIZATION

FOR factor prices to be equalized among countries it is necessary either that each country produce some of each commodity which is produced anywhere in the world or that factor endowments of countries be such as to lie on specialization boundaries. These boundaries, and the region they enclose, have been described only for those cases in which two factors and two commodities are assumed to exist. The object of the present chapter is to construct such regions for cases in which n commodities and r factors are distinguished, to make explicit the treatment of raw materials and specific factors of production, and to present an empirical example showing the equalization region and indicating the likelihood of complete specialization under free trade. The empirical equalization region, derived from statistics on factor intensities, suggests that under free trade many nations would specialize in relatively few commodities. This indicates too that full factor-price equalization would not take place without factor movements among nations. But international capital movements and free trade are probably sufficient, as in the two-factor examples of the first chapter, virtually to equalize factor prices and thus to make optimal the geographical distribution of world production.

The treatment can, despite the introduction of more factors and commodities, remain essentially geometric. The geometry is a simple adaptation of the diagrams in the preceding chapter. It will be useful, and for some purposes necessary, to present a parallel algebraic formulation.

THE MATRIX OF FACTOR INTENSITIES

Let the parallelogram $X_1PX_2'Q''$ in Figure II-1 be the world equalization region. This region shows all possible allocations of the world's fixed factor supplies among countries which leave the solution to the world production problem unchanged. It can be formulated algebraically as follows. Let F_1^W be the world endowment of factor 1, equal to the length X_1N in Figure II-1. Let $F_2{}^W$, equal to the length X_1M, be the world endowment of factor 2. Let $F_{12}{}^W$ indicate the amount of factor 1 which works in industry 2 in the world. In Figure II-1, this amount is equal to the distance X_1G or $G'N$. The superscript W refers to the world as an integrated economy.

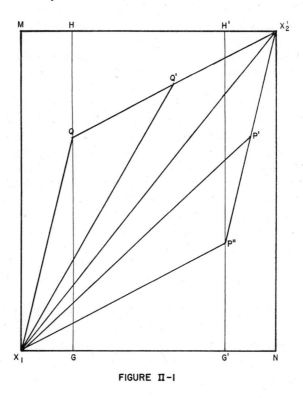

FIGURE II-I

Further, let $F_1{}^A$ be the amount of factor 1, and $F_2{}^A$ the amount of factor 2, allocated to country A. When country A's factor endowments are fixed within the equalization region, $X_1P''X_2'Q$, the amount of factor 1, $F_{12}{}^A$, which country A employs in industry 2 will be determined. The symbol $F_{kj}{}^A$ can represent the amount of factor k ($k = 1, \ldots, r$ where r is the number of factors) which industry j ($j = 1, \ldots, n$ where n is the number of commodities) employs in country A. Similarly, $F_{kj}{}^B$ is the amount of factor k which the other country, country B, employs in industry j. Figure II-1 requires that both r and n be equal to 2, but it is possible to change the diagram slightly so that n may be as large as desired.

For this purpose it will be more convenient to define factor intensity, as was done for Figure II-1, as the ratio of the amount of a factor employed by a given industry to the amount of another factor, used as a base, employed in the same industry, rather than as the ratio of factor use to gross output in an industry, as is usually done. The most convenient and natural bases for the ratios are the quantities of F_1 (labor), since every industry employs some labor. The symbol ρ_{kj} ($k = 1, \ldots, r$ and $j = 1, \ldots, n$) stands for the amount of F_k per unit of F_1 which industry j directly employs. Each ρ_{1j} is, of course, equal to one. In addition, ρ_{2j} is the ratio of capital to labor in industry j. In Figure II-1, the slope of X_1P'' is equal to ρ_{21} and that of X_2P'' to ρ_{22}. Factor-price equalization requires that $\rho_{kj}{}^A$ equal $\rho_{kj}{}^B$. When this assumption is made, ρ_{kj} will be written without a superscript.

With this notation, the equalization region $X_1P''X_2'Q$ of Figure II-1 may be represented by the equation

$$\begin{Bmatrix} F_1{}^A \\ F_2{}^A \end{Bmatrix} = \begin{Bmatrix} 1 & 1 \\ \rho_{21} & \rho_{22} \end{Bmatrix} \begin{Bmatrix} F_{11}{}^A \\ F_{12}{}^A \end{Bmatrix}$$

where $0 \leqq F_1{}^A \leqq F_1{}^W$, $0 \leqq F_2{}^A \leqq F_2{}^W$, $0 \leqq F_{11}{}^A \leqq F_{11}{}^W$, and $0 \leqq F_{12}{}^A \leqq F_{12}{}^W$.

In this formulation, as in the geometric one, $F_{11}{}^W$, $F_{12}{}^W$, ρ_{21}, and ρ_{22} are taken as given. Their values depend on world demand conditions, the two production functions, and world factor supplies, $F_1{}^W$ and $F_2{}^W$, also taken as given. The factor endowments of country A, $F_1{}^A$ and $F_2{}^A$, can thus assume any values which preserve the above inequalities without disturbing the equilibrium factor and commodity prices, world output, and employment prevailing before the world was divided up into separate but freely trading countries. This two-dimensional factor space describes all points within the parallelogram drawn in Figure II-1.

The slopes of the boundaries of this subspace are given by the two ρ's. If $\rho_{21} < \rho_{22}$, then country A can maximize the average

F_2-intensity of her two products by dropping altogether the production of x_1. The slopes of rays from the origin to points on the specialization boundaries are given by the maximum and minimum of the expression

$$\frac{F_2^A}{F_1^A} = \frac{\rho_{21}F_{11}^A + \rho_{22}F_{12}^A}{F_1^A}$$

considered as a function of F_1^A. The maximum of this expression

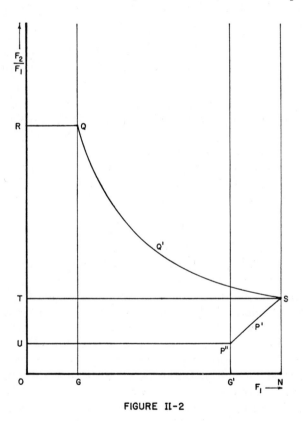

FIGURE II-2

will, of course, be less than ρ_{22} ($\rho_{21} < \rho_{22}$) if country A has more than F_{12}^W units of F_1.

Figure II-2 graphs the above relationship between F_2^A/F_1^A and

F_1[4]. The vertical axis of that diagram measures the ratio of the endowment of the two factors in one of the two countries, and the horizontal axis the amount of F_1 situated in that same country. The total world supply of F_1 is given by the length ON. The curve $RQQ'S$ shows the maximum F_2/F_1 ratio for one country compatible with factor-price equalization. The curve $UP''P'S$ gives the minimum ratio.

These curves can be derived directly from Figure II-1. In that diagram, the maximum amount of F_2 satisfying the above condition, for any amount of F_1 less than X_1G, is given by the slope of the line X_1Q. Let the distance OG in Figure II-2 equal X_1G in the first figure. Then, since the slope of X_1Q is everywhere constant, the segment RQ of the curve $RQQ'S$ will be a straight line, parallel to OG. Now imagine a point such as Q' in Figure II-1 which moves along the segment of the specialization boundary represented by QX_2'. The line connecting it with the origin, X_1, will have a constantly diminishing slope as Q' moves from Q to X_2'. This slope, measured along $QQ'S$ in Figure II-2, desribes a hyperbolic section. When Q' reaches X_2' in Figure II-1, the slope of X_1Q' is equal to the ratio of the world endowments of the two factors, F_2^W/F_1^W. This ratio is equal to the height OT in Figure II-2.

The curve $UP''P'S$ in Figure II-2, showing the minimum F_2/F_1 ratio when factor prices are equalized in the two countries, is derived in the same way. The horizontal segment of that curve, UP'', derives from the slope of the ray X_1P'' in Figure II-1. The height of the rising segment, $P''P'S$, measures the slope of the ray X_1P' in Figure II-1 as P' moves from P'' to X_2'.

The region $RQQ'SP'P''U$ in Figure II-2 is therefore an equalization region and corresponds exactly to the region $X_1QX_2'P''$ in Figure II-1. The advantage of Figure II-2 over Figure II-1 is that it can depict the equalization region even though more than two commodities are included.

Figure II-3 shows an equalization region for three commodities. The factor intensities of the three commodities, x_1, x_2, and x_3, are shown by the height of the three horizontal lines, RQ (or $R'Q'$), VW (or $V'W'$), and $U'P'$ (or UP). The length of each of these horizontal segments indicates the amount of the world's F_1 devoted, under full competitive equilibrium and factor-price equalization, to each of the three commodities. Thus RQ equals $F_{11}{}^w$, VW equals $F_{12}{}^w$, and UP equals $F_{13}{}^w$. Also, of course, RQ plus VW plus UP equals ON.

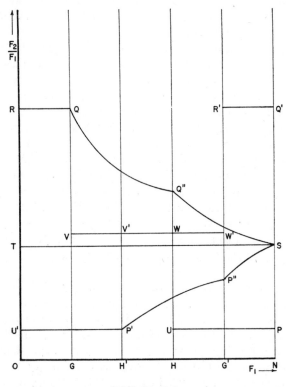

FIGURE II-3

Suppose that RQ, VW, and UP are arranged in descending order of their F_2/F_1 ratios, as illustrated in Figure II-3. The upper specialization boundary, $RQQ''S$, can now be easily derived, as before. Until country A has RQ units of F_1, it may have a maximum of OR units of F_2 per unit of F_1, if factor prices between countries A and B are to remain equal. In this case, it specializes entirely on the production of x_1. At point Q, country A produces the total world supply of that commodity.

If country A is now given a larger share of the world's supply of F_1, its maximum permissible F_2/F_1 ratio is diminished, for it must now begin to produce x_2, which has a lower F_2/F_1 ratio. In Figure II-3, suppose A has OH' units of F_1 and that GH' is equal to OG. The curve QQ'' will cut the vertical extension of $H'V'$ at a point half as far from V' as Q is from V. Similarly, if $H'H$ is equal to OG, the length $Q''W$ will be equal to one third of the length VQ. Thus for any amount of $F_1{}^A$ in country A, the height of QQ'' will be equal to the arithmetic average of the F_2/F_1-intensity of each unit of F_1 employed.

Country A continues to produce only x_1 and x_2 along $RQQ''S$ until it has OH units of F_1. At that point, it produces the entire world supplies of both x_1 and x_2. Therefore, beyond H, it must start to produce x_3 as well, and the relevant segment of her specialization boundary is $Q''S$, derived as above. The height of the point S is, of course, equal to $F_2{}^W/F_1{}^W$, or the world F_2/F_1 ratio.

The lower boundary for country A can be derived in a similar manner. The only difference is that now the three industries, x_1, x_2, and x_3, must be arranged in ascending order of their F_2/F_1 ratios. The height and length of the horizontal lines, $U'P'$, $V'W'$, and $R'Q'$, indicate respectively the equilibrium F_2/F_1 ratios and the equilibrium amount of F_1 devoted to the production of x_3, x_2, and x_1, in that order, in the world as a whole. Country A may have as little as OU' units of F_2 per unit of F_1 and still earn the same amount per unit of each factor as B does, so long as it has no more than OH' units of F_1. If it does have more, it must have more units of F_2 for each unit of F_1 if the equilibrium level of factor prices, identical in each country, is not to alter. If A has, say, OG' units of F_1, it must have at least $G'P''$ units of F_2 per unit of F_1, and so on.

The matrix ρ for this three-commodity, two-factor world may be written as follows:

$$\rho = \begin{bmatrix} 1 & 1 & 1 \\ \rho_{21} & \rho_{22} & \rho_{23} \end{bmatrix}.$$

The excessive number of columns of this matrix, relative to the number of its rows, indicates that unless the endowment point of one of the countries lies on a specialization boundary, the exact pattern of production in either country is indeterminate. In Figure II-3, let country A's endowment point lie at Q. It then must concentrate entirely on the production of x_1. At Q, A has OG units of F_1, so that country B must have the rest. Now let the diagram refer to country B. Then B's endowment point must lie at P'', where B has OG' units of F_1, since $G'N$ equals OG. At that point, B would produce only x_2 and x_3, and so its pattern of production would also be fixed. But the geographical distribution of production is not determinate if the endowment ratio of either country (and therefore of both countries) lies within the equalization region rather than on one of its frontiers. At the point V, for instance, it makes no difference to the equilibrium levels of world output already established whether country A produces one half of the world's output of x_2, or that combination of x_1 and x_3 which would also just exhaust her factor supplies at the established world factor prices.[1]

As many sectors as desired may now be considered. The ρ matrix gains a new column for each new sector. The specialization boundaries in Figure II-3 become smoother and more nearly continuous as each individual scallop becomes relatively less important, until finally they take on the smooth appearance of the curves shown in Figure II-4.

Suppose now, to illustrate another point, that the heights of RQ, VW, and UP in Figure II-3 are equal to ρ_{21}, ρ_{22}, and ρ_{23} in the three-column ρ matrix. It is only because these ρ's differ in magnitude that the equalization region shown in that diagram can exist. If two of the three sectors exhibited identical ρ_2's, it would be as though they were really one sector, and an equalization region shaped like that of Figure II-2 would appear. It is clear that if all three ρ_2's were identical, it would be impossible for any equalization region to exist. The assumption that at least two goods must exist in order to equalize prices for two factors should be amended to read that at least two of the ρ_2's must differ in magnitude. On the other hand, the number of sectors whose ρ_2's are the same is immaterial.

[1] See also Paul A. Samuelson, "Prices of Goods and Factors in General Equilibrium," *Review of Economic Studies*, 21:8–9 (1953–1954).

When there are more than two factors, the analogous condition is somewhat more difficult to state, and it is necessary to dwell for a moment on the purely mathematical requirements of the problem. For an equalization region to exist, it must have the same dimensionality as the factor space to which it belongs. The

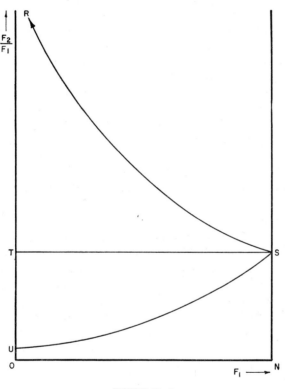

FIGURE II-4

ρ matrix maps the (column) vector, $F_1{}^A$, the elements, $F_{1j}{}^A$, of which represent the amount of F_1 devoted to each industry j in country A, into the (column) vector, F^A, which indicates the amount of each factor that must then be located in country A. For F^A to be a vector in r space, it is only necessary, then, for the rank of ρ to be equal to r.

INTERMEDIATE PROCESSES AND EQUALIZATION REGIONS

The production functions assumed in international-trade models are restricted by various formal properties, which were discussed in the first chapter. It was asserted that one of these properties, the ability to combine all stages of production into a single function, need not be assumed at all. The equipment is now available to show how easily this very restrictive assumption may be dispelled, as well as to indicate the degree of its former seriousness.

In Figures I-2 and II-1, the point P'' was described as a consumption point, because it showed the amounts of x_1 and x_2 which the world consumed. However, P'' is also a production point. Now, assume that x_1 is exclusively an input, and x_2 is the only final consumption good. The location of the production point, P'', is in this case determined not by demand conditions, but by the manner in which x_1 enters into the production of x_2. The equalization region still exists, nonetheless, so long as ρ_{21} differs from ρ_{22} and some positive amount of x_1 is required in the production of x_2.

It should be possible in this way to disintegrate vertically the production of any final good into its separate technological processes. For any n final goods, there are $n + n'$ final plus intermediate goods, or a total of $n + n'$ processes or activities. This means that, if the number of *commodities* is too small, separate *processes* can be distinguished, until the number of processes exceeds the number of factors. The ρ matrix will gain two new columns for each newly distinguished process, but will lose the column corresponding to the formerly integrated production process. The net gain is thus one column.

When this is done, the range of factor intensities among the intermediate processes will in general exceed the range among the original final products. This is because the factor requirements of a final good depend upon the factor requirements of each of its intermediate-good inputs. As long as all production functions are homogeneous of degree one, this dependence will be linear for any equilibrium set of factor and goods prices.

Therefore, the factor intensity of the integrated process will be a weighted average of the factor intensities of the subprocesses which it embodies. The more subprocesses distinguished, the greater will be the range of factor intensities among processes. This range, in turn, determines the vertical distance between the minimum and maximum specialization boundaries. Therefore, the general result of disintegrating production into separate processes is to enlarge the size of the equalization region.

There are, nonetheless, practical limitations upon the number of subprocesses that can be distinguished. All such processes must involve a transferable object in order to have any effect in equalizing factor prices interregionally or internationally. Moreover, it is conceivable that certain processes require factors in different proportions and yet, for reasons that lie on the borderline between economics and technology, must always be performed in conjunction with one another.

International trade, of course, practices precisely what the above theory prescribes. Suppose, for example, that country A's endowment ratio originally lay within the equalization region RSU in Figure II-4. Imagine that it acquires capital at a higher rate than rest of the world does. As the process of differential capital accumulation proceeds, its endowment ratio will eventually lie above the upper specialization boundary. But this process will set up forces causing the boundary itself to move outward. Entrepreneurs will look for subcontractors in country B to perform labor-intensive finishing and other operations that were previously performed within country A's own plants.

To appreciate how fine the subdivision of production processes among countries can be, one has only to inspect the tariff list of a country like the United States or France. Raw materials, for example, are listed separately for every conceivable stage of fabrication, indicating that the factor intensity of subprocesses among traded goods makes a substantial difference to someone in the recipient country. Thus, the extent to which production subprocesses can move among different countries, as a result of changes in factor proportions within countries, affects the possibility of achieving the equilibrium world trade solution.

GENERAL AND SPECIFIC FACTORS OF PRODUCTION

In order to apply this analysis to actual trade situations, it is necessary to define the ρ matrix in greater detail and to determine its actual structure. Any country has many different factors of production. There are different types of land, labor, machinery, buildings, education and training, and so on, and it is technically impossible to measure all of these in units of any one common factor, such as unskilled labor. Many of these factors, moreover, are specific: either they would yield so much less if transferred to another use (champagne land used to raise wheat) that they are not in fact transferred, or they can be used only for one purpose (a mine).[2]

Exactly which factors are specific and which are general depends partly upon the time horizon adopted. In the short run, such things as fixed plants and certain types of skilled labor are specific; in the long run, specific factors include mainly the various categories of land. Some types of land may be allocated to different crops and thus are specific only to agriculture, broadly defined. Natural-resource sites, on the other hand, are generally of value only in a single extractive type of activity.

This distinction between specific and general factors indicates that certain elements in the ρ matrix will be zero and that certain rows will be completely filled with positive, nonzero entries. The zero elements in a row reflect specific factors which do not enter certain production processes, while the filled rows correspond to general factors, of which, as asserted earlier, labor is the prime example.

But what sort of labor? It will obviously be meaningful in many instances to distinguish skilled labor of many degrees and types. Although some kind of labor is always present in pro-

[2] The distinction between specific and general (or nonspecific) factors, the latter being capable of employment in a number of different uses, was first introduced by Wieser, and has also been used by Bastable and others. Haberler used the distinction to explain the curvature of the transformation curve, and thus presented an explanation of that curvature which was essentially different from that based on variable proportions, used by Samuelson. See Gottfried von Haberler, *The Theory of International Trade with Its Applications to Commercial Policy* (London, 1936), pp. 175–176; and Richard E. Caves, *Trade and Economic Structure* (Cambridge, Mass., 1960), pp. 30–34.

duction, the levels and types of skills which accompany it vary with each production process. If, as others have suggested, a skilled laborer can be regarded as a combination of labor and capital, the latter representing the amount of resources sunk into training, gathering of experience, and education, there is no problem.[3] For long-run problems, the capital that education represents may be aggregated with other forms of capital and included in the capital (ρ_2) row of the ρ matrix. For short-run problems, separate rows can be distinguished for each type of skill considered economically important and for each specific type of capital — drilling machinery, turret lathes, milling machines, typewriters, trucks, cement mixers, and so on. For a short-run ρ matrix, therefore, there would be no single row for capital in which all elements were nonzero and positive, since in the short run all capital would be embodied in specific factors. The only complete row would be the one standing for labor, measured simply in terms of man-years or some other time unit.[4]

It may be helpful to illustrate these ideas by means of an expanded set of equations determining an equalization region. The notation corresponds to that used in the first section of this chapter. The first row of the ρ matrix shown below corresponds to labor, measured in man–time units. Every element in each column is, as already explained, divided by the first element of that column, so that the first row of the matrix consists entirely of one's. The example is assumed to cover a time sufficiently long for the marginal returns of each type of investment to be equalized in each sector and among sectors. Consequently, the second

---

[3] Diab has argued that the capital represented by the training of workers should be added to the physical capital with which they work in deriving estimates of the true capital intensity of processes or goods. I agree completely with this suggestion. See M. A. Diab, *The United States Capital Position and the Structure of Its Foreign Trade* (Amsterdam, 1956), pp. 52, 53.

Schultz estimates that the total cost of high school and college education in the United States in 1956 was equal to more than 24 percent of gross capital formation for that year. Thus this form of investment is not a negligible part of the total. See T. W. Schultz, "Capital Formation by Education," *Journal of Political Economy*, 68:572 (December 1960).

[4] Of course, all men are not equal even if allowance is made for differences in training. Whether the structure of natural gifts among the population differs from country to country is an interesting question, but one which the economist is not particularly well equipped to answer.

row, which records the amount of physical capital per worker in each activity, stands for the general factor, physical capital.

$$
\begin{bmatrix} F_1{}^A \\ F_2{}^A \\ F_3{}^A \\ F_4{}^A \\ F_5{}^A \\ F_6{}^A \\ F_7{}^A \\ F_8{}^A \\ F_9{}^A \\ \cdot \\ F_r{}^A \end{bmatrix} =
\begin{bmatrix}
1 & 1 & 1 & 1 & 1 & 1 & 1 & 1 & 1 & \cdot & 1 \\
\rho_{21} & \rho_{22} & \rho_{23} & \rho_{24} & \rho_{25} & \rho_{26} & \rho_{27} & \rho_{28} & \rho_{29} & \cdot & \rho_{2n} \\
0 & \rho_{32} & \rho_{33} & 0 & 0 & \rho_{36} & \rho_{37} & 0 & \rho_{39} & \cdot & \rho_{3n} \\
0 & 0 & \rho_{43} & \rho_{44} & 0 & 0 & \rho_{47} & \rho_{48} & \rho_{49} & \cdot & \rho_{4n} \\
\rho_{51} & \rho_{52} & \rho_{53} & \rho_{54} & 0 & 0 & 0 & 0 & 0 & \cdot & 0 \\
0 & 0 & 0 & 0 & \rho_{65} & 0 & 0 & 0 & 0 & \cdot & 0 \\
0 & 0 & 0 & 0 & 0 & \rho_{76} & 0 & 0 & 0 & \cdot & 0 \\
0 & 0 & 0 & 0 & 0 & 0 & \rho_{87} & 0 & 0 & \cdot & 0 \\
0 & 0 & 0 & 0 & 0 & 0 & \rho_{97} & 0 & 0 & \cdot & 0 \\
\cdot & \cdot & \cdot & \cdot & \cdot & \cdot & \cdot & \cdot & \cdot & & \cdot \\
0 & 0 & 0 & 0 & 0 & 0 & 0 & 0 & 0 & \rho_{rj} & 0
\end{bmatrix}
\begin{bmatrix} F_{11} \\ F_{12} \\ F_{13} \\ F_{14} \\ F_{15} \\ F_{16} \\ F_{17} \\ F_{18} \\ F_{19} \\ \cdot \\ F_{1r} \\ F_{1n} \end{bmatrix}
$$

This example may also illustrate a situation in which, in at least one country, investment in education, or human capital, is not everywhere governed by purely economic considerations— that is, when marginal returns to education are not equated to returns in other lines. The number of people studying science, for instance, may be restricted by social values deprecating such an activity, or perhaps there are restrictions upon entry into trades which require training of a special type. If only certain classes are considered eligible for, or are given the opportunity to acquire, education, then the marginal return to investment in education may be permanently greater than the return to other forms of investment. If this is so, it might be useful to differentiate this form of investment, even in the long run, by considering the skills in which it is embodied as separate factors.[5]

Let total investment in these types of training be represented by F_3 and F_4. In country A, these coefficients are, one way or another, affected by forces other than those governing purely

[5] Maurice Allais has commented upon a set of studies on social mobility in Italy, France, and the United States. Seven or eight social groups or stratifications were distinguished (the number apparently depended upon the country), and the probability that the son of a common laborer would pass into one of the two top groups was estimated. This probability was 2.6 percent for Italy, 4.1 percent for France, and 7.3 percent for the United States. See Maurice Allais, *L'Europe unie* (Paris, 1960), pp. 41, 42.

economic investment decisions. A nonzero ρ_{kj} will appear in each column corresponding to an activity that uses labor having the skills developed by these two types of training.[6]

Agricultural land could be represented in the example by F_5, which is used in several occupations, or by different types of crops, x_1 through x_4. Symbols F_6 through F_9 and F_r represent specific factors, each one being used in only one activity. By and large, each activity will depend upon only one specific factor. But in addition to, say, land on which a particular raw material is located, there may be other specific resources or factors that directly affect its extraction. For that reason, it is not possible to rule out cases such as x_7, in which more than one factor is specific to an activity. The typical secondary manufacturing sector will be like x_8 or x_9 in its primary factor requirements. It is chiefly engaged in transforming a raw material through general factors: labor and physical and human capital.

The rank of the ρ matrix in the example just illustrated is less than r because some industries use more than one specific factor. Thus no equalization region of dimensionality r can be constructed from it, as it stands.[7] Unfortunately the method of adding independent columns to the ρ matrix will not correct this situation so long as two or more factors remain specific to the same activity. Trade cannot equalize the returns to such factors, though it can those to the others. The separate factors in each such bundle must work together in fixed proportions, regardless of their geographical distribution, if the marginal returns to each are to be equalized.

In practice, the only way to measure the amount of such

[6] It may be emphasized at this point that it is perfectly consistent with the Heckscher-Ohlin theory that influences other than the simple quantities of factors of production affect the structure of production and of trade. Formally, these present no real problem and require only the addition of extra equations to express them. Practically, their importance may be considerable, and they form a reason why, in any particular case, it may be incorrect to infer factor endowments from observed patterns of trade.

[7] It is easy to prove that the determinant of any matrix which has at least one column (or row), with two or more positive elements appearing, respectively, in rows (or columns) whose other elements are all zeros, is equal to zero. (The row version of this theorem, it should be observed, cannot operate so long as every activity requires more than one factor.) Thus no r by r submatrix of the ρ matrix can be found whose rank is r.

bundles is to aggregate all factors specific to a single, integral activity into a single factor. It is impossible to measure quantities of such aggregate factors in any precise way, of course, and the concept of rent, as explained in the first chapter, must be invoked.[8]

SPECIALIZATION BOUNDARIES WITH TWO GENERAL FACTORS

Specialization boundaries may be graphed so long as only two general factors are assumed, no matter how many specific factors exist. In the long run, when all markets, including that for education, are assumed to be free, only two general factors, labor and capital, are significant. To see the manner in which specialization boundaries may be graphed when specific resources are taken into account, return to the example used to develop Figure II-3. There the equilibrium F_2/F_1 ratios for the commodities, x_1, x_2, and x_3, were given by the heights of the line segments RQ, VW, and UP. The amounts of F_1 devoted to the activities of producing those commodities were given by the lengths of the same line segments.

Now suppose that one of these commodities, say x_2, requires a specific factor, F_3, in addition to the general factors, F_1 and F_2. When two countries are distinguished, the world supply of F_3 may either be divided in some proportion between them or given entirely to one or the other. Figure II-5 is drawn on the assumption that the entire world supply of F_3 is given to country A. The solution to world equilibrium output cannot hold, now that separate nations with different factor proportions are recognized, unless country A is also given at least as much F_1 and F_2 as would be associated with F_3 in the production of x_2 in an undivided world.

The first segment of both specialization boundaries for A is therefore the line VW. But until $F_1{}^A$ is equal to OH' (VW), factor prices in the two countries cannot be equalized by free trade. Until that point is reached, the marginal productivity of $F_1{}^A$ will always exceed that of $F_1{}^B$. This is because country A specializes entirely in the production of x_2, but applies less F_1 to the given

[8] Generally, one of the factors will earn all of the rent, and the others will be free.

world supply of F_3 than was applied in the prenational solution, when national boundaries did not hinder factor movements.

The true equalization region in Figure II-5 therefore begins at W, where country A devotes OH' units of F_1 to x_2. Between H' and H on the horizontal axis, it may concentrate on the pro-

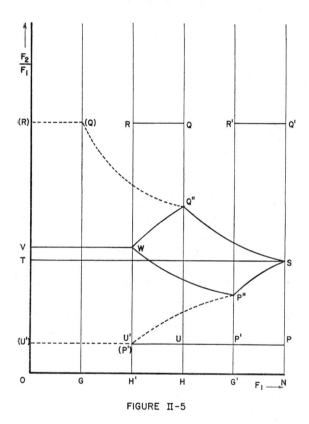

FIGURE II-5

duction of x_1, the most F_2-intensive good, upon the production of x_3, the least F_2-intensive good, or may produce a combination of both, depending upon the actual F_2/F_1 ratio. In the former case, its upper specialization boundary will be given by WQ'', showing the maximum ratio in country A which is consistent with the original world production equilibrium. The bottom boundary will be given by the line WP'', showing the minimum acceptable ratio.

The segments, $Q''S$ and $P''S$, are derived for Figure II-5 in exactly the same way as for Figure II-3, and they in fact coincide with their counterparts in the earlier diagram. The specialization boundaries of Figure II-3, where they fail to correspond with those of Figure II-5, are drawn in as dotted lines to facilitate a comparison of the two examples.

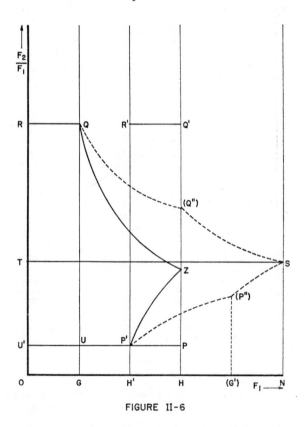

FIGURE II-6

Figure II-6 makes the opposite assumption about the distribution of F_3 between the two countries. Now the entire world

endowment of this factor is in country B. The first portions, RQ and $U'P'$, of country A's specialization boundaries will be the same as in Figure II-3, for the same reasons. If country A is on the upper boundary, RQ, producing x_1 only, and its share of the world supply of F_1 increases beyond G, it will start to produce x_3. This order of specialization is reversed if it is originally on the lower boundary, $U'P'$, producing only x_3. Both of these paths terminate at point Z, which is HN (VW) units from the right-hand vertical axis. Beyond this point, there would be insufficient F_1 in country B to produce the world's supply of x_2 using the same factor proportions as in the prenational solution. As a result, F_1's price in B would necessarily be greater than in A. Thus the equalization region in this figure is the area enclosed by the lines $RQZP'U'$ and the left-hand vertical axis.

One way in which to imagine the relationship between the situation illustrated in Figure II-3 and those shown in Figures II-5 and II-6 is the following. Suppose that all three diagrams represent the same world, in which x_1, x_2, and x_3 are the same commodities with the same production functions, and so on, and that tastes and factor endowments are the same in all three situations. In Figure II-3, however, it was not specified that x_2 required a third, specific, factor. In effect, Figure II-3 assumes that wherever it turns out to be advantageous to produce x_2, the required amount of F_3 is available for that activity. Consequently, the location of F_3 was not permitted to disturb the patterns of comparative advantage between the two countries as determined by their relative endowments of F_1 and F_2. In other words, Figure II-3 assumes that the specific factor, F_3, was perfectly mobile internationally and would always move between countries to equalize returns.[9] In Figures II-5 and II-6, however, the location of F_3 is allowed to play the same role in determining comparative advantage as that of the two general factors, F_1 and F_2. Here, then, the assumption was made that the specific factor was immobile internationally. This assumption obviously holds for such specific factors as natural resources. But since, in going

[9] Examples of such specific factors might include technicians, singers, patents, and prize fighters.

from Figure II-3 to Figures II-5 and II-6, the production relationship between F_3 and x_2 is unchanged, the specialization boundaries of Figure II-3 turn out neatly to include the other two.

The entire world supply of the specific resource, F_3, need not, of course, be found in one or the other country. Any particular

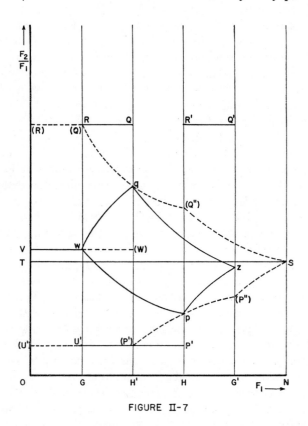

FIGURE II-7

distribution between the two is possible and can be represented by means of the same basic diagram. Figure II-7 shows the specialization boundaries when each country has one half of the world supply of F_3. Country A will now produce x_2, into which F_3 enters directly, exclusively until point w is reached. As explained in connection with Figure II-5, unless A has an amount of F_1 equal to at least OG units, factor prices will not be equalized. Factor-price equalization will occur only if A's endowments of F_1 and F_2 lie within the region bounded by the specialization boundaries, $wqzp$. This region will move to the left as country B is given more and more of the total supply of F_3 until, when B has all of the world's F_3, the situation will correspond to that of Figure II-6.

It will be observed that the equalization regions in Figures II-5, II-6, and II-7 are considerably smaller than those in Figure II-3. This is exactly what one would expect, given the location of F_3 as an additional constraint. This dictates that one of the commodities (x_2) has a priority claim to production, regardless of its actual order in the F_2/F_1 rank. In the three-commodity case, only two possible rankings, depending upon whether one follows the upper or the lower specialization boundary, are left to determine the equalization region. Another degree of freedom would be lost if one of the other commodities were made to depend upon another specific factor. In that case, the country's exact order of specialization would be determined by its endowments of the two specific factors. Consequently, no equalization region could exist.

On the other hand, any amount of new specific factors may be added, so long as each has its commodity. From this point of view, the distance VW in Figure II-5, or its variations, stands for the amount of F_1 which must be associated with all of the specific factors in production. The distance OV, by the same token, is the average F_2/F_1 ratio for all the activities which require specific factors.

Some factors, such as agricultural land, can be specific to more than one activity. How will this affect the appearance of the equalization region? In Figure II-5, the total amount of F_1 used to produce x_2 (OH') equals the amount used for x_3 ($H'G'$), and the combined amount equals OG'. Now, retaining this assumption, suppose that both x_2 and x_3 require the specific factor, F_3. Suppose further that $\rho_{32} = 2\rho_{33}$, or that, under equilibrium conditions, each unit of F_1 works with twice as many units of F_3 to produce x_2 as to produce x_3. Finally, suppose that country A has one half of the world supply of F_3. Figure II-8 illustrates the specialization boundaries under the above special assumptions.

Country A may pursue either of the activities requiring F_3 or a combination of the two, depending upon its F_2/F_1 ratio. The equilibrium F_2/F_1 ratio for x_2 is OV, and for x_3 is OU', where OV is greater than OU'. Consequently, country A's upper specialization boundary will begin at V. Since by assumption the world

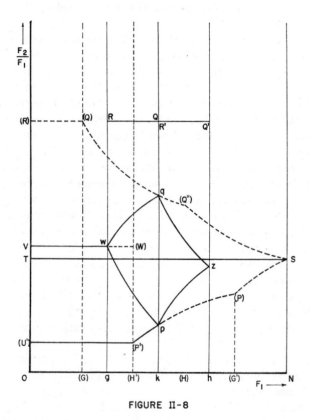

FIGURE II-8

devotes the same amount of F_1 to x_2 as to x_3, and since $\rho_{32} = 2\rho_{33}$, the total production of x_2 will use two thirds of the world's supply of F_3. Therefore, if country A exhausts its half of the world's F_3 in producing x_2, it will produce only three fourths of the world's x_2. The distance Vw in Figure II-8 shows this amount in terms of F_1.

Country A's lower specialization boundary begins at (U'). Since, by assumption, at equilibrium factor prices the total output of x_3 uses only one third of the world's F_3, A has more than enough F_3 to produce the entire world supply of x_3. This amount equals $(U')(P')$ F_1 units in Figure II-8. In order to employ the remainder of its F_3 at the world price for that factor, country A must produce $(H')k$ or $w(W)$ F_1 units of x_2, or one fourth of the world's output of that commodity. Thus, fully to employ its F_3, A must produce $O(H')$ F_1 units of x_3 and $(H')k$ F_1 units of x_2, with an average F_2/F_1 ratio equal to kp.

If country A now receives more F_1 than it needs to work with its F_3, it will begin to produce x_1, whose F_2/F_1 ratio is $O(R)$. As a result, A's upper specialization boundary moves up the line wq, and its lower boundary moves along pz. If A's factor endowments are at point q, it will produce the entire world supply of x_1, in addition to three fourths of the world's x_2. If its factor endowments are at point z, it will produce all of the world's x_1 and x_3 and one fourth of its x_2 output.

The section qz of country A's upper specialization boundary is analogous to the section qz in Figure II-7, where it began to produce x_3. Because, however, it no longer has any free F_3, it cannot move onto this section directly from q by producing x_3. Nonetheless, it can attain any point on it indirectly by altering the composition of its total output in the following manner. By producing some combination of x_2 and x_3 until its supply of F_3 is exhausted, country A can attain any point along the line wp. Then, by producing the total world output of x_1, it will move along a curved line in the area $wqzp$ to a point on qz.[10] It is obvious that if the combination of x_2 and x_3 consists heavily of x_3, then the point on wp will lie close to p, and the corresponding point on qz will lie close to z; and vice versa if the combination consists primarily of x_2. Points q and z, then, merely describe the limiting cases where the combinations of x_2, x_3, and the world output of x_1 which A produces contain no x_3 or no x_2.

If country A's factor endowments lie within or on the boundary of the area $wqzp$, factor prices will be equalized, as in earlier illustrations. It is important, however, to notice that the area

[10] In the special case in which $\rho_{32} = \rho_{33}$, wp and qz will be vertical straight lines.

$V(U')(P')pw$ is not an equalization region. In this area, A will be unable fully to employ its F_3 at given world input proportions, and consequently the price of F_3 there will fall below the world price.

It is also worth noticing that the equalization region in Figure

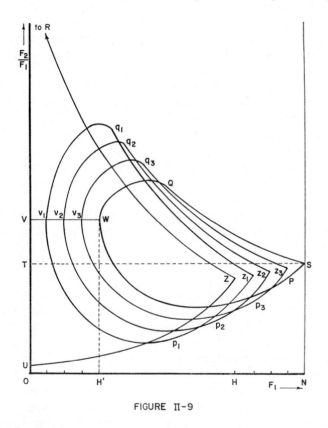

FIGURE II-9

II-8 is similar in general configuration to that in Figure II-7. In order to illustrate this, the equalization regions in both diagrams were drawn inside the superimposed specialization boundaries of Figure II-3. These last boundaries, it will be recalled, were drawn on the assumption that the specific factor or factors were perfectly mobile internationally, whereas Figures II-5 through II-8 are drawn on the much more realistic assumption that specific factors are immobile. As long as immobility is maintained, any further assumptions regarding the identification of specific resources, and their distribution between countries A and B, will lead to equalization regions lying entirely within, but touching in at least two points (such as q and p in Figures II-7 and II-8), the specialization boundaries drawn on the former assumption.

If many activities, or industry sectors, are distinguished, these equalization regions will have smooth-looking specialization boundaries, such as those drawn in Figure II-9. This figure assumes that in equilibrium, under free trade, OH' units of F_1 are employed in conjunction with an average bundle of specific factors. The average F_2/F_1 ratio for this bundle is OV. The equalization region is $v_1q_1z_1p_1$ if country A possesses Vv_1 units of the specific factors. The other regions, beginning at points V, W, v_2, and v_3, are drawn on corresponding assumptions. If in Figure II-9 all specific factors are perfectly mobile internationally, the equalization region (the boundaries of which are not drawn in) would enclose the area $Rq_1q_2q_3QSPp_3p_2p_1U$. This envelope specialization boundary is in fact the one which Figure II-4 shows.

EMPIRICAL SPECIALIZATION BOUNDARIES

Are equalization regions in reality as full and chunky as those of Figure II-9, or do they lie close about the line of average capital-labor intensity (TS in the diagrams)? This question might seem unanswerable, since it requires a knowledge of the structure of the world economy under conditions of perfect international factor mobility. In fact, however, such information is unnecessary. Take, instead of the entire world, a single country as a model. This country alone will be an adequate substitute for the world, provided only that it is quite nearly self-sufficient and that factors within it move fairly freely so that their prices are nearly uniform throughout its territory. It would be extremely useful in addition if the economy of such a country were highly developed, competitive, and modern.

Leontief has presented the required data in his studies on the structure of United States foreign trade. They present the direct capital-labor (F_2/F_1) ratios for 192 industry and service sectors and the amount of labor employed by each sector.[11] The first task in using them is to determine which of the 192 sectors depend upon specific factors and so must be performed where those factors are found. Into this group go all agricultural and extractive industries.[12] Those activities which do not depend directly upon any specific resource, and which give rise to products or services that can move in trade, belong in a second group. The remaining sectors do not fit either of the above classifications, and yet they account for almost half of the total labor employed. The activities of this group, mainly various services and utilities, do not give rise to any traded commodity or service: their products must be consumed where production takes place.[13]

These immobile goods (and services) have not yet entered the analysis, but it is easy to appreciate that their existence will reduce the area in which factor-price equalization is possible. Therefore, in constructing an actual example of such an area, they must be explicitly taken into account. One way of considering the workers who produce goods and services that cannot be traded is as the unproductive workers of whom Adam Smith was fond of speaking. Like the menial servant's, their "services generally perish in the very instant of their performance, and seldom leave any trace or value behind them, for which an equal quantity of service could afterwards be procured."[14] Smith tended to think of all such laborers as servants to those who

---

[11] Wassily Leontief, "Factor Proportions and the Structure of American Trade: Further Theoretical and Empirical Analysis," *Review of Economics and Statistics*, 38.4:386–407, appendix 3 (November 1956). The amount of labor per sector was computed by multiplying the direct labor coefficients by the gross output of each sector, as given in the 1947 B.L.S. input-output table.

[12] Fishing depends upon a natural, and therefore specific, resource which in practice *can* migrate freely from country to country. Since, however, fishing was lumped together with hunting, forestry, and agriculture in the data, this intriguing property of its specific resource had to be ignored.

[13] In most cases no good reason exists why the equivalent of foreign trade should not occur in this group: why, for instance, professionals of one country should not export their services to another, why foreign airlines, truck companies with foreign personnel, etc., should not operate domestically.

[14] Adam Smith, *An Inquiry into the Nature and Causes of the Wealth of Nations* (New York, 1937), p. 315.

produced material or vendible commodities. It is convenient here to think of them in the same way and to imagine that they are always in attendance upon such producers, wherever and in whatever occupation they may be found. If the Air Force sets up a base in the desert, for instance, or if an oil well is found there, the community which springs up will contain a certain number of barbers, launderers, garage mechanics, school teachers, in addition to the workers actually employed in the activity that determined the location of the community. Even where the base activities may be more diffuse and hard to isolate from the unproductive ones, the same thing occurs.

Moreover, although earlier and poorer societies have more servants, later and richer ones more repairmen, salesmen, agents, teachers, doctors, lawyers, and government officials, the ratio of unproductive to productive workers seems to be roughly constant, at least for nonagricultural workers, over both time and space.[15] Therefore, the simplest and most realistic assumption about employment in sectors whose products cannot be traded seems to be that such employment represents a constant fraction of the total.

Appendix I at the back of the book lays out the information and the methods used to construct Figure II-10. In this example, the United States data prepared by Leontief describe a world economy consisting of member countries which trade freely together. Figure II-10 shows only two sets of specialization boundaries: that representing the situation in which country A, one of the trading partners, has all $(VWPSQ)$ and that in which it has none of the world's specific factors (RZU). The reader may, with the aid of Figure II-9, imagine boundaries corresponding to other possible distributions of natural resources between country A and the rest of the world.

Notice how narrow are the equalization regions for country A

[15] For data on the relative constancy of the ratio of employment in services, trade, and transportation to total employment, see Simon Kuznets, "Quantitative Aspects of the Economic Growth of Nations, II: Industrial Distribution of National Product and Labor Force," *Economic Development and Cultural Change*, 5:3–111, supplement (July 1957). For Kuznets' explanation of why income per capita does not seem to affect the percentage of the labor force engaged in services, see esp. pp. 13–17.

in this empirical example. They would, it is true, be somewhat wider if it were possible to construct Figure II-10 from as many subprocesses as in fact exist. Particularly striking is the narrowness of the equalization region $WQSP$. Table II-A, in Appendix II, shows that the regions' narrowness does not stem from a small

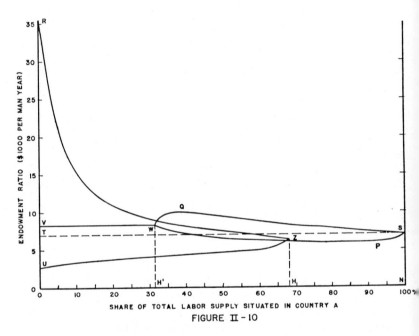

SHARE OF TOTAL LABOR SUPPLY SITUATED IN COUNTRY A

FIGURE II - 10

range of capital-labor intensities, nor from the insignificance of employment in sectors exhibiting extreme ratios, but rather from the large employment in the Group III activities, the products of which cannot be traded and which therefore must be performed in each country regardless of its capital-labor endowment.[16]

The narrowness of the equalization regions indicates that if endowment ratios of capital to labor differ very much, specialization should occur. Since the range of endowment ratios among nations is considerable, it is safe to conclude that, under free

[16] This indicates, in accordance with note 3, that trade in these products would be very beneficial.

trade, much more specialization and foreign investment would occur. The chapters to follow attempt to show that the manner in which commercial policies are applied prevents this from happening.

III

RELATIVE FACTOR ENDOWMENTS
AND AMERICAN FOREIGN TRADE

THE preceding chapters concentrated upon a particular presentation of the Heckscher–Ohlin trade theory. I have attempted to provide a simple yet comprehensive way of handling problems involving many goods, many factors, and many different kinds of factors. It should be possible to measure relative factor endowments of countries and to apply the Heckscher–Ohlin theory to indicate the lines of comparative advantage, which public and private intervention so often obscures, and of advantageous factor movements. This and the following chapters attempt to apply this idea. My purpose, then, is to help bridge the frustrating gap between theory and reality and to show that the Heckscher–Ohlin theory is not only realistic, but also leads to useful and perfectly straightforward conclusions.

THE LEONTIEF TEST

The only extensive attempt to test empirically the Heckscher–Ohlin theory has been made by Wassily Leontief.[1] He began with the following hypothesis: a country will tend to export commodities which are intensive in its relatively abundant factors and to import those which are intensive in its relatively scarce ones. Leontief observed that the United States, by common consent, has more capital per worker than its trading partners and reasoned that it must therefore export capital-intensive, and import labor-intensive, commodities.

Leontief tested this hypothesis by measuring the amounts of capital and labor services in American exports and competitive imports. He found that each million dollars' worth of exports con-

[1] "Domestic Production and Foreign Trade: The American Capital Position Re-examined," *Economia internazionale*, 7:9–38 (February 1954); and "Factor Proportions and the Structure of American Trade: Further Theoretical and Empirical Analysis," *Review of Economics and Statistics*, 38.4:386–407, appendix 3 (November 1956).

tained more labor services, and less capital services, than a million dollars' worth of competitive imports would require if they were produced in the United States. From this, he concluded that the United States must have less capital per worker than the rest of the world. The paradox caused an uproar similar in both tone and content to that which accompanied the factor-price equalization theorem. All of the important theoretical explanations were advanced early in the controversy and, since about 1956, no significant new ones have appeared. Although the old explanations have been abundantly reworked, no systematic attempt has been made even to eliminate those which are mutually inconsistent. The result has been, instead, a surprising and, in view of its importance, disappointing readiness to accept any explanation whatsoever. As a result, an admirable theory and method of empirical study stand in jeopardy.

In the present relative calm of this almost entirely theoretical controversy, the most respectable opinion seems to be that more empirical work is required. But what kind of further verification is wanted? Caves, the modern reviewer of general-equilibrium trade theory, praises the "excellence of Leontief's work as far as it goes," but goes on to say that "the Heckscher–Ohlin model has not yet come close to having a full-scale testing. Perhaps some day a supercharged economist with supersonic calculating equipment backed by a supersaturated foundation will perform this task." Until this happens, he claims, "there is no deprecating the sort of look-see verification of the Ohlin model done by Ohlin himself."[2] This position ignores, on the one hand, the magnitude of the effort already made and pretends, on the other, that a tiny, or look-see, assessment (such as, tropical countries export tropical commodities) is quite safe and even commendable, that only a gigantic effort can equal it, and that anything in between is destined to fall into error.

Despite the large number of words written on the subject, the exact nature of Leontief's test and of what it tested has not been well understood. The many fallacies and implausibilities of the current explanations bear witness to this statement. It is best,

[2] Richard E. Caves, *Trade and Economic Structure* (Cambridge, Mass., 1960), p. 282.

therefore, to begin with a discussion of the pure logic of the test and of the nature of the inferences that can be drawn from it. The simple two-commodity, two-factor case helps to introduce the subject, though it must give way finally to more general assumptions. The diagrams and discussion of the last two sections of the first chapter can therefore serve as the starting point.

Figure III-1 essentially repeats Figures I-3 and I-7; it shows, as they did, the factor space $X_1^A M X_2^B N$, for a hypothetical world possessing $X_1^A M$ units of F_2 (capital) and $X_1^A N$ units of F_1 (labor). In addition, the factor space is divided into regions which reveal the distinctive patterns of production in the two countries, A and B. If the world is an integrated economy, with free factor movements and trade, its transformation curve, derived from the world contract curve as explained in the last section of Chapter One, is $(a'')(p'')(b'')$. If world tastes are such as to establish production at the point (p'') on the world transformation curve, they will also establish production at the point P'' on the world contract curve. The equalization region is the parallelogram, $X_1^A P'' X_2^B Q''$. So long as the division of factors between countries A and B, as indicated by a point such as $X_2^A \ (= X_1^B)$, falls within the equalization region, $(a'')(p'')(b'')$ will continue to be the world transformation curve, and (p'') or P'' the world consumption and production points.

The Leontief test infers from a country's trade structure, and from the capital-labor intensities of its industries, its relative endowments of capital and labor. Suppose that production takes place within the world equalization region and that tastes are the same in country A and country B. If X_1^B lies above the diagonal, $X_1^A X_2^B$, but still within the equalization region, $X_1^A P'' X_2^B Q''$, both countries will produce x_1 and x_2, but country A will export x_2, the relatively capital-intensive commodity in Figure III-1. If X_1^B lies below the diagonal, so that A is the relatively F_1 (labor)-rich country, it will export the labor-intensive commodity x_1. Thus the diagonal of the equalization region distinguishes two separate areas with different patterns of trade, as a result of different factor endowments in each country. If factor endowments coincide with any point on the diagonal, no trade will take place.

Leontief's test will correctly infer the relative factor endowments of the countries if the point dividing the world's factors
falls anywhere within the equalization region. In the two-

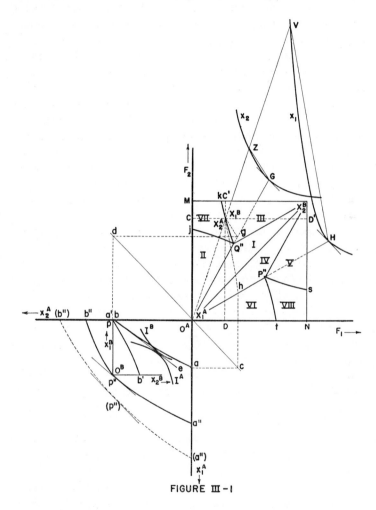

FIGURE Ⅲ−I

commodity case, however, if tastes in the two countries are not
identical, this statement must be altered. The indifference curves
in the third quadrant of Figure III-1 are drawn so that country

A prefers x_1, the labor-intensive good, while country B prefers x_2, the capital-intensive good. Therefore, unless these differences in taste are exactly reflected in the factor endowments of the two countries, trade will take place. In general, trade may proceed between two countries with different tastes even if factor endowments lie along the diagonal, $X_1{}^A X_2{}^B$. As a result, the Leontief test would indicate that the factor proportions differ between the countries when in fact they are the same.

A curved line (not shown), lying entirely on one side or the other of the diagonal, $X_1{}^A X_2{}^B$, will be the no-trade line when tastes in the two countries differ. It will still divide, of course, all points at which one country is in fact labor-rich from those at which it is capital-rich, relative to the other country. There will be consequently a crescent-shaped area to one side of the diagonal in which the Leontief test will give the false inference.[3]

Suppose that $X_2{}^A$ lies on the segment $X_1{}^A Q''$ of the specialization boundary $X_1{}^A P'' X_2{}^B Q''$. Country A will produce only and therefore export x_2, the F_2-intensive commodity. Country B, however, will produce both x_1 and x_2. If $X_2{}^A$ lies on the segment $Q'' X_2{}^B$, country B will produce only and export x_1, while country A produces both commodities and continues to export x_2. At Q'', both countries will specialize completely.

Now suppose that $X_2{}^A$ moves outside the equalization region toward the point M. The world transformation curve then becomes $a'' p'' b''$, rather than $(a'')(p'')(b'')$, and shrinks toward the origin O^A as factor prices diverge more and more in the two countries. As it separates from the original world transformation curve, it also breaks into two discontinuous segments, $a'' p''$ and $p'' b''$, as the last section of Chapter One explained. In Figure III-1, the dotted construction lines show how the position of point p and therefore of p'' derives from the position of $X_2{}^A$.

As long as the world terms-of-trade line pe intersects country A's and country B's transformation curves, ab and $a'b'$, at their extremities, b and a', country A will specialize on x_2 and country B will specialize on x_1. Whenever pe becomes tangent to country

---

[3] Other consequences of relaxing the assumption of identical tastes are examined below.

A's transformation curve ab at b, country A will start to produce x_1 as well. The line $Q''k$ is the locus of all points at which country A is operating at point b on its transformation curve producing only x_2 but, because of its increased size relative to country B, is on the verge of producing x_1 as well. In the same way, whenever pe becomes tangent to country B's transformation curve $a'b'$ at a', country B will cease to specialize. The line $Q''j$ is the locus of all points at which country B is on the verge of producing x_2 because of its increased size relative to country A. So throughout the region $Q''jMk$, marked VII in the diagram, each country specializes on one commodity, just as at Q''. The region fans out toward M because, as factor endowments become more and more extreme, the transformation curves' slopes at point b, or a', where each country specializes, diverge more and more.

The half of the factor space, $X_1{}^A M X_2{}^B N$, lying above the diagonal is therefore divided into four distinct regions. In region I, country A and country B both produce some of each commodity. If tastes are the same in both countries, A will export x_2 and import x_1 everywhere in that region. In region II, country A will produce, and therefore export, only x_2. Country B will produce both commodities and will export x_1. In region VII, country A will produce only, and will export, x_2; country B, only x_1. In region III, country A will produce something of each commodity, and will export x_2; country B will produce and export x_1 only. Identical reasoning indicates the patterns of specialization and trade that will prevail in the four regions below the diagonal, as shown in Table 1.

If factor endowments are distributed anywhere in regions I or IV, and tastes are identical, the Leontief test will correctly infer the relative factor endowments of either country from its exports and imports, and from the observed factor intensities of its domestic industries. It will prove impossible to make the test in regions VII and VIII because the investigator will have capital and labor coefficients only for exports; there will be no import-competing industry to provide coefficients for the sectors whose products are imported. Whether the test is possible in the other regions depends upon which country is being tested. If country A

TABLE 1. *Patterns of Specialization and Trade*

Region of Figure III-1	Country A products	Country B products	Country A exports
I	x_1, x_2	x_1, x_2	x_2
II	x_2	x_1, x_2	x_2
III	x_1, x_2	x_1	x_2
IV	x_1, x_2	x_1, x_2	x_1
V	x_1, x_2	x_2	x_1
VI	x_1	x_1, x_2	x_1
VII	x_2	x_1	x_2
VIII	x_1	x_2	x_1

is being tested, and the point describing its factor endowments lies in regions III or V, so that it is producing both goods, the test will be possible and will give the correct inferences. The corresponding regions for country B are II and VI.

In all regions in which the test is possible, therefore, it responds correctly in the above two-commodity, two-factor case when tastes are identical. Obviously this will hold true only under the assumption that the governments of both countries pursue neutral commercial, monetary, fiscal, and antitrust policies. Either country could export either good, regardless of its relative factor endowments, if it were willing to apply a sufficiently high subsidy to either its production or its exportation. In some instances, a domestic excise tax would have the effect of similarly altering the trade pattern. On the other hand, tariffs or other import restrictions could not, in the world of Figure III-1, upset the validity of the Leontief test. Rather, they would very likely render it possible in those regions in which, under free trade, the country being tested would completely specialize. If country A's factor endowments lay within region II, for example, the Leontief test would normally fail, as explained above, for lack of an import-competing industry. But a protective tariff policy would remedy that shortcoming. The investigator would then have the customs officials to thank for artificially encouraging the inappropriate industry, thereby enabling him to know something about his country's relative endowments of capital and labor.

CHANGES IN FACTOR-INTENSITY RANKING
AND THE LEONTIEF TEST

Many theorists have suggested that isoquants display such wide variations in the elasticity of factor substitution that the ranking of commodities by factor intensity will vary in different countries with changes in relative factor prices. Rice is among the most capital-intensive goods in the United States economy, they may point out, where capital is cheap and labor dear, and yet it is among the most labor-intensive in Asia, where labor is relatively cheap. These writers have emphasized that such a consideration may well explain Leontief's paradox.[4] The impression is rife that if commodities change factor-intensity ordering when factor prices change, the Leontief test is likely to be falsified.

In reality, special assumptions have to be made in order to obtain that outcome, and it is extremely improbable on purely theoretical grounds that intensity changeovers can have been responsible for Leontief's results. To illustrate this, it is necessary to begin with the two-commodity case, into which mold, unfortunately, the main theoretical controversy has been forced. The method here can be the same as that used above: it consists in dividing the factor space into various zones or regions and examining the results of Leontief's test in each one of them.

The relevant factor space was shown in Figure I-4. The particular examples in that figure showed two different worlds, one capital-rich and the other labor-rich, lying on either side of the ray X_1T, whose slope gave the critical factor-intensity ratio where the production isoquants for both goods, x_1 and x_2, have identical slopes. In Figure III-2, the F_2/F_1 ratio for the world exceeds the critical ratio, X_1^4T, and so x_1 is the capital (F_2)-intensive good if there is only one country. It is not necessarily true, however, that the F_2/F_1 ranking of goods will be the same

[4] See R. W. Jones, "Factor Proportions and the Heckscher–Ohlin Model," *Review of Economic Studies*, 24:1–10 (1956–1957); Kelvin Lancaster, "The Heckscher–Ohlin Trade Model: A Geometric Treatment," *Economica*, n.s., 24:32–39; H. G. Johnson, "Factor Endowments, International Trade and Factor Prices," *Manchester School*, 25:270–283 (September 1957); and R. F. Harrod, "Factor-Price Relations under Free Trade," *Economic Journal*, 68:245–255 (June 1958).

in each of all pairs of countries. The various possibilities are illustrated in Figure III-2. The slope of $X_1{}^A T$, as that of $X_1 T$ in Figure I-4, gives the critical ratio and is equal to the slope of $X_2{}^B V'$. If the point $X_2{}^A (=X_1{}^B)$ (not shown in Figure III-2), dividing world factor supplies, lies anywhere between these two

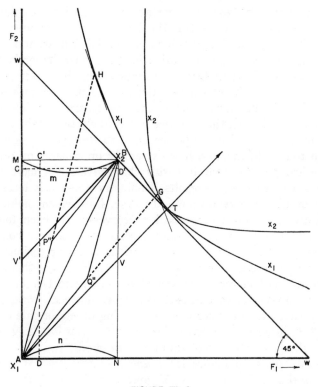

FIGURE III-2

lines, the F_2/F_1 ratio in each country will exceed the critical ratio. Therefore, within the area $X_1{}^A V' X_2{}^B V$, the ordering of goods by factor intensity will be identical for both countries. That area can be divided into the same eight regions as the entire factor space in Figure III-1, and the Leontief test will produce the same results in those regions.

But what of the space outside $X_1{}^AV'X_2{}^BV$? In the region $V'MX_2{}^B$, country A sees x_1 as the F_2-intensive commodity, but country B sees it as F_1-intensive, relative to x_2. It is clear that ambiguities could arise if one applies Leontief's test to one or the other country in this region. Whether or not the test actually yields erroneous inferences in this area, or for that matter in the correspondent area $VNX_1{}^A$, will depend upon the pattern of trade between the two countries. The easiest way to visualize the various possibilities is probably, as Lancaster suggests,[5] to begin with the set of cases in which (1) units are so chosen that the critical ratio is equal to one; (2) isoquants of x_1 and x_2 are chosen which are tangent to one another at the point T; and (3) the two sets of isoquants are assumed to be perfectly symmetrical about the ray, $X_1{}^AT$.[6] These conditions are fulfilled in Figure III-2.

A Theorem of Inverse Points must be substituted in this instance for the Theorem of Corresponding Points, which has formed the basis of the discussion so far. Figure III-3 shows Edgeworth boxes for two countries, A and B. These boxes are arranged so that their corresponding sides are parallel. The sum of the factor supplies, indicated by the lengths of those sides, is equal to total world supplies. The isoquant maps are those of Figure III-2; that is, they are symmetrical about the critical ratio. Further, the factor-endowment ratios of the two countries lie on opposite sides of the critical ratio (not shown), so that Figure III-3 refers to the *critical region* of Figure III-2, $V'MX_2{}^B$, if X_1 corresponds to $X_1{}^A$, or $VNX_1{}^A$ if X_1' corresponds to $X_1{}^A$.

Let P' be a point on the contract curve of, say, country B. Draw, in the box X_1CX_2D then representing country A, a ray, X_1H, whose slope is equal to the inverse of the slope of ray $X_1'P'$ in country B's box. Angle HX_1C in A's box will then be equal to angle $D'X_1'P'$ in B's. Also draw a ray, X_2G, inverse to $X_2'P'$; that is, so that angle GX_2C equals angle $P'X_2'D'$. Then the point P, lying at the intersection of X_1H and $X_1'G$, is the inverse point of P' in country B and has the following properties.[7]

[5] Lancaster, p. 23.

[6] If one folds Figure III-2 along the ray $X_1{}^AT$, the left-hand segment of each isoquant will be juxtaposed to its right-hand segment.

[7] See Lancaster, p. 37.

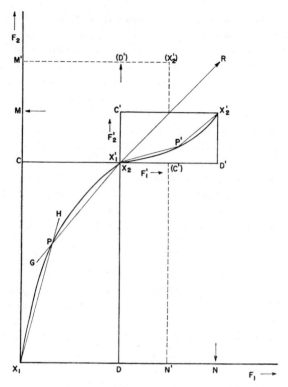

FIGURE III - 3

(i) If P' is on the contract curve of country B, then P is on the contract curve of country A.

(ii) The marginal productivity of F_1 in the production of both commodities at point P in country A is equal to the marginal productivity of F_2 in the production of both commodities at point P' in country B, and a similar inverse relationship holds between the marginal productivity of F_2 at P' and the marginal productivity of F_1 at P.

(iii) The commodity price ratio is the same at P as at P'.

Property (ii) above follows directly from the properties of inverse rays through the origin when isoquants are symmetrical.

In Figure III-3, imagine for a moment that X_1' is superimposed on X_1, and therefore that the ray $X_1'P'$ passes through X_1. Since the F_2/F_1 ratio along the ray X_1P is equal to the F_1/F_2 ratio along X_1P', the critical ratio, which was made equal to one by a felicitous choice of units, bisects the angle formed by these two rays. By symmetry, tangents to the x_1 isoquants at the points where they are cut by X_1H in Figure III-2 form the same angle with the F_2 axis as do the tangents, at points where those isoquants are cut by X_1P', with the F_1 axis. Thus, since the slope of one country's tangent to the x_1 isoquant is the inverse of the other's, the ratio of marginal productivities in one country will also be equal to the inverse of that ratio in the other. The same is true of x_2 and can be proved in a similar manner. It also follows directly because, by definition, the ratio of marginal productivities is the same in either industry all along the contract curve of either country.

Property (i) above holds because, if P' is on the contract curve of country B, then the ratio of the marginal productivity of F_1 to that of F_2 in x_1 is the same as the ratio of the marginal productivity of F_1 to that of F_2 in the production of x_2. Since each of these ratios at P' is the inverse of its value at P, the equality still holds at P, which therefore must be on A's contract curve. The commodity-price ratio in either country is given by the ratio of the marginal physical productivity of one of the factors in one industry to that factor's marginal physical productivity in the other industry. Since P is on A's contract curve, the above ratio will be the same for either factor at P; that is, $MPPF_{11}/MPPF_{12} = MPPF_{21}/MPPF_{22}$. By property (ii), $MPPF_{21}/MPPF_{22}$ is equal to $MPPF_{11}'/MPPF_{12}'$, the primes denoting values at P'. Consequently, $MPPF_{11}{}^A/MPPF_{12}{}^A = MPPF_{11}{}^B/MPPF_{12}{}^B$.[8]

The above theorem yields the necessary first clue about the way in which the two critical regions, $V'MX_2{}^B$ and $X_1{}^ANV$, in Figure III-2 are structured. In Figure III-3, the F_2/F_1 ratio in one country is the inverse of that ratio in the other country, so that $X_1C/X_1D = X_2D'/X_2C'$. Since the production isoquants for x_1 and x_2 are symmetrical, $F_1{}^A$ does the same work as $F_2{}^B$, and $F_2{}^A$

---

[8] This proof is essentially the same as Lancaster's on pp. 37–38.

as $F_1{}^B$.[9] In all other respects, the assumptions of the two diagrams are the same. As a result, countries A and B in effect have the same factor proportions. If in addition they also have identical tastes, they will have no occasion to trade. In Figure III-2, any point along the diagonal, $X_1{}^A X_2{}^B$, divides the world box into two similar rectangles, or two countries with identical factor proportions. If the two countries also have identical tastes, then, the diagonal is a *no-trade line*. In the same way, X_1' in Figure III-3 is a *no-trade point*, formed by two similar but *inverse* rectangles.

By geometry, whenever the division of world factors creates two inverse rectangles, the point describing this division lies in one of the critical regions where factor-intensity crossovers can occur. The locus of all points which divide the world into two inverse rectangles is a hyperbola. Examples of such hyperbolae are indicated by the curves, $MmX_2{}^B$ and $X_1{}^A nN$, in Figure III-2.[10]

The following construction should help to clarify this. Take a point, X_2 in Figure III-4, which divides the world factor space, $X_1 M X_2' N$. Draw a line through this point at an angle of forty-five degrees. Let this line meet the horizontal boundary, $X_2'M$, at R. Through R, draw a vertical line which meets the forty-five-degree line, $(X_2')X_2'$ at (X_2'). The rectangle $X_2(D')(X_2')(C')$ will then be the inverse of the rectangle $X_1'C'X_2'D'$. The new box, $X_1M'(X_2')N'$, defines a *pseudo-factor space*. Draw the diagonal, $X_1(X_2')$, of this pseudo-factor space. If X_2, the given point, lies on this diagonal, as it must if it divides the pseudo-factor space into similar rectangles, it lies on the no-trade line. The locus of the no-trade line in the original factor space can now easily be determined from the construction. Let (X_2') slide along the forty-five-degree line, $X_2'(X_2')$. The no-trade line is traced out by the intersection of the forty-five-degree line, Rqp, as point R moves along MX_2', and the line $X_1(X_2')$. This locus is represented by $MmX_2{}^B$ in Figure III-2, if the primed variables of Figure

---

[9] It also follows, of course, that one unit of capital in one country earns what one unit of labor does in the other.

[10] Let A and B stand for the lengths of the sides of any rectangle, and let these sides lie along the x and y axes, respectively. The two curves, giving all points which divide the world box into two inverse rectangles, are then described by $y/x = (A - x)/(B - y)$. In general, this will describe an hyperbola; in the special case where A equals B, it describes the diagonals of a square.

III-4 refer to country B, or by $X_1{}^AnN$ if they refer to country A.

The next problem is to see what happens on either side of these hyperbolic no-trade lines.[11] Which country will export which product? Lancaster suggests that trade patterns, when the factor

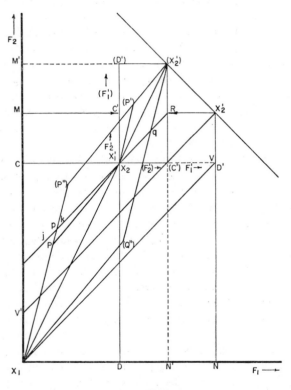

FIGURE III-4

proportions of one country are the inverse of those of the other, can be analyzed conveniently by reference to one country and the inverse of the other; that is, to the symmetrical case.[12] Rotate the Edgeworth box for one country about the forty-five-

---

[11] They are no-trade lines, analogous to the diagonal, $X_1{}^AX_2{}^B$, of Figure III-1 on the assumption of identical tastes.

[12] Lancaster, p. 39. They could also be analyzed by means of diagrams like those of Figures I-5, I-6, I-7, and III-1.

degree line through X_1' $(=X_2)$, as explained above, and in addition, using the isoquants of Figure III-2, construct a *pseudo-equalization region*, such as $X_1(P'')(X_2')(Q'')$ in Figure III-4, within the pseudo-factor space. Then the Theorem of Corresponding Points indicates which country will export which good in exactly the same manner as in the normal cases.

If the point describing the division of the world's factors between countries A and B lies to the left of the diagonal, but within the pseudo-factor space, reference to Figure III-1 and Table 1 shows that the country with X_1 as its origin will export x_1, its capital- or F_2-intensive good, and the other country will export x_2, its labor- or F_1-intensive good. Because in the inverse case F_1^A corresponds to F_2^B, the second country effectively exports its F_2-intensive good as well.

Consider now points p and q in Figure III-4 and what happens when X_2 coincides with either, or lies between them. Notice first that since they lie on the boundaries of the pseudo-equalization region, $X_1(P'')(X_2')(Q'')$, they must lie outside the true equalization region; in fact, they must, by construction, lie within the critical region,[13] $V'X_2'M$. Second, notice that they lie at the intersections of the pseudo-equalization-region boundary and the forty-five-degree line Rqp. Now let (X_2') again slide along $X_2'(X_2')$. Once more, the intersection of Rqp and $X_1(X_2')$ will trace out the no-trade hyperbola. At the same time, q and p trace out their own curves. Since within the pseudo-equalization region neither country specializes on either good, the segment qp, excluding its termini, must be a nonspecialization locus. By the same reasoning, q and p, lying on the specialization boundaries, must be specialization points. Thus the loci of points traced out by p and q as (X_2') moves along $X_2'(X_2')$ must represent specialization boundaries in the critical region, $V'X_2'M$, of the true factor space, $X_1MX_2'N$. Since qp must lie everywhere between these loci, the area between them must be a nonspecialization region. This nonspecialization region may also be styled, in the symmetrical case, an *alter-equalization region*, because within it the price of capital in one country is equal to the price of labor in the other and neither country specializes completely.

[13] This corresponds to the critical region, $V'X_2^BM$ of Figure III-2.

These loci are shown in Figure III-5. The line $MmX_2{}^B$ in that diagram is one of the no-trade lines, while $Mk'pkX_2{}^B$ is the p locus, and $MqX_2{}^B$ the q locus. Because of the assumed symmetry of the x_1 and x_2 isoquants, it is perfectly legitimate to draw the corresponding loci on the other critical region, $X_1{}^A VN$, of Figure III-5. If $X_1{}^A$ is the origin for the capital-rich country, country A in Figure III-4, the portion of Figure III-5 above the diagonal

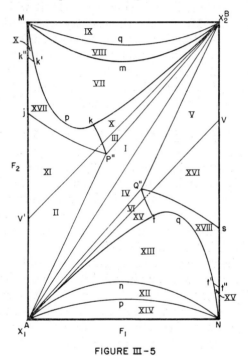

FIGURE III-5

is obtained; if $X_1{}^A$ refers to the labor-rich country, the section below the diagonal is mapped out.[14]

[14] Although the boundaries of the alter-equalization regions and their no-trade lines are analogous to the corresponding specialization boundaries and diagonal of Figure III-1, there are important differences between the sets of curves. Relative factor prices, for example, remain the same in each country along the normal no-trade line of the earlier diagram, whereas they change along those of the latter. As $X_1{}^B$ moves along $X_2{}^B mM$ of Figure III-5, the price of F_2, say, starts out equal in both countries. At M, however, it has become zero in country A and infinite in B. Similar things happen along all the curves between $X_2{}^B$ and M, $X_1{}^A$ and N.

Now suppose that p originally lies along $(P'')(X_2')$ in Figure III-4 and that $X_2 (=X_1')$ coincides with p. As X_2 moves away from p and outside the pseudo-equalization region, the transformation curve for the country whose origin is at X_2 will move out from its origin. For a while, that country will continue to specialize on x_2, but at some point, j on Rqp, when the slope of its transformation curve at the x_2 axis becomes equal to the slope of the world terms-of-trade line $a'e$ (Figure III-1), it will take up the production of x_1. Meanwhile, the country whose origin is at X_1 originally produced both x_1 and x_2. As its transformation curve contracts, however, it will produce a larger quantity of x_1 relative to x_2, until finally it specializes entirely on x_1. This will happen at some point, k on Rqp, which will be located between p and j if p lies along $(P'')(X_2')$, or will coincide with p if p lies along $X_1(P'')$.

The lines $P''j$ and $P''kpk'k''$ in Figure III-5 show the loci of these points, j and k. How far the alter-equalization region, $X_2{}^Bkpk'Mq$, intrudes into the area $P''jk''k'pk$, or whether it even reaches it, is determined by the shape of the market-demand curves and production functions in the two countries, and by the factor endowments of the world. In the other critical region, $X_1{}^AVN$, of Figure III-5, there are corresponding loci, marked $Q''s$ and $Q''tqt't''$. Along the line $Q''s$, country A produces only x_2, but it is on the verge of producing x_1, which it will do the moment relative factor endowments place X_1' (in Figure III-4) above the line $X_1{}^AQ''s$. Country A's position along $Q''s$ is thus identical to that of B's along $P''j$; just below that line B begins to produce x_1. Meanwhile, country B concentrates on x_1 as long as X_2 (in Figure III-4) lies above $Q''tqt't''$ and to the right of $X_2{}^BQ''$, but undertakes the production of x_2 the instant that point crosses $Q''tqt't''$. So between the lines $Q''tqt't''$ and $Q''s$, as well as between jP'' and $P''kpk'k''$, each country specializes.

The various zones, in which distinctive trading patterns emerge when a single factor-intensity crossover is assumed, are indicated by Roman numerals and separated by solid lines in Figure III-5. If the assumption of mirror-symmetrical isoquants, under which Figure III-5 is drawn, is relaxed, the shapes of the various regions will change, but their identity and general character will not.

For example, the no-trade lines, MmX_2^B and $X_1^A nN$, will no longer describe sections of hyperbolae, and the factor space of Figure III-5 will no longer be divided into regions perfectly symmetrical about the diagonal, $X_1^A X_2^B$. These properties are not essential, however.

TABLE 2. *Patterns of Specialization and Trade with Their Leontief Test Inferences*

Region of Figure III-5	Country A products	Country B products	Country A exports	Leontief test		
				Correct	Incorrect	Impossible
I	x_1, x_2	x_1, x_2	x_1	A, B		
II	x_1	x_1, x_2	x_1	B		A
III	x_1, x_2	x_2	x_1	A		B
IV	x_1, x_2	x_1, x_2	x_2	A, B		
V	x_1, x_2	x_1	x_2	A		B
VI	x_2	x_1, x_2	x_2	B		A
VII	x_1, x_2	x_1, x_2	x_1	A	B	
VIII	x_1, x_2	x_1, x_2	x_2	B	A	
IX	x_1, x_2	x_1	x_2		A	B
X	x_1, x_2	x_2	x_1	A		B
XI	x_1	x_1, x_2	x_1		B	A
XII	x_1, x_2	x_1, x_2	x_1	A	B	
XIII	x_1, x_2	x_1, x_2	x_2	B	A	
XIV	x_1	x_1, x_2	x_1		B	A
XV	x_2	x_1, x_2	x_2	B		A
XVI	x_1, x_2	x_1	x_2		A	B
XVII	x_1	x_2	x_1			A, B
XVIII	x_2	x_1	x_2			A, B

Table 2 summarizes the patterns of production and of trade according to the different regions of Figure III-5. The last three columns indicate the expected results of Leontief's test if it were applied in each of the regions which Figure III-5 distinguishes. By a kind of Abelardian *sic et non* process, one can judge the test by counting the number of regions in which it either gives the correct, or abstains from giving any, answer, against the number of regions in which it gives a false answer for one or the other of the two countries.

In regions I–VI, X, and XV, if the test responds, it always gives the correct answer, although in X and XV this is only because the specializing country happily disqualifies itself from the test. It is precisely regions I–VI, X, and XV, moreover, which expand in size at the expense of all others, as the world F_2/F_1 ratio diverges more and more from the critical ratio. A sufficient divergence of these two ratios, with appropriate demand conditions, could eliminate regions XI and XVI which, along with IX and XIV, are the most troublesome, since they either give the wrong answer or none at all.

In all regions where an answer emerges for both countries, at least one will be correct. This means that the test can never say, for example, that country A is F_2-rich and country B is F_1-rich when in fact the opposite is true. If applied in both countries, the test will either be correct for both or give an inconsistent set of answers. In only two cases would the existence of import restrictions further reduce the test's score. If in region XV, country A restricted imports of x_2 sufficiently to allow a domestic x_2 industry to grow up, the test would give the wrong answer for A, whereas without such restrictions it would give no answer at all. The same would hold in XV if country B restricted imports of x_1, and of course similar results would prevail in region X. In both regions XVII and XVIII, import restrictions could make the test possible in either country, and in that case the test would give correct answers.

Suppose for the moment that country A is the only country in which the test is applied. Under free trade, even though factor intensities do cross over with changes in relative factor prices, the test could mislead only if the world factor space were divided in region VIII, IX, XIII, or XVI. Of these, XIII and XVI are eliminated if A is capital-rich.

Two secondary considerations reduce the likelihood that falsification could occur. One is the possible existence of more than one critical ratio. This would increase the number, and total size, of areas in which the factor-intensity ranking is the same as in the area $X_1^A V' X_2^B V$, and thus would reduce the area within which the Leontief test can go astray. The second is the possibility of factor migration. Around points M or N, factor prices will diverge fiercely between the two countries, resulting in strong migratory pressures. Mobility of either factor between countries will tend to move the point dividing the factor space into the equalization region where, of course, the Leontief test will always give correct answers. In the real world, factors never move with perfect mobility among countries, but they move. The migrating factors will tend to avoid frontier areas such as regions IX and XI. Those who claim that Leontief's paradoxical findings are attributable to factor-intensity crossovers must also justify the unlikely argument that the test was applied in one of these frontier regions.

The likelihood that factor-intensity crossovers explain the Leontief paradox suffers even more when the confines of the two-commodity case are sundered. The previous analysis carries over into the many-commodity cases only under the assumption that one critical ratio serves for all possible crossovers. Now, consider cases in which any given pair of isoquants may cross or be tangent in more than one place — that is, cases in which they exhibit more than one critical ratio. If all such ratios lie very close to one another, they may be considered the same, and the above analysis will still apply. In other words, where the critical ratios are identical or nearly so, Leontief's test will either be correct, if the point distributing factors lies inside the equalization region or in some other region that checks out in Table 2; impossible, because of complete specialization and lack of import-competing industries; or incorrect, because the point lies in one of the frontier regions previously described.

The weakest assumption is that critical ratios occur at widely varying angles when many commodities are considered, and that the isoquants for these commodities exhibit a multitude of factor-substitution elasticities. Figure III-6 samples the variety that one might find. For graphical simplicity, it has been made symmetrical about the forty-five-degree line, OT, but this does not amount to a special assumption.

The isoquants for x_1 and x_5 have high factor-substitution elasticities along certain portions and lower elasticities along others. This pair of isoquants has two critical ratios, one between the point v and OT, the other between v' and OT. The other five isoquants are cornered, but nothing essential is changed if one imagines the corners to be slightly rounded. Further, imagine that world tastes and factor endowments are such that, if no separate countries existed or if all factors were perfectly mobile among countries, the world F_2/F_1 ratio would be as indicated by the slope of OT, and the world equilibrium factor-price ratio by the slope of ww. Finally, let two countries be distinguished such

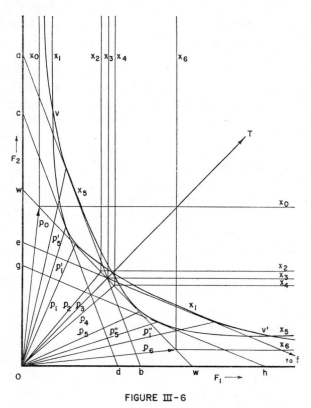

FIGURE III-6

that factor prices in one equal the slope of the tangents, ab (or cd), and in the other the slope of ef (or gh). The factor intensities of the various goods in the two countries are indicated by the slope of the rays marked with ρ's through the origin. If unprimed, the ρ's refer to the value of the F_2/F_1 ratio in a world undivided; if primed, to their value in the capital-rich; and if double-primed, to their value in the labor-rich country. When the ρ's remain the same in all three circumstances, they are not distinguished separately.

TABLE 3. *Commodities by F_2 rank*

F_2 rank	0	1	2	3	4	5	6
F_2-rich country	x_0	x_5	x_1	x_2	x_3	x_4	x_6
Undivided world	x_0	x_1	x_2	x_3	x_4	x_5	x_6
F_2-poor country	x_0	x_2	x_3	x_4	x_5	x_1	x_6

The rank of the commodities by their F_2 intensity in these three situations is shown in Table 3. Imagine first that only x_1 and x_5 exist, and that x_5 is the relatively F_2-intensive good in both the F_2-rich and F_2-poor countries. The Leontief test would always yield the correct inference in this case, even though, because of the multiplicity of critical ratios between x_1 and x_5, for the world as a whole x_5 is F_1-intensive relative to x_1. Now consider x_3 along with x_1 and x_5. In this case, the F_2 rank of the three goods is different in all three rows. As a result, the test may give an incorrect inference.

If the value of x_3 per million dollars of trade is small relative to that of x_1 and x_5, however, it is obvious that its ability to reverse the test findings based on the other two goods alone is also small. If, for instance, x_1 accounts for 90 percent, and x_2 for 10 percent, of the imports of the F_2-rich country, and this country exports x_5 exclusively, the Leontief test would correctly conclude that it was in fact F_2-rich, even if the test used the commodity F_2 ranking of the F_2-poor country. If, on the other hand, x_3 is an important part of world trade, the ambiguity remains. Since, however, x_1 and x_5 enjoy the same rank relative to each other in both the F_2-rich and F_2-poor countries, they can be treated as one aggregate commodity for comparison with x_3. Now x_5-x_1 is F_2-intensive relative to x_3 in the F_2-rich country, and vice versa in the F_2-poor country. But exactly the same problem arose in the two-commodity case, analyzed earlier in this chapter, so its treatment here bears no further elaboration.

Next, introduce x_2 and x_4. Since they always bear the same close F_2-rank relationship to x_3 in all three rows of Table 3, x_2, x_3, and x_4 may also be considered as a single aggregate commodity. Thus, whenever separate commodities appear close together and in the same order in all F_2 ranks, they may be treated as a single commodity, thereby simplifying the problem.

Finally, admit x_0 and x_6. They maintain the same ranking throughout the table, basically because their cornered isoquants have the same factor intensities for all relevant factor-price ratios. The Leontief test would always give the correct inference on the basis of x_0 and x_6 alone. In addition, since their factor proportions differ by such a marked degree, this will be true despite the introduction of goods exhibiting factor-intensity crossovers, unless x_0 and x_6 are quite small fractions of world trade. So those who advance intensity crossovers as an explanation of the Leontief paradox are also making another implicit assumption: either the isoquants of goods whose factor proportions are relatively constant over wide ranges of relative factor prices tend to cluster near some central ratio, such as OT, or goods with relatively constant factor proportions are an unimportant fraction of world trade. Otherwise, the inclusion of these goods will lend a crucial stability to the Leontief results.

Actually the first assumption is implausible: cornered isoquants tend to exhibit extreme factor proportions. Much raw-material preparation and processing, for example, is everywhere performed by heavy and expensive machinery, with a few skilled technicians providing the labor services required. Oil is refined, and most basic chemicals are processed, in large plants, into which raw materials flow in steady streams and out of which the finished product flows continuously. The intermediate processing is largely automatic. Most products with fixed coefficients require such equipment; in addition, the requirements of heat, pressure, speed, or electrical current are such as to render impossible any but a highly capitalized method of fabrication. At the same time, processes such as finishing, designing, engineering, tailoring, fitting, inspecting, adjusting, and the like, require the diligent attention of human operatives. Products requiring many such operations will be universally labor-intensive. In many cases, as urged in the preceding chapter, several processes can be distinguished in the production of a given final good, and these intermediate processes may exhibit more extreme factor intensities. In addition, certain final goods may become profitable only when factor prices reach certain extreme ratios. These will add exports intensive in the abundant factor to the trade of each country, thereby increasing the presumption that the Leontief test will respond correctly.

EMPIRICAL STUDIES BEARING ON FACTOR-INTENSITY RANKING

The preceding section has provided a strong theoretical presumption that factor-intensity crossovers among countries with different relative factor prices could not have been responsible for Leontief's perverse results. At this point it would be desirable to present detailed empirical evidence to support the theoretical conclusions. Unfortunately, the empirical work on this subject is not, so far, conclusive by itself. Two studies, admittedly incomplete, do tend to corroborate rather than contradict my theoretical analysis.

M. A. Diab cites a study which attempted to rank comparable industries in four countries according to their capital-labor ratios. The results, presented in Table 4, indicate that, in spite of a considerable variation in capital-labor ratios employed by the same industries in different countries, the ranking of these industries according to their ratios is similar.

Leontief measured the factor endowments of the United States relative to its trading partners by comparing the factor content of its exports and import-competing industries. Presumably, he could also have compared the factor content of its cheap and expensive goods, relative to those of other countries, for where trade is restricted the price of the same good in countries with different factor endowments will not be the same. For instance, if international commerce encounters resistance,[15] capital-intensive goods will be cheaper in capital-rich than in capital-poor countries. Lorie Tarshis has made this alternative study for the

[15] Such resistance includes primarily shipping and transport costs, tariffs, import quotas, exchange restrictions, and the like. Import and export subsidies should also be included if they act against the natural direction of trade, as when a capital-rich country subsidizes exports of labor-intensive, or imports of capital-intensive, goods.

TABLE 4. *Capital-Labor Ratios in Various Industries in Various Countries*
(in thousands of dollars per man)

Industry	U.S.A.		Mexico		Colombia		India	
	Ratio	Rank	Ratio	Rank	Ratio	Rank	Ratio	Rank
Flour and grist- mill products	39.1	1	10.4	2	19.9	1	5.6	4
Iron and steel	32.1	2	10.8	1	5.4	6	5.7	3
Sugar refining	26.8	3	8.2	5	12.4	3	2.6	6
Alcoholic beverages	16.0	4	6.6	6	18.0	2	6.1	2
Starch	—	—	9.4	—	3.8	—	3.3	—
Tobacco	12.4	5	8.6	4	2.0	9	—	—
Woodpulp, paper, paper products	10.2	6	8.9	3	4.8	8	6.6	1
Cotton yarn and cloth	8.7	7	2.1	9	6.2	4	1.8	7
Rubber products	7.0	8	3.4	8	6.1	5	—	—
Printing and publishing	5.1	9	3.5	7	5.1	7	—	—
Bread and bakery products	5.0	10	1.7	10	1.3	10	3.5	5

Source: M. A. Diab, *The United States Capital Position and the Structure of Its Foreign Trade* (Amsterdam, 1956), p. 36.

United States, the United Kingdom, the Soviet Union, and Japan.[16] He compared the prices of a large number of commodities in each of the countries, then calculated the average United States labor-capital ratio for the relatively cheap and relatively expensive categories. His results, shown in Table 5, indicate that, of the four countries studied, the cheap goods in the United States use the least labor per unit of capital, whereas, with the dubious exception of England (which has relatively high wages), its expensive goods use much more.

Tarshis, unlike Leontief, obtained the expected result — that the United States is capital-rich relative to other countries. But like Leontief, Tarshis used United States factor proportions throughout. If factor-intensity crossovers did occur between the United States and the other countries, his results would have

[16] Lorie Tarshis, "Factor Inputs and International Price Comparisons," *The Allocation of Economic Resources*, ed. Moses Abramovitz and others (Stanford, 1959), pp. 236–244.

TABLE 5. *Average Value of the Ratio of Man-years per Unit of Capital
($10,000) for Commodities According to Their Comparative Prices*

Commodity prices	U.S. ratio of labor to capital	Ratio of ratios
Expensive in U.S.	1.416	
Cheap in U.S.	0.842	1.682
Expensive in U.K.	1.426	
Cheap in U.K.	1.026	1.390
Expensive in U.S.S.R.	0.889	
Cheap in U.S.S.R.	1.070	0.831
Expensive in Japan	0.844	
Cheap in Japan	1.477	0.571

Source: Lorie Tarshis, "Factor Inputs and International Price Comparisons," *The Allocation of Economic Resources*, ed. Moses Abramovitz and others (Stanford, 1959), p. 241.

been falsified in the same way as Leontief's. Factor-intensity crossovers are more likely to occur the more widely relative factor endowments differ. Since Japan is the most labor-rich of the four countries he compared, and since Tarshis' study correctly indicated that Japan was substantially labor-rich relative to the United States, it provides a compelling argument that factor-intensity crossovers are not sufficiently important in other countries to have falsified Leontief's test. Tarshis commented on his findings as follows:

I believe the results are significant, partly because they suggest, unlike Leontief's, that the factor to which Heckscher and Ohlin first drew attention is indeed relatively important, even though its influence in specific instances may be offset by other factors. . . . Our attention is directed to differences in patterns of prices rather than to trade flows. In this connection, it is worthwhile to point out that, insofar as it is possible to locate trade figures for items for which prices in the United States are unusually high or low, there is no evidence for the relationship between prices and trade that we should normally expect. Instead, a number of high priced items are exported— commonly to Canada, Latin America, Japan, and the Philippines, while a number of distinctly low priced items are imported.[17]

Here is a truly curious phenomenon. Tarshis observed that in some instances the pattern of trade is not only independent of, but in some cases directly contrary to, the pattern which relative

[17] Tarshis, pp. 238 and 244.

goods prices would indicate. The correspondence he found between goods prices and factor endowments means that Leontief was mistaken in assuming that trade flows resulted primarily from differences in those factor endowments. It follows that Leontief's results were falsified not by any failure of the theory he set out to verify, but by forces which artificially distort the trading patterns predicted by the theory. These artificial forces are, of course, the very trade restrictions which permitted Tarshis to observe substantial differences in the prices of the same good in different countries. This explanation will be thoroughly examined later. First it is necessary to review the other conventional rationalizations of Leontief's paradox.

COMPLEMENTARY FACTORS AND THE LEONTIEF TEST

The two most prevalent explanations of the Leontief paradox are probably the one discussed in the preceding sections and one centering on the importance of factors of production not included in the test. This section will continue in the vein of the preceding and show that, according to the Heckscher–Ohlin theory, excluded factors alone could not have caused the results Leontief obtained.

One version of the argument, advanced by M. A. Diab and by Jaroslav Vanek, points out that activities depending upon natural resources generally employ considerably more capital per worker than other activities do, and that the United States is a net importer of the products of such activities.[18] An inspection of Figure II-10 and Appendix Table II-A will reveal that such activities are indeed capital-intensive. Moreover, if such activities are eliminated from Leontief's classification, so that imports corresponding to them are considered noncompetitive, the test applied to the remaining sectors gives the expected answer — that

[18] Diab, *The United States Capital Position and the Structure of Its Foreign Trade* (Amsterdam, 1956), pp. 46–50. Vanek, "The Natural Resource Content of Foreign Trade, 1870–1955, and the Relative Abundance of Natural Resources in the United States," *Review of Economics and Statistics*, 41:152–153, chart 3 and conclusions (May 1959).

United States imports are more labor-intensive than its exports.[19]

Diab explains that "the *differential* in the capital intensities of import replacements and exports in general . . . is only due to the fact that the highly capital-intensive non-manufacturing group of industries enjoys, percentage-wise, a higher weighting in import replacements than in exports, namely sixty-five percent versus fifteen percent respectively."[20] But why do these products constitute so much higher a percentage of competitive imports? Diab explains this in part by invoking the United States's supposed poverty of relevant natural resources.[21]

Vanek measured the resource-product inputs (it proved unfeasible to measure natural-resource inputs directly) of United

TABLE 6. *Domestic Capital, Labor, and Natural-Resource Requirements per Million Dollars' Worth of American Exports and Competitive Import Replacements, 1947*

Requirement	Exports	Imports
Capital (dollars)	2,550,780	3,091,339
Labor (man-years)	182.313	170.004
Natural-resource products (dollars)	340,000	630,000

Source: Jaroslav Vanek, "The Natural Resource Content of Foreign Trade, 1870–1955, and the Relative Abundance of Natural Resources in the United States," *Review of Economics and Statistics*, 27:152 (May 1959).

States imports and exports. His results, shown in Table 6, lend credence to Diab's suggestion. Vanek comments as follows:

The results [in Table 6 here], plus the fact that capital appears strongly complementary to, and labor substitutable for, the natural resource factor in the cross-section of American industries, lead to an important conclusion: it may well be that capital is actually a relatively abundant factor in the United States. Yet relatively less of its productive services is exported than

[19] Leontief, "Factor Proportions," calculation D, table 1, p. 398. Calculation D has been made for roughly the same sectors as are included in Groups II and III in Appendix II at the end of this book.

[20] Diab, p. 50.

[21] Diab, p. 50. The other part of his explanation is that the vastness of United States territory makes it more profitable in some cases to import raw materials, etc., from overseas than to ship the long distances overland. But this argument cuts both ways: distance should lead to more exports of such materials as well.

would be needed for replacing our imports, because resources, which are our scarce factor, can enter productive processes only in conjunction with large amounts of capital.[22]

Diab's and Vanek's explanation of the Leontief paradox touches as much at the roots of the entire Heckscher–Ohlin theory as does Robinson's attack on the ambiguity of the concept of production factors. They say in effect that, if a country lacks certain factors, it may be obliged also to import services of other factors that it may possess in abundance. This in turn would mean that, even if one knew the relative factor endowments of countries, he would have to know the whole complicated system of complementarities and substitutabilities among factors and products in order to predict trade patterns. In other words, he would need little less than perfect knowledge of all economic processes. Such an explanation resolves the paradox by eliminating the theory, rather than by explaining Leontief's results.

But factor endowments, according to the Heckscher–Ohlin theory, determine the level as well as the composition of trade. Each unit of a raw material may require a large amount of capital per unit of labor employed in its production — but this does not mean that each million dollars' worth of imports necessarily does. Thus, if certain products which must be imported contain the services of its abundant factor, a country need only increase its imports of products containing the services of its scarce factor (and export more products containing its abundant factor) in order to obtain the proper factor ratios in its trade flows. For instance, if the working up of the raw material into finished products is relatively capital-intensive, re-exportation of the final product will carry out more capital relative to labor than the original importation and there will be no problem. If the contrary is true, the country could reduce the average capital intensity of its imports by importing the raw material in finished form. It could also dilute whatever capital-intensive raw materials it continued to import directly by expanding its imports of labor-intensive products while exporting more of its most capital-intensive products.

This much follows from Chapter Two, which formulates the

[22] Vanek, p. 153.

Heckscher–Ohlin theory in terms of the equalization region using two general and any number of specific factors (including natural resources). An equalization region would exist, moreover, even if all activities not depending on specific resources were less capital-intensive than those which did. Refer again to Figure II-10. The equalization region for the United States would be *RZU*, while that for the rest of the world, possessing all of the specific resources, would be *VWQSP*. In the case just cited, however, the horizontal line *VW* will lie above point *R* on the vertical axis. The area *WQSP* will then slope downward from *W* to *S*, which meets the right-hand vertical axis at the world capital-labor ratio. If United States factor proportions are represented by a point within the area *RZU*, the theory will of course correctly infer its relative factor endowments from its trade structure, even though its imports include the capital-intensive specific resources. On the contrary, even if the point lies outside the equalization region, as the second section of this chapter shows, the theory would correctly infer actual endowments from the trade structure unless substantial factor-intensity crossovers occurred. But the second and third sections of this chapter effectively eliminate that possibility.

The existence of complementary third factors does not, therefore, destroy the ability of the Heckscher–Ohlin theory to explain a country's production and trade structure. Because Leontief was obliged to use the American input-coefficient matrices rather than those of the world as a whole, third factors could theoretically have falsified his calculation. This circumstance could arise when a country specializes because its relative factor endowments lie outside the specialization boundaries. It would arise if the industries using its specific resources and whose products it imported were more capital-intensive, on the average, than the Group I and Group II products exported. Any industry based on a specific factor would continue to operate at some level in the country despite foreign competition, since its production function would be homogeneous of degree less-than-one in the allocable factors. But the same is not true of Group II industries. If there are two allocable factors, for instance, and if factor endowments lie on a specialization boundary or outside the equalization region or any possible alter-equalization regions, none of the Group II industries will exist in country A, except the least labor-intensive one, to give rise to any competitive imports.[23] The noncompetitive imports of their products will nonetheless represent imports of the labor and capital that the rest of the world devotes to them. Leontief's calculation, by eliminating noncompetitive imports, will miss these factor service imports. If the competitive Group I imports happen to be capital-intensive and are imported because of the country's paucity in their specific resources, the Leontief calculation will be incorrect.

These circumstances cannot be responsible for Leontief's results, however, because they do not all hold. All Group II products, including the most labor-intensive, showed competitive imports, whereas the explanation requires that no more than one competitive Group II sector exist. Moreover, the noncompetitive products he excluded — tropical commodities like tea, bananas, coffee, jute, and ores not found in American mineral deposits — are clearly not Group II but rather Group I products depending on natural resources lacking in the United States.[24]

The capital-labor intensities of these noncompetitive Group I products are still relevant, however, as the next section shows more clearly. Even though their imports bring in the services of resources unavailable in the United States, they also bring in labor and capital services and these, just as much as those brought in by competitive imports, affect the relative scarcity of factors in the United States. If noncompetitive Group I products are capital-intensive, their imports would cause the United States to export capital-intensive products and to import labor-intensive products. But Leontief's calculation, since it cannot observe the amount of capital and labor services hitching rides on noncompetitive imports, cannot indicate the direction in which observable competitive trade is being affected.

Competitive Group I products are capital-intensive, on the average. If noncompetitive ones are also, Leontief's actual calculation would have tended to come out in the expected way. If noncompetitive Group I imports explain the paradox, therefore,

[23] Cf. Figures II-5 through II-9 and Chapter Four.
[24] See Leontief, "Factor Proportions," pp. 392, 395.

it can be only because they are strongly labor-intensive and would be so in the United States if the United States had the specific resources to produce them. This explanation amounts to another special assumption, because only the accidental lack of the required specific resources, and not the labor intensity of the noncompetitive Group I products, can account for their non-competitiveness. If competitive Group I industries are capital-intensive, there is a presumption that noncompetitive ones are as well. There is no reason to suppose, for instance, that a tin mine is more labor-intensive than a copper mine simply because tin ore is not found in the United States while copper ore is. It is nonetheless necessary to recognize that noncompetitive imports have perhaps affected Leontief's results one way or the other, because he could not observe their labor and capital content, and to qualify his statement that ignorance of production methods not actually used in the United States cannot affect the ability of his calculation to explain the observed situation.[25] The next chapter considers the possible effects of noncompetitive imports on Leontief's findings.

FACTOR ENDOWMENTS AND TRADE FLOWS

Answering Leontief's remaining critics requires formulating the equalization region in terms of domestic commodity outputs. While this necessitates an algebraic formulation,[26] it also permits generalizing the equalization region to include any number of allocable and specific factors.

The net output, q_j of commodity j in any economy is equal to:

$$q_j = \psi_j(F_{1j}, \ldots, F_{rj}; x_{1j}, \ldots, x_{nj}) - \sum_{i=1}^{n} x_{ji} \ (j = 1, \ldots, n) \quad \text{(i)}$$

where F_{kj} $(k = 1, \ldots, r)$ is the amount of factor k and x_{ij} $(i = 1, \ldots, n)$ is the amount of commodity i which industry j uses directly, and x_{ji} is the amount of commodity j which industry i uses. The production function

[25] Leontief, "Factor Proportions," p. 392.
[26] Appendix I explains the system of notation and gives definitions of all newly introduced variables in detail.

$$x_j = \psi_j(F_{1j}, \ldots, F_{rj}; x_{1j}, \ldots, x_{nj}) \quad (j = 1, \ldots, n)$$

gives the gross output of commodity j and is assumed to be homogeneous of degree one and the same in every country. The Leontief system,

$$q = (I - A')x \qquad (1)$$

where q and x are, respectively, column vectors of the n-net and n-gross commodity outputs, A' is the $n \times n$ matrix of coefficients $a_{ij}' = x_{ij}/x_j$, and I is the identity matrix, relates the net to the gross outputs.

Because each production function in (i) is homogeneous of degree one, it is possible, according to Euler's theorem, to multiply each of its arguments and x_j by the same constant. Multiplying by $1/x_j$ expresses the production function in terms of its unit isoquant:

$$1 = \psi_j(F_{1j}', \ldots, F_{rj}'; a_{1j}', \ldots, a_{nj}') \quad (j = 1, \ldots, n) \quad \text{(i)}'$$

where $F_{kj}' = F_{kj}/x_j$. The optimal coefficients which enter (i)' at equilibrium depend on the relative input prices:[27]

$$F_{kj}' = F_{kj}'(p_{o1}, \ldots, p_{or}; p_1, \ldots, p_n) \quad \text{and}$$
$$a_{ij}' = a_{ij}'(p_{o1}, \ldots, p_{or}; p_1, \ldots, p_n) \quad (i = 1, \ldots, n),$$
$$(j = 1, \ldots, n), (k = 1, \ldots, r).$$

These coefficients will accordingly be the same in every country facing the same relative input prices.

Factor supplies must equal factor demands in every country making the best use of its resources. Therefore,

$$F_k = \sum_{j=1}^{n} F_{kj} = \sum_{j=1}^{n} F_{kj}'x_j \quad (k = 1, \ldots, r). \qquad \text{(ii)}$$

Let F be the column vector of the r elements F_k and let F' be the $r \times n$ matrix of input coefficients F_{kj}'. Equations (ii) may then be rewritten as follows:

$$F = F'x = F'(I - A')^{-1}q. \qquad \text{(ii)}$$

Any two countries constitute an integrated economy only if

[27] See below, Chapter Four, for the formal demonstration of this and for a complete exposition of the world general equilibrium underlying the trade model.

their input coefficient matrices are identical, that is, only if $A'^A = A'^B$ and $F'^A = F'^B$. This simply states the Theorem of Corresponding Points in the general case of intermediate goods, r factors, and n commodities. Each country's share in the common supply of each factor and its output of each commodity will not affect total joint output of any commodity in the two countries so long as it can produce, according to (ii), nonnegative amounts of each commodity under the common set of optimal input coefficients applying to both countries. Thus, if the superscript W refers to the world as to an integrated national economy, the world equalization region can be derived from the vector:

$$F^A = F'^W x^A \qquad (1)$$

where $0 \leqq x_j^A \leqq x_j^W$ and $0 \leqq F_k^A \leqq F_k^W$. System (1) describes the equalization region lying in r-dimensional factor space.

Inverting system (1) shows how country A's production structure varies with its factor endowments under factor-price equalization:

$$x^A = (F'^W)^{-1} F^A \qquad (2)$$

where $(F'^W)^{-1}$, or simply F'^{W-1}, is the inverse of the matrix F'^W. If commodities are more numerous than factors, country A's production structure will be partly indeterminate. Therefore, to obtain a square, invertible, submatrix of F'^W, outputs of $n - r$ commodities must be assigned either to country A or to country B. The assignment of outputs is perfectly arbitrary within the limits set by the fixed common output of each commodity, the countries' fixed amounts of each factor, and the fixed input coefficients. Country A's net-output vector, as a function of its factor supplies, will be:

$$q^A = (I - A'^W) F'^{W-1} F^A.$$

Notice that the net outputs of some commodities could well be negative.

Country A's imports or exports, t_i^A, of commodity i equal the difference between its net output, q_i^A, and its final demand, r_i^A:

$$t_i^A = r_i^A - q_i^A = r_i^A - x_i^A + \sum_{j=1}^{n} a_{ij}'^W x_j^A \qquad (i = 1, \ldots, n).$$

Let r^A be the column vector of the amounts of the n commodities going to final demand, $r_i{}^A$. Country A's trade flows vary with r^A and F^A alone when F'^W and A'^W are fixed; that is, when factor endowments lie within the equalization region:

$$t^A = r^A - (I - A'^W)F'^{W^{-1}}F^A. \tag{3}$$

The n equations in system (3) are simply balance equations which hold when factor endowments lie within the world's equalization region. Premultiplying system (3) by $F'^W(I - A'^W)^{-1}$ yields r balance equations expressing country A's foreign trade in terms of the physical amounts of the various primary factors' services that it trades with the rest of the world:

$$F'^W(I - A'^W)^{-1}t^A = F'^W(I - A'^W)^{-1}r^A - F^A. \tag{4}$$

System (4) may be abbreviated by defining $F_{t_k}{}^A$ as the amount of factors k's services which country A imports (exports are negative imports) and by defining $F_{r_k}{}^A$ as the amount of factor k's services which A's final demand contains. Let $F_t{}^A$ equal $F'^W(I - A'^W)^{-1}t^A$ and $F_r{}^A$ equal $F'^W(I - A'^W)^{-1}r^A$. They are the column vectors corresponding to these two definitions. Notice that the vector $F_r{}^A$ does not distinguish the national origin of the factor services which country A consumes; $F_r{}^A$ really contains the total amounts of each factor working for A. The factor-service trade vector, $F_t{}^A$, measures country A's net trade in the factor services. It and country A's factor endowment vector, F^A, show how A's own factor supplies and those of the rest of the world enter its final demand.

Suppose the vector $F_r{}^A$ to be proportional to the world endowment vector F^W (or the world vector of primary factor consumption, $F_r{}^W$) so that $F_r{}^W$ equals diag wF^W where diag w is a scalar matrix of the coefficient w, equal to the ratio between country A's national income and that of the world. The factoral balance of trade vector, $F_t{}^A$, then gives an accurate indication of country A's factor endowments relative to those of the world as a whole. Because the separate factor-service trade accounts in $F_t{}^A$ derive from the independent balance equations of (4), they accurately measure the factor content of competitive imports despite any possible complementarities among the various factors in production. It is perfectly legitimate, therefore, to look at the trade balance in any factor's services (in that of labor or capital, for instance) without bothering with any of the other accounts. Country A's endowment vector F^A is presumably known, and $F_t{}^A$ is easily calculated. Thus the crucial term in judging relative factor endowments is $F_r{}^A$, the estimate of world relative factor endowments.

Leontief's measurement of American factoral trade was essentially identical to that of system (4). He was unable to use the physical input coefficients, $F_{kj}{}'$ and $a_{ij}{}'$, and had instead to use observable input coefficients in value terms. Instead of $a_{ij}{}'$, he used a_{ij}, equal to $p_i a_{ij}{}'/p_j$. The matrix A of these coefficients is equal to diag pA' diag p^{-1} where diag p is a diagonal, $n \times n$, matrix of the commodity prices. Instead of $F_{kj}{}'$, Leontief used the coefficient $f_{kj}{}'$, equal to $F_{kj}/x_j p_j$, which in turn equals $F_{kj}{}'/p_j$. The matrix f' of these coefficients is equal to F' diag p^{-1}. Substituting these matrices into system (3) and expressing trade flows and consumption in value units at world prices transforms (3) into:

$$\text{diag } p^W t^A = \text{diag } p^W r^A - (I - A^W) f'^{W^{-1}} F^A. \tag{5}$$

Premultiplying system (5) by $f'^W (I - A^W)^{-1}$ yields system (4):

$$F_t{}^A = F_r{}^A - F^A. \tag{4}$$

Leontief begins with the balance equation

$$(I - A)x = \text{diag } yb - \text{diag } zc + r$$

where diag y is a diagonal matrix of the scalar y and diag z a diagonal matrix of the scalar z.[28] These scalars represent, respectively, the value, in 1947 United States dollars, of total United States exports and competitive imports. The coefficient b_i in the column vector b is the proportion which exports of commodity i bear to total exports, and the coefficient c_i in the column vector c is the proportion which imports of commodity i bear to total competitive imports. The vector (diag zc − diag yb) is therefore equivalent to diag $p^W t^A$ if the difference between

[28] Cf. "Factor Proportions," p. 402. In comparing his formulation with the one presented here, I have changed his notation slightly to make the two consistent.

American and world prices can be ignored. The vector x contains the gross domestic commodity outputs and the vector r the domestic final consumption, both valued at United States prices. They are thus equivalent to diag $p^W x^A$ and diag $p^W r^A$ if the difference between American and world prices can be ignored. Finally, if American and world prices are the same or, alternatively, if their differences do not affect the value input coefficients, Leontief's matrix A is equivalent to A^W. Premultiplying system (2) by diag p^W shows that diag $p^W x^A$ equals $f'^{W^{-1}} F^A$. Leontief's trade-balance equation is then essentially system (5), but with diag $p^W x^A$ substituted for $f'^{W^{-1}} F^A$. Leontief multiplies his balance system by $(I - A)^{-1}$ and by the rows of direct capital and labor coefficients. This double multiplication is, of course, equivalent to multiplying through once by $f'^W (I - A^W)^{-1}$ if the input coefficients in f'^W are the same as those observed in domestic production.

Leontief's test is therefore capable of unraveling the factor content of a country's trade — provided that the country's factor endowments lie within the equalization region and that trade is free so that domestic and world prices, and domestic and world input coefficients, are the same or at least comparable. The test measures relative factor endowments under these assumptions, in addition to the assumption that F_r^A is an unbiased estimate of relative world factor endowments and that noncompetitive imports can be ignored.

This conclusion eliminates the possibility that some characteristic of input-output analysis falsified Leontief's results. Stefan Valavanis-Vail claims that the assumption of fixed input coefficients, in physical terms, makes input-output analysis inappropriate for the study of international trade, where all countries gain and employ their resources fully.[29] Although this assertion is true, it is irrelevant here since Leontief did not need to assume input proportions fixed; his test merely observes an equilibrium which has been established and makes no statement

---

[29] "Leontief's Scarce Factor Paradox," *Journal of Political Economy*, 62:523–524 (December 1954); and "Comment on Leontief's Factor Proportions and American Trade," *Review of Economics and Statistics*, 40:111–113 supplement (February 1958).

regarding any other configuration. It requires only the assumptions of the equalization region and can take prevailing factor proportions for granted.

Diab has criticized Leontief for not eliminating from United States imports the value which its factors might have added in the form of prior raw-material exports.[30] He suggests reformulating international trade theory in terms not of the products, but of the units of each nation's factor services that are traded. He would not count, for example, the total value of an exported United States automobile tire, but only the value which its factors added to it directly and indirectly. If the tire used natural rubber, all of which was imported, the value of the rubber would not be counted. If it used cotton cord produced overseas from American raw cotton, the value of the raw cotton would be included, but not that created by transforming it into cotton cord. Diab claims that this method, which unfortunately he does not formulate precisely, would yield results different from Leontief's.[31]

But the above comparison also effectively dispenses with Diab's criticism by showing that Leontief's calculation actually does accomplish this task. System (4) records trade flows in terms of the domestic factor services which country A and the rest of the world exchange. American capital services that are exported in raw cotton, for example, are counted when the cotton leaves the United States. If it is reimported in the form of more nearly finished products, the use of direct-plus-indirect coefficients automatically ensures that the capital exports originally counted will be netted out on the import side so that no double counting takes place.

Finally, several writers have stressed that trade patterns will not accurately reflect relative factor endowments if the structure of final demand differs among countries.[32] In the two-commodity case this is always true. Where many goods and factors are involved, however, the argument is far less compelling.

---

[30] Diab, chap. iv.

[31] Diab, pp. 59–60, 63–65, 67.

[32] Robinson, "Factor Proportions: I," pp. 184–87; Valavanis-Vail, "Leontief's Scarce Factor Paradox," p. 525; and Jones, pp. 2–5.

First, when countries consume a multitude of commodities, tastes may vary among them, as they obviously do among different cultures at different levels and distributions of income, without causing differences in the demand for the broad generic factors, capital and labor. Second, even in the two-commodity case, factor endowments would have to be similar in the two countries, or tastes would have to vary greatly, in order to falsify the results of the test. In fact, however, the United States has much more capital per worker than any other country. Further, if United States final demand is factor-biased, there is reason to believe that this bias is toward labor rather than capital.[33]

A slightly different form of the Leontief test completely eliminates the possible influence of tastes. Instead of examining the factor content of traded items, one can compare directly the factor content of production among countries. If, on the one hand, the test based on production structures contradicts the results of Leontief's test, there is strong presumptive evidence that a marked preference in the United States for capital-intensive products explains it. If, on the other hand, the production test corroborates Leontief's findings, factor-biased tastes must be ruled out, for the United States would not maintain a labor-intensive production structure if it in fact preferred capital-intensive products and was capital-rich.

I tested these alternatives by comparing the factor contents of United States and French production. The known factor endowments of the United States (country A), F^A, are always equal to f'^A, its matrix of primary-factor input coefficients per dollar's worth of gross output, times the vector, diag $p^A x^A$, of its domestic gross output at its own prices. This in turn is also equal to its matrix of capital-labor ratios ρ^A, times its labor allocation

---

[33] A. J. Brown claims that United States consumption may be biased in favor of labor-intensive commodities. See Caves, *Trade and Economic Structure*, p. 275, n. 25. Romney Robinson points out that even if tastes are identical in two countries, but if indifference maps are not homothetic, differences in per capita national income may alter the factor content of consumption ("Factor Proportions: I," pp. 185–187). Since agricultural products, which are capital-intensive, weigh heavily in low-income consumption, it is likely that United States consumption is at least as labor-intensive as that of the rest of the world. If it is more so, the bias should have given the Leontief test a fillip in the right direction.

vector, $F_1{}^A$. A parallel situation exists for France (country B), and the following system emerges:

$$F^A = f'^A \operatorname{diag} p^A x^A = \rho^A F_1{}^A$$
$$F^B = f'^B \operatorname{diag} p^B x^B = \rho^B F_1{}^B. \tag{6}$$

It is now a simple matter to compare the capital and labor contents of United States and French production, using the right-hand expressions in system (6). For the United States, Leontief's data give the direct capital- and labor-input coefficients for 192 economic sectors, and these capital-labor ratios, $\rho_{2j}{}^A$, are reported in Appendix Table II-A. Detailed labor-input coefficients for France are also available.[34] If the ranking of industries by capital-labor ratios is approximately similar in the two countries, it is permissible, for the purposes of this test, to compute the implied French capital-input coefficients using the United States capital-labor ratios.[35] It was impossible to compare the two countries' production structures for the same year because the United States data are available only for 1947 and the French employment statistics were not compiled before 1956. This difference in time is probably not important, however, especially since the results are so striking that they can absorb a considerable margin of error.

Table 7 gives the essential results of the test (details are found in Appendix Table III). The French employment figures by industrial sectors were made, insofar as possible, to conform to the United States classification reported in Appendix II. In other instances, it was necessary to combine two or more United States sectors to correspond to the more aggregative French figure. It proved impossible to disaggregate Leontief's agricultural sector and impracticable to disaggregate the Group III services, owing to wide differences in classification between the United States and French sources. But the manufacturing and processing sectors were generally comparable, as were the mining activities.

The last line in Table 7 states that the average United States

[34] Ministère des Finances, "Les Salaires déclarés en 1957," *Statistiques et études financières*, 122:160–185 (February 1959).

[35] Since Tarshis' study found no significant factor-intensity crossovers between the United States and England, Japan, and Russia, it seems safe to rule out this possibility for France as well.

TABLE 7. *American and Implied French Capital-Labor Ratios*

	U.S. in 1947		France in 1956	
Group	Man-years	Capital (units of $10,000)	Persons employed	Imputed capital (units of $10,000)
Group I				
Agriculture, fishing, hunting	6,926,002	6,469,682	4,684,500	4,375,861
Capital-labor ratios	0.9341		(0.9341)	
Mining	886,921	1,179,952	337,300	249,460
Capital-labor ratios	1.3304		0.7396	
Total, Group I	7,894,027	7,695,021	5,021,800	4,625,321
Capital-labor ratios	0.9748		0.9210	
Group II				
Manufacturing and processing	17,132,831	10,980,856	4,966,360	2,940,684
Capital-labor ratios	0.6409		0.5921	
Group III				
Nontradables	22,246,668	14,176,042	9,580,840	6,105,112
Capital-labor ratios	0.6372		(0.6372)	
Totals	47,273,526	32,851,919	19,569,000	13,671,117
Capital-labor ratios	0.6949		0.6986	

Source: Appendices II and III.

capital-labor ratio is 0.6949 while that of France is 0.6986. The similarity of these ratios corroborates Leontief's paradoxical results. Factor-biased tastes cannot explain them. From Leontief's results alone, it is just barely possible that the average capital-labor ratio of United States final demand was greater than its average capital-labor endowment. If so, it would be obliged to import capital-intensive goods in return for more labor-intensive exports, even though it possessed relatively more capital per capita than its trading partners. This argument assumes nonetheless that the United States maintains the capital-intensive production structure consistent with its resource endowments. In fact, it appears that France, an important trading partner, possesses a relatively more capital-intensive production structure, even though it is indisputably less capital-rich than the United States. The best available estimate states that the stock of productive capital (not including residential housing) in France in 1950 was 18,500 billion 1950 francs.[36] This amount of capital was worth, at the maximum, about 62 billion 1947 U.S. dollars. Leontief's data state that the productive capital stock in the United States was 328 billion dollars, which in 1947 was associated with about 47 million man-years. The active population in France in the period 1944–1958 was 19,575,000,[37] which means that there was less than one-half as much capital per worker in France in 1956 as in the United States in 1947.

Table 7 shows that France has a much larger proportion of its working population engaged in agriculture. Since United States agriculture is highly capital-intensive, France's disproportionately large agricultural sector is entirely responsible for its higher average capital-labor ratio. Within the disaggregated manufacturing and mining sectors, on the other hand, France's capital-labor ratio is slightly lower than that of the United States. This means, of course, that within these sectors France produces a slightly more labor-intensive bundle of goods. This is what one would expect. It is surprising, however, that the tendency is not more pronounced. It is even more surprising that the United States devotes a larger, and France a smaller, proportion of its labor force to the Group II manufacturing sector, whose products on the average tend to be more labor-intensive than those of the rest of the economy.

France's relative abundance, and the United States's relative poverty, of resources specific to the capital-intensive Group I products does not readily explain these results. Mining in France not only employs a smaller proportion of the working population but, according to United States factor proportions, employs less capital per man-hour as well. Therefore it appears that France has a relatively smaller endowment of resources specific to mining in general, and especially of resources specific to the most capital-intensive forms of mining. Nor can the availability of agricultural land provide an explanation for France's much larger agricultural

[36] Jean Bénard, *Vues sur l'économie et la population de la France jusqu'en 1970* (Paris, 1953), p. 254.

[37] United Nations, Food and Agricultural Organization, *Production Yearbook* (Rome, 1959), p. 19.

population. There is little doubt that the United States possesses at least twice as much agricultural land per worker as France and that the United States's land is of at least comparable quality, especially for the major staple crops such as wheat, rice, and corn.

If one assumes that both France and the United States are producing almost entirely for the home market, Engel's law may help to explain their perverse production structures. It may well be that France's lower incomes imply a much larger percentage of agricultural products in consumption, while the United States's higher living standard permits a larger proportion of manufactured goods. In other words, France has relatively capital-intensive tastes and the United States has relatively labor-intensive tastes. But notice that this factor bias in consumption is the opposite of that proposed above to explain Leontief's results[38] and only serves to intensify the basic dilemma: because the United States is relatively capital-rich and France is relatively labor-rich, the United States should supply France (and other countries) with agricultural products in exchange for relatively labor-intensive manufactures.

OTHER EXPLANATIONS OF THE LEONTIEF PARADOX

Diab mentions that many of the United States's capital-intensive imports are in fact produced abroad with American capital equipment and productive techniques, and that this production should therefore be counted as part of the output of the domestic, rather than of the foreign, economy.[39] But, if the domestic economy were already highly endowed with capital, why would American capital, once overseas, not go into the most labor-intensive activities, where its productivity would be so much higher? It would seem, for instance, more profitable for the exported capital to engage cheap foreign labor to provide the home market with textiles, radios, clothing, and the like, along with petroleum, ore, and tropical commodities. Since exported

---

[38] By contrast, this explanation agrees entirely with Brown's and Robinson's reasoning. See above, note 33.

[39] Diab, pp. 53–56.

American capital goes primarily into capital-intensive activities, its existence compounds, rather than explains, Leontief's paradox.

Leontief explained his own results by claiming that one American worker is so far superior to his foreign counterpart that the United States actually possesses more labor than the rest of the world.[40] This explanation resolves some difficulties, but raises others. It could, for instance, explain the results obtained above by comparing the American and French production structures. On the other hand, it contradicts Tarshis' findings. If Leontief's explanation were correct, moreover, then according to the assumptions of the Heckscher–Ohlin theory the rate of interest on invested capital in the United States would have to be higher than in the rest of the world. The interest rate on capital is equal to its marginal physical productivity in producing capital goods. If production functions are the same, or differ only by a multiplicative constant, among countries, it is impossible for the interest rates in a capital-rich country to exceed those in a capital-poor country. Since the rate of interest in the United States is comparatively low, and since the United States has been an important net exporter of capital since the First World War, it is difficult to see how it could actually have less capital per unit of labor than the rest of the world.

The Leontief paradox, then, is still unresolved. None of the various explanations examined above provides a completely satisfactory solution; nor can these explanations be combined to dress a list of influences all working together to cause the phenomenon which Leontief observed. Suppose that common consent, which accords the United States much more capital per man-hour than the rest of the world, is correct. Does the United States really export more capital services than it imports, and does the Leontief test simply fail, because of some undetected fluke, to observe this? Or does the Leontief test correctly perceive that the United States really imports more capital services than it exports?

The analysis of this chapter rules out the first possibility. If relative factor endowments are the ultimate causes of international trade, Leontief's calculations are perfectly tailored to

[40] Leontief, "Domestic Production," pp. 25–29.

unravel their effects.[41] Tarshis found that, although differences in factor endowments among countries are accurately reflected in different goods prices, they do not in every case produce the trade flows which the theory predicts. The comparison of the production structures of France and the United States confirmed that relative factor endowments are not the main determinants of the direction of trade between these two countries. This supposition, then, appears to have been the common mistake in all previous investigations of Leontief's paradox. The lesson of that paradox is that some other force can play a more important role in determining the commodity and factoral composition of international trade. The next chapters will demonstrate how commercial policy plays precisely that role.

[41] Except for his unavoidable exclusion of noncompetitive imports.

IV

PROTECTION AND THE STRUCTURE OF PRODUCTION AND TRADE

THE preceding chapters have concentrated on the relationship between relative factor endowments and the structure of production and trade. This chapter and those to follow will consider commercial policy and factor endowments as codeterminants of the actual division of production among nations.

The application of protection responds to motives lying deep in the national consciousness. Every new state willingly sacrifices its trade with foreign nations in order to foster a budding domestic commerce. Old and established nations trade freely only with those areas which are either subject to their own laws, customs, and commercial practices or willing to adopt a common set of economic policies. The universality of protection testifies to its power effectively to divert trade from foreigners and to serve the sentiments of national, imperial, or, in some cases, international unity.

The most powerful rationalizations for protection reside in motives of national development and independence. The common aim of national commercial systems is self-sufficiency, achieved by producing domestically a greater number of goods which each nation consumes. Any industry, which the scarcity rather than absence of a factor of production would eliminate under free trade, can be established through the simple application of a duty on the imports of its products. Whether capital or labor is relatively abundant, therefore, any country can produce most manufactures. Unless its endowments of these two factors are extreme, moreover, it can do so with quite low tariffs and a comparatively small loss of economic efficiency.

It is quite easy to explain the tariff histories of most countries in these terms. Commodities may be ranked, at least roughly, according to the ability of developing countries to produce them. At the top of the list are textiles, handicrafts, apparel, toys, and the like, and at the bottom products requiring more capital and more technique. As new economies emerge, they will concentrate on the products at the top of the list. These industries in the older, more developed countries will then be subject to increased competition, and the people engaged in them will demand protection. This demand is all the more urgent since the factors engaged in the old industries in the developed country will be discouraged from entering the production of the newest goods at the bottom of the list. First, they and their equipment will be particularly unsuited to produce the newest goods. Second, the emerging nations, while attempting to usurp the market for the older goods, will often discourage imports of the newest products in order to establish domestic production of these goods as well. Nationalism, often the most developed attribute in these countries, requires that they be, above all, independent of the industrial countries for the most recent and thus the most prestigious items.

Subtler variations on the same theme also exist. Labor is more organized in the old than in the nascent economies, as is the political power of the established manufacturers. Restricting imports of labor-intensive and well-established products is a way of acceding to the interests of vociferous political sectors, by maintaining or raising their incomes without obliging them to adjust to changing economic conditions. The establishment of capital-intensive industries in underdeveloped and capital-poor countries, on the other hand, undoubtedly favors the most politically mature classes by providing opportunities to invest profitably without requiring that they break in a large and perhaps refractory labor force.

The aim of national self-sufficiency ultimately accentuates a country's dependence on the materials which it cannot produce at home. Securing these residual items becomes essential to satisfy that part of final consumption which cannot forgo them, or to feed the secondary industries established on national soil to work them up. Countries universally refrain from impeding these so-called essential imports, and the powerful countries expend great efforts to secure their foreign sources of supply and to keep them out of the hands of enemies and commercial rivals.

The instruments of protection are numerous but may be conveniently divided into two main types. The first contains all devices which tend to establish and maintain a differential between the home-market and foreign prices of articles: quantitative and selective exchange restrictions, customs duties and import subsidies, multiple exchange rates, administrative protection, export subsidies, private market restrictions, and export restrictions of various kinds. Public export subsidies require tariffs or other import restrictions to prevent reimports. Private producers, if they have a degree of monopoly over the home market, often provide their own export subsidies through price discrimination, but this too requires a tariff or other import restriction in order to work. The tariff thus permits such producers to sell at a higher domestic price than they could without it.[1]

The second type of protection consists of measures which encourage directly some domestic industries at the expense of others, but which do not in themselves create a disparity between the domestic and foreign prices of the affected commodities. Direct production subsidies and tax rebates are the simplest forms of such discrimination (and the only ones the following discussion treats). But other common policies, such as low-interest loans, liberal depreciation policies, subsidized or de-taxed inputs, and the like, obviously have effects similar to the payment of direct subsidies. Monopoly profits, moreover, are like

---

[1] Milton Gilbert found that export-price discrimination is fairly widespread and thus a confirmation of Yntema's theory that higher elasticities of demand in world than in domestic markets make dumping profitable: "In many cases it was stated that while some export sales would be possible at the domestic price, the lower export price results in so large an increase in sales that total profit on export is enhanced." Quoted in Richard E. Caves, *Trade and Economic Structure* (Cambridge, Mass., 1960), p. 281. See also Adam Smith: "That bounties upon exportation have been abused to many fraudulent purposes, is very well known. But it is not the interest of merchants and manufacturers, the great inventors of all these expedients, that the home market should be overstocked with their goods, an event which a bounty upon production might sometimes occasion. A bounty upon exportation, by enabling them to send abroad the surplus part, and to keep up the price of what remains in the home market, effectually prevents this. Of all the expedients of the mercantile system, accordingly, it is the one of which they are the fondest. I have known the different undertakers of some particular works agree privately among themselves to give a bounty out of their own pockets upon the exportation of a certain proportion of the goods which they dealt in. This expedient succeeded so well, that it more than doubled the price of their goods in the home market, notwithstanding a very considerable increase in the produce" (*Wealth of Nations*, p. 484).

discriminatory taxes which the monopolist levies on his own products and which he pays to himself.

The use of such fiscal methods to protect and encourage some industries, necessarily at the expense of others, is probably growing, even while the traditional use of tariffs and other trade restrictions may be diminishing somewhat. It is therefore necessary to show the relationship between the two main types of protection.

WORLD GENERAL EQUILIBRIUM UNDER PROTECTION

The introduction of protection changes the equilibrium production and consumption patterns, trade flows, and factor prices of the countries it affects. It does so by causing the relative prices facing producers and consumers to vary from country to country. Restrictions and encouragements acting directly on trade flows through tariffs, trade subsidies, or quantitative limitations make the common set of relative prices facing consumers and producers in one country differ from those of its trading partners. Discriminatory production taxes and subsidies produce the same relative prices for consumers in each country, but they introduce a divergence in prices faced by producers in different countries.

Figure III-1 presented in the last chapter can be adapted to show the effects of different commercial policies in the two-factor, two-commodity case. In that figure, under free trade country A will always specialize in the production of x_2, the F_2-intensive commodity, while country B will produce x_1 exclusively. Country A might decide to establish the production of x_1, or country B might decide to produce x_2. Figure IV-1 reproduces the third quadrant, the commodity space, of Figure III-1. It depicts a situation in which protection has caused the two countries to stop specializing completely as they did in Figure III-1 under free trade. Line pe of Figure III-1, the slope of which indicates the common commodity-price ratio in the two countries under free trade, has been replaced in Figure IV-1 by two lines whose divergent slopes indicate the price disparities imposed by protection. The slope of puc gives the ratio of the domestic price of

x_2 to that of x_1 in country A, and the slope of *pire* gives the corresponding ratio in country B.

Producers of either country, in maximizing their profits, adjust their outputs until the price lines are tangent to the country's

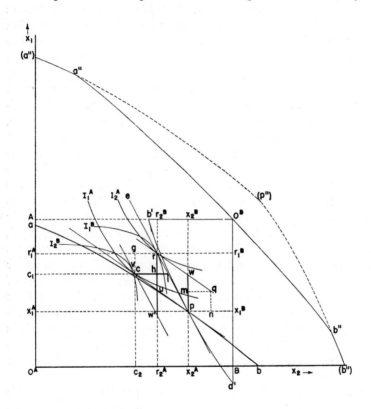

FIGURE IV-I

transformation curve. The common production point p on the transformation curve apb of country A and $a'pb'$ of country B indicates where internal production equilibrium occurs in each country. Country A produces $O^A x_2^A$ units of x_2 and $O^A x_1^A$ units of x_1, while country B produces $O^B x_2^B$ units of x_2 and $O^B x_1^B$ units of x_1. Consumers in country A trade from point p to point c, where puc is tangent to their market-demand curve, $I_1{}^A$. They demand O^Ac_1 units of x_1 and O^Ac_2 units of x_2. Consumers in country B meanwhile trade along $pire$ to its tangency with their market-demand curve, $I_1{}^B$, at r. There they consume $O^Br_1{}^B$ units of x_1 and $O^Br_2{}^B$ units of x_2. The failure of the two consumption points to coincide, as the production points do, derives from the governments' collection of customs duties or other trade taxes. Thus, if country B's people and government consume jointly at r, country A's people and government must consume at r as well and absorb $O^Ar_1{}^A$ units of x_1 and $O^Ar_2{}^A$ units of x_2. The determination of the two governments' shares will be explained later.

The transformation curve $(a'')a''O^Bb''(b'')$ in Figure IV-1 shows how much of each commodity the two countries will produce in common when the relative prices facing producers in each country differ constantly by the same factor, as at p. As p moves along apb and the slope of puc, kept tangent to apb, thus alters, that of $pire$ alters also, so that their slopes always differ by a constant factor. Country B's transformation curve, $a'pb'$, meanwhile slides up or down $pire$ until it is tangent to it at p. Its origin, O^B, then traces out the world transformation curve under the protection implied in the difference between the slopes of puc and $pire$. The coordinates of O^B, A and B, give the joint production of x_1 and x_2 respectively. The curve $(a'')a''(p)''b''(b'')$ in Figure IV-1 is the free-trade world transformation curve; it is the same curve as $a''p''b''$ in Figure III-1 and is included here to show the effects of protection in reducing the world's production possibilities.[2]

Notice that the disparity between country A's and country B's prices in Figure IV-1 is insufficient to make their common production possibilities less than under free trade, if the joint demand for their products places O^B on either the segment $(a'')a''$ or the segment $b''(b'')$ of the world transformation curve. The higher the degree of protection, however, the shorter those segments become until (a'') and (b'') become the only points com-

---

[2] The curve $(a'')(p'')(b'')$ in Figure III-1, it will be recalled, is the world transformation curve when the factor supplies of the two countries lie within the equalization region.

mon to the free-trade and the protection transformation curves of country A and country B combined.

The point on $(a'')a''O^Bb''(b'')$ at which equilibrium occurs depends upon the shapes of each country's indifference or market-demand curves, of which $I_1{}^A$, $I_2{}^A$, $I_1{}^B$, and $I_2{}^B$ are examples, and also in general upon which country levies the tariffs responsible for the price disparity and upon how the governments spend their customs revenue.

In Figure IV-1, the slope of line *pire* gives the world terms of trade and country B's internal price ratio on the assumption that country A imposes the only trade restraints. Let country A apply the tariff rate which causes *puc*, the slope of which gives its own internal price ratio, to diverge from *pire* by the amount shown in the figure. Country B's consumers will trade from point p on their transformation curve to point r, at which point *pire* is tangent to their market demand curve, $I_1{}^B$. The customs authorities of country A will collect ru units from the total amount, equal to $r_1{}^A$ units minus $x_1{}^A$ units, of x_1 which A imports. Country A's consumers will want to trade along *puc* from point p to point c, where *puc* is tangent to their market-demand curve, $I_1{}^A$. Assume that their government trades hu units of its x_1 for hc units of x_2 and thus consumes hr units of x_1 and hc units of x_2. The same amount and distribution of the two commodities would occur if the government collected its duty in the form of an export tax of the same *ad valorem* amount and spent it in the same way. In that event, it would collect ci units of x_2. The government benefiting from its privilege of trading at the more favorable external price ratio would trade hi units of x_2 with country B for rh units of x_1 and, under the same government and consumer consumption preferences, end up as before. Any combination of import and export exactions yielding the same price distortion would leave the distribution of the commodities and therefore the internal and external terms of trade the same.[3]

If the government remits the tariff revenue to the people, their preferences will determine the government consumption schedule assumed above. Suppose that after the government has collected

[3] See A. P. Lerner, "The Symmetry between Import and Export Taxes," *Economica*, n.s., 3:306–313 (August 1936).

the ru units of x_1 it gives them to all citizens, not just importers, according to some neutral consideration, perhaps by income, in such a way as not to affect the market-demand curves. Country A's consumers, after the distribution of x_1, will be able to trade from point w above point p, where pw equals ru. Draw qwr through point w parallel to puc to indicate that relative prices in country A still diverge from those of country B by the same amount as before. The consumers will trade from w along qwr to r, where qwr is tangent to their market-demand curve, $I_2{}^A$. The diagram, as it is drawn, is in equilibrium because r is also country B's consumption point and there is neither a deficit nor a surplus of either commodity. Country A's citizens demand directly rh additional units of x_1 and hc additional units of x_2, just as if their government had bought these quantities for them and they had traded from q (where qm equals ch and pm equals rh in rectangle $qnpm$) rather than from w.[4]

Now suppose that country A abolishes its tariff, reverting to free trade, while country B introduces the same *ad valorem* tariff that A previously applied. Country B's government now collects ci units of x_2 as an import duty. When it remits this to consumers, they trade from w' along $w'cv$, always parallel to $pire$, to the point v where $w'cv$ is tangent to their market-indifference curve, $I_2{}^B$. As Figure IV-1 is drawn, v does not coincide with c, for x_2 is in deficient supply and x_1 in surplus. The price of x_2 will therefore rise relative to that of x_1. The slopes of $w'cv$, puc, and $pire$ will all increase by the same amount. The point v where $w'cv$ is tangent to country B's market-demand curves will move toward c as $w'cv$ rotates clockwise, and c will move toward v as puc rotates in the same direction. The production point p, meanwhile, will move toward b along country A's transformation curve, apb, and country B's transformation curve, $a'pb'$, will correspondingly move to intersect p at its point of tangency with $pire$. As a result O^B will move toward (b'') along $(a'')a''O^Bb''(b'')$. Each country's market-demand curves maintain their positions with respect to

[4] Notice that the government could not collect ci units of the export commodity, x_2, and remit them directly to the people and achieve the same results, because exports are worth less in terms of x_1 at domestic than at world prices. The government has to allow citizens to trade hi units of x_2 freely with country B to make them as well off as they are with ru units of x_1.

the country origins, so that as O^B moves toward (b''), country B's market-demand curves, and consequently the points at which they are successively tangent to $w'cv$, move downward and to the right. Thus as the rise in its price curtails world demand for x_2, it also increases its output. The opposite holds for x_1 until equilibrium is established when v and c coincide. In the new equilibrium every variable, including the amount of tariff revenue collected, will have changed.

It is possible to describe by the same methods a situation in which each country collects part of the world tariff revenue responsible for the given disparity in their relative prices. If this price disparity remains the same, the world transformation curve $(a'')a''O^Bb''(b'')$ will remain the same also. The common equilibrium consumption point of the two countries will fall somewhere between $pire$ and puc at a point where lines corresponding to qwr and $w'cv$ are tangent to the market-demand curves of the two countries. The location of this new point depends on the exact distribution of tariff revenue. Each change in the distribution would, in general, lead to a change in the slope of puc and $pire$ and therefore in the position of their tangency with the two transformation curves.

One could also imagine that only one country collected tariff revenue and transferred all or part of it to the other. If, for instance, country B collected all of the tariff revenue but gave it entirely to country A, the equilibrium would be the same as if country A had imposed and collected the tariff. Nothing essential changes, moreover, if the tariff revenue is negative; that is, if subsidies have to be paid in order to maintain the desired price disparity. The point corresponding to, say, q, from which consumers in country A are imagined to trade, would then simply lie below their actual production point p, rather than above it, and the rectangle $pmqn$ would indicate the amount of x_1 and x_2 which they must pay to the government, but which they would get back in the form of more favorable prices.

Tariffs or trade subsidies are not the only means, of course, by which countries can alter their production structures. Country A, say, might leave trade itself nominally free but use direct production subsidies or discriminatory internal taxes to encourage the production of one or the other commodity. It might, for instance, subsidize producers of x_1 by taxing producers of x_2. In this case the line *pire* in Figure IV-1 will indicate the relative prices faced by consumers in both countries and by producers in country B. Country A's producers, however, will face the relative prices indicated by the slope of *puc*. The world transformation curve, $(a'')a''O^Bb''(b'')$, will be the same as when tariffs were the cause of the price disparity if that price disparity itself remains unchanged. The world equilibrium will be different, however. If country A switches from the tariff assumed in Figure IV-1 to a production subsidy having the same effect on relative producer prices, its consumers will want to consume at the point on *pire* where one of their market-demand curves lying above I_2^A is tangent to it, while consumers in country B will continue to be in equilibrium at r. The change in relative prices to consumers in country A will lead to an excess world demand for x_2 and a deficient world demand for x_1. The resulting increase in the relative price of x_2 entails a decrease in the slopes of *pire* and *puc* until *pire* is tangent to market-demand curves of the two countries at the same point.

If the market-demand curves are interpreted as community-welfare curves, it can be seen that the new consumer equilibrium involves an increase in the welfare of both countries. Meanwhile the production point p will have moved even closer to a along apb, so that a production subsidy is more effective than a tariff creating the same price disparity in protecting country A's x_1 industry. At the same time, since the new equilibrium increases the total world output of x_1 beyond its free-trade level, rather than restricting it as the tariff does, the subsidy reduces country B's output of x_1 less than the tariff does. Therefore, because it disturbs the other country's production structure less and leaves consumers in both countries better off, production subsidies and discriminatory internal taxes are better instruments of protection than tariffs and trade subsidies are. This conclusion, however, widely accepted among trade theorists, does not hold if commodities are inputs into other production sectors. It will be necessary to return to it later.

As soon as the world equilibrium is worked out for any set of commercial policies, and the point p on the transformation curves of the two countries is established, relative factor prices in each country can also be determined. Figure I-5 in the first chapter shows the derivation of each country's transformation curve from its factor endowments and production functions. If Figure I-5 stands, say, for country A, another similar to it could represent country B. The two figures could then be juxtaposed so that their transformation curves have the same positions relative to one another as those of Figure IV-1. From the combined diagram, one can establish the complete trade equilibrium under protection, including the relative factor prices of both countries.

Figure I-5 makes it apparent that as a country protects its labor-intensive commodity, x_1, and thus moves its production point from point p to point p', the relative price of labor (F_1) increases. At p the ratio of the price of labor to that of capital (F_2) is equal to the slope of the x_1 and x_2 isoquants at H and G, while at p' it is equal to their slopes at H' and G'. The relative distribution of income to suppliers of the two factors will be equal to the slope of the isoquants, tangent at the given production point, times the inverse slope of X_1X_2, which gives a country's endowment ratio of the two factors, or to

$$\frac{Y_1{}^A}{Y_2{}^A} = \frac{p_{o1}{}^A F_1{}^A}{p_{o2}{}^A F_2{}^A}$$

where $Y_1{}^A$ and $Y_2{}^A$ are the incomes of suppliers of $F_1{}^A$ and $F_2{}^A$, respectively, in country A.

As Stolper and Samuelson have shown, a reduction in protection that does not cause a country to specialize will reduce the real income, in terms of either commodity, of the factor which the protected commodity uses relatively intensively.[5] The loss in real income of the heretofore protected factor, despite the general increase in world real income accompanying the trade liberalization, occurs simply because its marginal physical productivity has fallen in both industries, not because the country's terms of trade have deteriorated as a result of liberalization. Once the country specializes, however, further reductions in tariff

[5] Wolfgang F. Stolper and Paul A. Samuelson, "Protection and Real Wages," *Review of Economic Studies*, 9:70–73 (November 1941).

protection will not lower the formerly protected factor's share in national income, since that share can only change with changes in production structure. Total national income will continue to increase, nevertheless, as the separate trading partners' indifference curves in Figure IV-1 become tangent. Consequently any increase in the freedom of trade which leads a country to specialize in the commodity in which it has a comparative advantage may increase the real income of the protected, as well as that of the unprotected, factor.

Figure IV-1 indicates that when the government redistributes its tariff revenue, rather than destroying it as so much tariff analysis implicitly assumes, the loss in consumption efficiency is not likely to be very great. Consider the market-demand curves in that diagram to be community-indifference curves. Consumer welfare would be only slightly increased, for instance, if the consumption point were moved from r, where the market-demand curves of the two countries intersect, to a point where they were tangent to one another and to a common price line between *pire* and *qwr*. If the production point of country A were at b, both countries would be on higher indifference curves than those intersecting at r, because of the increase in productive efficiency, but further tariff reductions would have only marginal effects in increasing consumer welfare.

Movements along the transformation curve, on the other hand, can have large effects on relative factor shares. Suppose that factor units in Figure I-5 are defined so that the isoquants of the two production functions are tangent to factor-price lines with a negative slope of one at the point where they are intersected by the rays X_1H and X_1G, the slopes of which indicate the factor proportions of the two goods when factor prices equal one. In Figure I-5, X_1H and X_1G are symmetrically placed with respect to the forty-five-degree line, X_1X_2.

The relative shares of the two factors in national income, and thus their absolute incomes, vary greatly as p moves from a'' to b'' along the transformation curve of Figure I-5. If two countries' factor endowments are in the same range — that is, if X_2 lies between X_1H and X_1G — the chances are small that either country will specialize under free trade. Therefore, within this range, protection will almost surely increase the real income of the scarce factor. As factor endowments become more extreme, protection will become less advantageous to the scarce factor, not only because free-trade specialization is more likely, but also because the divergence in factor-price ratios in going from one specialization point to another becomes smaller. Assume that the factor endowments of one of the countries lie to the left of the ray $X_1^A G$, as in Figure III-1. Then if country A produces at either a or b on its transformation curve, apb, the corresponding factor-price ratios will be given by the tangents to the isoquants at V and Z, respectively. The slopes at both points exceed unity. If $X_1^A X_2^A$, in Figure III-1, were more nearly vertical, if the isoquants were more nearly cornered, or if they were closer together, the slope of the x_1 isoquant at V would be more nearly equal to that of the x_2 isoquant at Z. If the two isoquants became vertical after a certain point, the slopes at V and Z would become identical and both equal to infinity. As the slopes of the isoquants become more similar, the transformation curve itself becomes more nearly a straight line and its slope becomes more and more extreme. As soon as it becomes a straight line, of course, relative factor prices do not change along it: one factor is free and protection unambiguously harms the nonfree factor.

If, on the other hand, factor endowments lie along either the ray $X_1^A G$ or $X_1^A H$, in Figure III-1, relative factor prices will vary from equality, at the specialization points a and b, to whatever the slope of the other isoquant is along $X_1^A G$ or $X_1^A H$ projected. Since this slope may vary from something exceeding unity to infinity along $X_1^A G$ projected to something between unity and zero along $X_1^A H$ projected, depending upon the shape and position of the isoquants, considerable factor-price variability exists even under relatively extreme factor endowments. Moreover, the transformation curve will always be the most bowed near its extremity corresponding to the commodity intensive in the same factor in which the country is rich. Bowed sections of the transformation curve also are sections in which changes in the output of one commodity with respect to those in the other imply relatively sharp changes in relative factor prices. Consequently, specialization may not be complete when free trade is attained in a given case, and, even if it is, a large change in relative factor prices will have preceded it.

The introduction of free trade is liable, therefore, to increase the real income of both factors only to the extent that protection is slight to begin with, that the country in question nearly specializes anyway, and that factor endowments are extreme with respect to the shape and position of the isoquants.

There is an empirical check on the latter possibility: if extreme factor endowments cause the transformation curve to be flat, the abundant factor will be free. If the transformation curve is only relatively flat, the abundant factor will merely be excessively cheap. If world factor endowments are extreme but nearly identical among trading partners, specialization will not occur despite the flatness of the transformation curves, and tariff protection will alter neither relative factor prices nor relative outputs very much. The world admitting this possibility would be a one-factor world, which is contrary to fact.

It is entirely possible that any given country's relative factor endowments are so extreme that its transformation curve is flat. Labor in many underdeveloped countries is probably, from a strictly economic viewpoint, a free factor, and only the lack of capital prevents higher output. Protection unambiguously lowers the real income of capital in such countries by a considerable amount, thereby considerably lowering national income as well. But it is probably safe to conjecture that if the ratio of the price of labor to that of capital is, say, 1 in one country and 10 in another, or if the ratios fall within those limits when they apply protection, the abolition of protection would harm the scarce factor in each country.

THE INDETERMINACY OF THE DOMESTIC PRODUCTION STRUCTURE

Factoral distribution of income has occasionally been an issue in tariff controversies, especially in the United States with its extreme relative factor endowments. Even in this country, however, the protection of high wages does not seem to be the main motive for protecting separate industries. A given disparity from free-trade factor prices can be achieved at minimum cost by maintaining only selected industries. When a nation establishes and maintains every possible industry, on the other hand, this indicates that maximum self-sufficiency is the prime objective of its commercial policy.

Economic theory cannot justify this motive on rational grounds. Given a country's relative input prices, however, it can show how much protection each industry requires to remain in that country. The following section will show that the tariff structures obtained in this way must conform to a definite pattern. This determinacy greatly facilitates and clarifies an empirical study of protection. The common, necessary features of protectionist policy derive in turn from the indeterminacy of the domestic production structure of homogeneous economic systems.

Indeterminacy has already been encountered in the multi-commodity equalization regions of Chapter Two. It was seen there that, whenever the number of commodities exceeded the number of primary factors, the domestic and foreign output of several sectors could change without altering factor proportions in any industry in the world as a whole or the total world output of any industry. The location of any given industry, and therefore the production structure of the country, was found to be indeterminate. It is easy to see why this free-trade indeterminacy occurs; simultaneous variations in the outputs of several industries, each using a common set of factors, can be made in such a way that the group will continue to employ the same amount of each factor, and each industry, despite the variation in its output, will employ them in the same proportions. It is only necessary, in general, that the number of industries varying in size exceed the number of factors they employ and that outputs vary within ranges in which returns to scale are constant.

It is not intuitively clear that indeterminacy exists under protection, which causes the input coefficients of primary factors and intermediate commodities to vary from country to country. The resulting transfer of some or all of the output of an industry from one country to another, in such a way as to leave all input coefficients and factor employments in each country the same as before, cannot be affected without changing the world output of at least r industries. This variation might conceivably render the division of world output among countries determinate. The next section will show that the indeterminacy does in fact remain. It depends upon a property of the transformation function of homogeneous economic systems and is therefore independent of particular sets of factor endowments or commodity demands. The assumptions of the equalization region — free trade and no specialization — made it unnecessary completely to describe multi-dimensional transformation functions, but the further discussion of protection now requires such a description.

The transformation function, $T(F_1, \ldots, F_r; q_1, \ldots, q_n) = 0$, where the q_i's are net outputs of commodities, is a production function; it differs from the customary production function only in giving the outputs of several commodities, rather than of only one, as a function of one or more primary-factor inputs. Figure IV-2 illustrates the simplest transformation among two commodities, x_1 and x_2, neither of which is considered to be an input in production, and their single primary factor, F_1. The figure is drawn in perspective to represent the three-dimensional space in which the transformation function, $T(x_1, x_2, F_1) = 0$, lies. The vertical F_1 axis is the factor space, analogous to the F_1, F_2 space of Figure I-6, for example, and the x_1, x_2 base plane is the commodity space, which is the same as the commodity space of the earlier diagrams. The production function for x_1 is $F_{11}'x_1 - F_{11} = 0$ where F_{11} is the amount of F_1 working to produce x_1. The production function for the other commodity is $F_{12}'x_2 - F_{12} = 0$. The lines Ors, lying in the F_1, x_1 space, Ouv, lying in the F_1, x_2 space, represent these production functions: their slopes are respectively equal to F_{11}' and to F_{12}'.

The locus of optimal transformation of x_2 into x_1 is obtained by adding to the restriction constituted by the separate production functions the condition that factor usage must not exceed factor supply: $F_{11} + F_{12} \gtrless F_1$. The output of x_1 is then maximized over every value of x_2, considered as a constant, for a given amount of F_1. This can be done by finding points, v and s, which correspond to the same fixed amount of F_1 on the production function rays, Ors and Ouv, and by finding the locus of all linear combinations of the resulting production vectors. In Figure IV-2, *vb* equals *sa*, *Ou* equals *rt*, and *Or* equals *ut* so that *tp* equals *sa* and the output of the two commodities at point *t* also exhausts the fixed amount of F_1. Other linear combinations of the vectors *Ov* and *Os* similarly give other output combinations which fully employ all of the available factor. All such combinations lie on

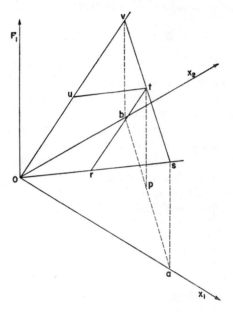

FIGURE IV-2

the straight-line segment, *stv*, and $F_{11}'x_1 + F_{12}'x_2 - F_1 = 0$ is the transformation function in this instance. The line segment *stv* cannot extend into negative regions of the commodity space because, by definition, amounts of primary factors cannot be negative. The projection *apb* of the locus *stv* onto the commodity space is the ordinary two-commodity transformation locus for a given factor input.

Although transformation functions in higher dimensions cannot be represented geometrically, the geometric example illustrates all of their essential aspects. Let

$$x_j = \psi_j(F_{1j}, \ldots, F_{rj}; x_{1j}, \ldots, x_{nj}) \quad \text{and}$$

$$q_j = x_j - \sum_{i=1}^{n} x_{ji} \quad (j = 1, \ldots, n) \tag{i}$$

be the production functions for the commodities. The expressions

$$F_k \geqq \sum_{j=1}^{n} F_{kj} \quad (k = 1, \ldots, r) \tag{ii}$$

are the constraints on factor usage relative to factor supply. The existence of more than one input complicates the conditions which ensure that any given transformation locus is optimal. Full employment of every factor is no longer sufficient to ensure optimality since factor proportions count as well. It may be impossible or nonoptimal to employ fully every factor, moreover. One must find the conditions which ensure the maximum output of any commodity when all primary-factor inputs and all other commodity outputs are specified.

The optimality conditions can be found by maximizing the expression

$$\sum_{j=1}^{n} \lambda_j \left\{ \psi_j(F_{1j}, \ldots, F_{rj}; x_{1j}, \ldots, x_{nj}) - \sum_{i=1}^{n} x_{ji} - q_j \right\}$$

$$+ \sum_{k=1}^{r} \phi_k \left(F_k - \sum_{j=1}^{n} F_{kj} \right)$$

in which all the F_k's and q_j's except one are taken as constant and the remaining q_j or F_k is set equal to zero. The ψ_j's and ϕ_k's are undetermined Lagrangian multipliers. The expression is maximized by taking its partial derivatives with respect to the inputs, F_{kj} and x_{ij}, and setting them equal to zero. This gives the following conditions for optimal resource employment:

$$\lambda_j \frac{\partial \psi_j(F_{1j}, \ldots, F_{rj}; x_{1j}, \ldots, x_{nj})}{\partial F_{kj}} = \phi_k \quad \text{and}$$

$$\lambda_j \frac{\partial \psi_j(F_{1j}, \ldots, F_{rj}; x_{1j}, \ldots, x_{nj})}{\partial x_{ij}} = \lambda_i$$

$$(i = 1, \ldots, n), (j = 1, \ldots, n), (k = 1, \ldots, r). \tag{iii}$$

Ratios of the undetermined Lagrangian multipliers give the slopes of the transformation function. Suppose, for example, that all inputs and all commodity outputs except q_1 and q_2 are held constant. The change in q_2 with respect to a change in q_1 is equal to

$$\frac{\partial q_2}{\partial q_1} = -\frac{\lambda_1}{\lambda_2}.$$

The change in q_1 with respect to F_1 is

$$\frac{\partial q_1}{\partial F_1} = \frac{\phi_1}{\lambda_1}.$$

These relationships, well known for cases in which intermediate goods are not considered, hold also when there are intermediate goods. The total differential of q_j is equal to:

$$dq_j = \sum_{k=1}^{r} \frac{\partial \psi_j}{\partial F_{kj}} dF_{kj} + \sum_{i=1}^{n} \frac{\partial \psi_j}{\partial x_{ij}} dx_{ij} - \sum_{i=1}^{n} dx_{ji}.$$

Therefore, because of (iii),

$$\lambda_j \, dq_j = \sum_{k=1}^{r} \phi_k \, dF_{kj} + \sum_{i=1}^{n} \lambda_i \, dx_{ij} - \sum_{i=1}^{n} \lambda_j \, dx_{ji}$$

$$(j = 1, \ldots, n).$$

Summing this expression over all j yields:

$$\sum_{j=1}^{n} \lambda_j \, dq_j = \sum_{k=1}^{r} \phi_k \, dF_k$$

because $dF_k = \sum_{j=1}^{n} dF_{kj}$, from (ii), and therefore

$$\phi_k \, dF_k = \sum_{j=1}^{n} \phi_k \, dF_{kj} \qquad (k = 1, \ldots, n),$$

and because all the terms $\lambda_i \, dx_{ij}$ and $\lambda_j \, dx_{ji}$ cancel out in the summation over j.[6] Holding all q_j's and all F_k's but two constant by letting their total differential equal zero now shows that

---

[6] This rather amazing canceling out of all the intermediate-commodity differentials accounts for the failure of intermediate goods to affect the formal results of many theorems, notably those of the factor-price equalization theorem.

$$\frac{\partial q_1}{\partial q_j} = -\frac{\lambda_j}{\lambda_1}, \frac{\partial F_1}{\partial F_k} = -\frac{\phi_k}{\phi_1}, \text{ and } \frac{\partial q_j}{\partial F_k} = \frac{\phi_k}{\lambda_j}$$

$$(j = 1, \ldots, n) \text{ and } (k = 1, \ldots, r)$$

so that the partial derivatives of the transformation function are inversely proportional to the Lagrangian undetermined multipliers. By the same token, of course, they are equal to minus the ratios of the marginal physical products of the inputs:

$$\frac{\partial \psi_1(F_{11}, \ldots, F_{r1}; x_{11}, \ldots, x_{n1})/\partial F_{k1}}{\partial \psi_j(F_{1j}, \ldots, F_{rj}; x_{rj}, \ldots, x_{nj})/\partial F_{kj}} = \frac{\lambda_j}{\lambda_1} = -\frac{\partial q_1}{\partial q_j},$$

$$\frac{\partial \psi_1(F_{11}, \ldots, F_{r1}; x_{11}, \ldots, x_{n1})/\partial x_{i1}}{\partial \psi_j(F_{1j}, \ldots, F_{rj}; x_{1j}, \ldots, x_{nj})/\partial x_{ij}} = \frac{\lambda_j}{\lambda_1} = -\frac{\partial q_1}{\partial q_j},$$

$$\partial \psi_j(F_{1j}, \ldots, F_{rj}; x_{1j}, \ldots, x_{nj})/\partial x_{ij} = \frac{\lambda_i}{\lambda_j} = -\frac{\partial q_j}{\partial q_i}, \text{ and}$$

$$\partial \psi_j(F_{ij}, \ldots, F_{rj}; x_{1j}, \ldots, x_{nj})/\partial F_{kj} = \frac{\phi_k}{\lambda_j} = +\frac{\partial q_j}{\partial F_k}$$

$$(i = 1, \ldots, n), (j = 1, \ldots, n), (k = 1, \ldots, r).$$

The desire of entrepreneurs to maximize profits causes them, under perfect competition, to produce goods in such proportions that the λ_j's are equal to the commodity prices which they face and the ϕ_k's to the factor prices. Let p_j be the price at which producers must sell x_j and let p_{ok} be the price they must pay for services of factor k. Total profits in the economy are then equal to:

$$\sum_{j=1}^{n} p_j q_j - \sum_{k=1}^{r} p_{ok} F_k.$$

Entrepreneurs maximize their profits within the same constraints of production function and factor supply as those which constitute the transformation function. Let

$$V = \sum_{j=1}^{n} p_j q_j - \sum_{k=1}^{r} p_{ok} F_k + \sum_{j=1}^{n} \lambda_j \left\{ \psi_j(F_{1j}, \ldots, F_{rj}; x_{1j}, \ldots, x_{nj}) \right.$$
$$\left. - \sum_{i=1}^{n} x_{ji} - q_j \right\} + \sum_{k=1}^{r} \phi_k \left(F_k - \sum_{j=1}^{n} F_{kj} \right)$$

and maximize V by setting its partial derivatives equal to zero. Setting its partial deriviatives with respect to the primary factor and intermediate commodity inputs to the various industries gives the same marginal productivity relationships as those derived above. Setting its partial derivatives with respect to q_j and F_k equal to zero yields:

$$\frac{\partial V}{\partial q_j} = p_j - \lambda_j = 0 \quad \text{and} \quad \frac{\partial V}{\partial F_k} = -p_{ok} + \phi_k = 0.$$

This shows that the Lagrangian multipliers are equal to the perfectly competitive prices of all goods that are actually produced.

There is an infinity of goods which no economy produces, however, because their production costs would exceed the price anyone was willing to pay. When countries trade with one another and their cost structures differ, the production cost of a commodity in one country may exceed its import price, in which case domestic production will normally shut down. Such cases correspond to sets of factor and commodity prices under which the objective profit function of V is maximized only by eliminating certain industries, those for which λ_j exceeds the import price even at zero output. Some factor or commodity prices, moreover, may settle at levels precluding the profitable use of the respective inputs in some industries. The full conditions for profit maximization must include the possibility of not producing all goods and of not using all factors in every production process:

$$p_j \gtreqless \lambda_j, \; p_{ok} = \phi_k \gtreqless p_j \frac{\partial \psi_j(F_{1j}, \ldots, F_{rj}; x_{1j}, \ldots, x_{nj})}{\partial F_{kj}}, \quad \text{and}$$

$$p_i = \lambda_i \gtreqless p_j \frac{\partial \psi_j(F_{1j}, \ldots, F_{rj}; x_{1j}, \ldots, x_{nj})}{\partial x_{ij}}$$

$$(i = 1, \ldots, n), (j = 1, \ldots, n), \text{and} (k = 1, \ldots, r). \quad \text{(iii)}$$

The above discussion has assumed only that production functions are continuously differentiable. Indeterminacy, like factor price-equalization, depends upon degree-one homogeneity of the production functions. Under this assumption, the scale of output does not affect the marginal productivities in (iii), and all price relationships depend therefore only on input proportions. A production function is homogeneous of degree k if, for any scalar t,

$$t^k \psi_j(F_{1j}, \ldots, F_{rj}; x_{1j}, \ldots, x_{nj})$$
$$= \psi_j(tF_{1j}, \ldots, tF_{rj}; tx_{1j}, \ldots, tx_{nj}) \qquad (j = 1, \ldots, n).$$

Differentiating both sides of this identity partially with respect to any argument, say F_{kj}, and dividing through by t gives:

$$t^{k-1} \frac{\partial \psi_j(F_{1j}, \ldots, F_{rj}; x_{1j}, \ldots, x_{nj})}{\partial F_{kj}}$$
$$= \frac{\partial \psi_j(tF_{1j}, \ldots, tF_{rj}; tx_{1j}, \ldots, tx_{nj})}{\partial tF_{kj}}$$
$$(j = 1, \ldots, n) \text{ and } (k = 1, \ldots, r).$$

This shows that partial derivatives of functions homogeneous of degree k are, by the definition of homogeneity, themselves homogeneous of degree $k - 1$. Therefore, if $k = 1$, $F_{kj}' = F_{kj}/x_j$, $a_{ij}' = x_{ij}/x_j$, and $t = 1/x_j$, then

$$\frac{\partial \psi_j(F_{1j}, \ldots, F_{rj}; x_{1j}, \ldots, x_{nj})}{\partial F_{kj}}$$
$$= \frac{\partial \psi_j(F_{1j}', \ldots, F_{rj}'; a_{1j}', \ldots, a_{nj}')}{\partial F_{kj}'} = \frac{\phi_k}{\lambda_j} \quad \text{and}$$
$$\frac{\partial \psi_j(F_{1j}, \ldots, F_{rj}; x_{1j}, \ldots, x_{nj})}{\partial x_{ij}}$$
$$= \frac{\partial \psi_j(F_{1j}', \ldots, F_{rj}'; a_{1j}', \ldots, a_{nj}')}{\partial a_{ij}'} = \frac{\lambda_i}{\lambda_j}$$
$$(i = 1, \ldots, n), (j = 1, \ldots, n), (k = 1, \ldots, r).$$

Degree-one homogeneity of the economic system has two important consequences, both of which depend on Euler's theorem. The former is that national profit, $\sum_{j=1}^{n} p_j q_j - \sum_{k=1}^{r} p_{ok} F_k$, is necessarily equal to zero, that is, national income at producer's prices, under perfect competition, is automatically equal to national income at factor cost. According to Euler's theorem,

$$k\psi_j(F_{1j}, \ldots, F_{rj}; x_{1j}, \ldots, x_{nj})$$

$$= \sum_{k=1}^{r} \frac{\partial \psi_j(F_{1j}, \ldots, F_{rj}; x_{1j}, \ldots, x_{nj})}{\partial F_{kj}} F_{kj}$$

$$+ \sum_{i=1}^{n} \frac{\partial \psi_j(F_{1j}, \ldots, F_{rj}; x_{1j}, \ldots, x_{nj})}{\partial x_{ij}} x_{ij} \qquad (j = 1, \ldots, n).$$

Let k be equal to unity. Apply this theorem to the production functions in (i) and substitute ϕ_k/λ_j and λ_i/λ_j for the corresponding partial derivatives, according to (iii). Multiplying every equation by λ_j then gives

$$\lambda_j q_j = \sum_{k=1}^{r} \phi_k F_{kj} + \sum_{i=1}^{n} \lambda_i x_{ij} - \sum_{i=1}^{n} \lambda_j x_{ji} \qquad (j = 1, \ldots, n).$$

Summing over j and inserting (ii) give

$$\sum_{j=1}^{n} \lambda_j q_j = \sum_{k=1}^{r} \phi_k F_k.$$

Because whenever λ_j is not equal to p_j the corresponding q_j is zero, and because whenever ϕ_k is not equal to p_{ok} none of the corresponding factor k finds employment, the above expression is equivalent to

$$\sum_{j=1}^{n} p_j q_j - \sum_{k=1}^{r} p_{ok} F_k = 0.$$

The second important property of any homogeneous economic system is that all of its prices, under perfect competition, depend on any r goods or factor prices, where r is the number of factors primary to the system.[7] This property also follows from Euler's theorem. The gross output of commodity j is equal to

$$x_j = \sum_{k=1}^{r} \frac{\phi_k}{\lambda_j} F_{kj} + \sum_{i=1}^{n} \frac{\lambda_i}{\lambda_j} x_{ij} \qquad (j = 1, \ldots, n),$$

and so

$$\lambda_j = \sum_{k=1}^{r} \phi_k F_{kj}' + \sum_{i=1}^{n} \lambda_i a_{ij}' \qquad (j = 1, \ldots, n). \qquad \text{(iii)}'$$

[7] Paul A. Samuelson, "Prices of Factors and Goods in General Equilibrium," *Review of Economic Studies* 21:18–19 (1953–1954).

Equations (iii)′ are n simultaneous, linear equations in the n λ_j's and r ϕ_k's. They can be solved for any n of the $n + r$ Lagrangian multipliers in terms of any r of them. It is probably most natural to express the λ_j's, which correspond to commodity prices, in terms of the ϕ_k's, which correspond to factor prices. Let λ stand for the column vector of n elements λ_j, and ϕ for the column vector of r elements ϕ_k, and let F' be the $r \times n$ matrix of optimal input coefficients F_{kj}' and A' the $n \times n$ matrix of optimal input coefficients a_{ij}'. Then, in matrix form, the relationship (iii)′ among prices in the homogeneous system is:

$$\lambda = [F'(I - A')^{-1}]^T \phi. \tag{iii}′$$

When equations (ii) are expressed in terms of the input coefficients F_{kj}' and a_{ij}', they closely resemble equations (iii)′. Let F be the column vector of elements F_k, the supplies of the kth primary factor, and let x and q be, respectively, the column vectors of gross and net outputs of the n commodities which the economy can produce. Then

$$F = F'x = F'(I - A')^{-1}q. \tag{ii}$$

Thus (ii) is a set of r equations in the $n + r$ primary-factor inputs and final-commodity outputs, while (iii)′ is a set of n equations in the prices corresponding to each of those variables. Both sets of equations utilize the same set of input coefficients, the F_{kj}' and the a_{ij}'. Imagine for a moment that these optimal input coefficients have been somehow determined, as they must be in any economic system, and assume that the economy is found actually to produce more commodities than it uses primary factors. Then (ii) has fewer equations than unknown q_j's, more than one set of which will satisfy (ii) for any set of fixed factor endowments and input coefficients. Thus more than one set of outputs will yield the same maximum value of national income and minimum value of national cost under any given set of factor and commodity prices. In fact, an infinite number of output combinations will satisfy (ii) and all the optimality conditions, although not every possible combination will do so. The r equations in (ii) will finally require a definite relationship among at least r outputs, when all the rest are prescribed along with the factor endowments, if the input coefficients are to remain the same. For this reason, one can say that an $n - r$ infinity of output combinations are compatible with any set of revenue-maximizing input coefficients and that production structure is indeterminate to this extent.

The input coefficients in equations (ii) and (iii)′ depend in turn only on the production functions and, through the marginal productivity conditions, on relative input prices. Dividing the production functions in (i), assumed to be homogeneous of degree one, by their gross outputs gives the following n relationships:

$$\psi_j(F_{1j}', \ldots, F_{rj}'; a_{1j}', \ldots, a_{nj}') - 1 = 0$$
$$(j = 1, \ldots, n). \qquad \text{(i)}'$$

Each equation in (i)′ is merely that of the unit isoquant of x_j. The marginal productivity conditions in (iii) — with the marginal productivities taken with respect to the input coefficients, F_{kj}' and a_{ij}', of the functions in (i)′ — give an additional $n(n + r)$ relationships in the input coefficients. Equations (i)′ and (iii) therefore lack only r prices to determine the remaining n prices and all $n(n + r)$ input coefficients.

The input coefficients depend now only on relative prices and would be the same even if each price in the system were multiplied by the same arbitrary constant. So the input coefficients depend on only $n + r - 1$ price ratios, $r - 1$ of which the homogeneous system requires to determine all the rest. In this sense, one can say that a homogeneous system has $r - 1$ degrees of freedom in its prices and input coefficients.

The existence of only $r - 1$ degrees of freedom means that more than that number of price ratios cannot be arbitrarily imposed on the system without causing it to close down all but r of its industries. Suppose that the $r - 1$ ratios of primary-factor prices were given. Then, by (iii)′, all relative commodity prices would be determined. If one then tried to impose another set of relative commodity prices while maintaining the factor prices, certain industries would close down because their λ_j's would exceed the imposed corresponding p_j's. Certain other imposed p_j's would presumably exceed the corresponding λ_j's and positive profits would appear in those industries. The profits would signal their expansion and the absorption of the primary factors which the closed industries released. The bidding for factors and for employment would entail a change in the initially prescribed relative factor prices and would in turn make some industries unprofitable. Finally, the set of at least r commodity prices maximizing national income would determine a new set of factor prices and input coefficients.

The existence of only $r - 1$ degrees of freedom implies further that, in certain circumstances, any two countries not sharing a common set of relative prices can share in the production of at most only $r - 1$ tradable commodities and that their production structures will therefore be determinate. The necessary circumstances involve what corresponds to the absence of factor-intensity cross-overs in the two-commodity cases. Since all prices depend on any set of r prices or $r - 1$ price relatives, commodity prices can be said to depend only on the r factor prices, considered as known. Let p be the vector of commodity prices and p_o the vector of factor prices. Then, in the most general terms, $p = g(p_o)$ where $g(p_o)$ is the mapping of factor prices into commodity prices. If two trading countries share the same commodity-price vector for at least r commodities they have the same factor prices provided that the mapping $g(p_o)$ is univalent, that is, that it is one-to-one. The well-known sufficient condition for the local univalence of $g(p_o)$ is that the determinant of its Jacobian matrix, $g'(p_o) = \partial g/\partial p_o = (\partial g_j/\partial p_{ok})$, be nonzero at $p_o{}^o$. This condition implies that $p_o{}^1 = p_o{}^o$ when $g(p_o{}^1) = g(p_o{}^o)$. It does not guarantee global univalence, however, even though the determinant, $|g'(p_o)|$, does not vanish at any set of factor prices. Gale and Nikaido have recently shown that $g(p_o)$ is globally univalent if all the principal minor determinants of $g'(p_o)$ are nonnegative.[8] The set of simultaneous equations in (iii)$'$ is the mapping $g(p_o)$ when conditions are such that $\lambda_j = p_j$ $(j = 1, \ldots, n)$ and $\phi_k = p_{ok}$ $(k = 1, \ldots, r)$ in both countries. The elements of $g'(p_o)$ are those of the coefficient matrix $[F'(I - A')^{-1}]^T$, which may be abbreviated F''^T. Thus $p = F''^T p_o$ where the elements of F''^T are functions only of the r factor prices:

[8] John S. Chipman, "Factor Price Equalization and the Stolper-Samuelson Theorem," mimeographed paper presented at the Econometric Society meetings, Cleveland, September 6, 1963, p. 3.

$$F_{kj}' = F_{kj}' \, (p, \, p_o),$$
$$a_{ij}' = a_{ij}' \, (p, \, p_o), \quad \text{and}$$
$$F_{kj}'' = F_{kj}'' \, (p_o)$$

because equations (i)' and (iii) have together only $r - 1$ degrees of freedom and because the coefficients in (iii)' derive from them alone via Euler's theorem. If the equations in (iii)' constitute a univalent mapping and if both countries have the same factor prices, they can produce all n commodities at the same prices. Any r commodity prices in (iii)' are sufficient, however, to determine the set of r factor prices which can be found by inverting the relevant r equations in (iii)'. Therefore the divergence of factor prices in two countries implies, under global univalence, that they produce less than r commodities in common.

One would expect indeterminacy to occur as a matter of course in classical trade theories, which assume a single primary factor and many commodities. The case involving a single factor and two commodities indeed gives an example of indeterminacy that can be illustrated very easily. When r equals 1, the homogeneous economic system has no degree of freedom; input coefficients and relative prices are rigidly fixed even though production functions might well allow substitution among intermediate-commodity inputs and between intermediate inputs and the primary factor if relative prices could change. This is Samuelson's substitution theorem. The constancy of relative prices implies a straight-line transformation locus, exactly like locus apb of Figure IV-2. If production functions were everywhere the same, each country's transformation locus would have the same slope as that of every other country's and only their distances from the origin, depending on the supply of the single factor, would differ among countries. Imagine two such transformation curves placed in the same relationship to one another as are the normal transformation curves, apb and $a'pb'$, of Figure I-6. They would then lie tangent in a straight-line segment, the length of which would depend on the fixed quantities of the two commodities which the two countries jointly produce. The production point p (Figure IV-2) could assume any position on the line segment of tangency without altering the total world output of either commodity. Each position would correspond to a different commodity trade pattern and yet to precisely the same factoral trade pattern, since no factoral trade can occur when there is only one homogeneous factor.[9] Whether or not the countries traded would not matter, therefore, and the slightest transport costs would eliminate all trade.

Indeterminacy in the simplest example thus turns on the straightness of the transformation curve and on the identity of its slope in different countries. It is hard to imagine how these same characteristics can occur when more than one factor exists and when the transformation locus consequently curves through the commodity space. Figure IV-3 attempts to illustrate how they can occur by means of a perspective drawing of a three-dimensional curved transformation locus. The three axes, q_1, q_2, and q_3, corresponding to three commodities, define the commodity space on which the three-dimensional transformation curve is projected from the five-dimensional commodity-factor space. This five-space, if it could be drawn, would include axes for the two primary factors, F_1 and F_2, which are postulated. The surface *abc* in Figure IV-3 represents the commodity transformation locus. Notice that it extends into the negative region of each commodity. This occurs because, when intermediate goods exist, an economy can produce negative net amounts of commodities by importing them to produce commodities in which it tends to specialize. The edges of the transformation surface therefore correspond to zero *gross* outputs of the commodities. The curves *rr'p's's* and *a'a''pb''b'* are level curves, the former corresponding to a zero net output of q_3. The curves *tt'a''r'r''* and *t''t'p''s's''* are also level curves and correspond respectively to zero net outputs of q_2 and of q_1.

The plane *efg* in Figure IV-3 is the highest price plane that touches the transformation surface. The price plane's equation is:

[9] For this reason, in order to explain trade, the classical economists had to assume that nationality somehow affects production functions. The assumption is therefore not a general and desirable one, as modern critics of the Heckscher–Ohlin theory suppose, but merely an *ad hoc* assertion necessary to explain observable facts in the absence of any trade theory. For, in the most fundamental sense, the classical single-factor assumption is incompatible with a systematic explanation of foreign trade.

$$p_1q_1 + p_2q_2 + p_3q_3 = \text{national income.}$$

Like the transformation surface, it also extends into the negative net-output regions of the three commodities if there are inter-mediate goods, although to make its depiction clearer only its

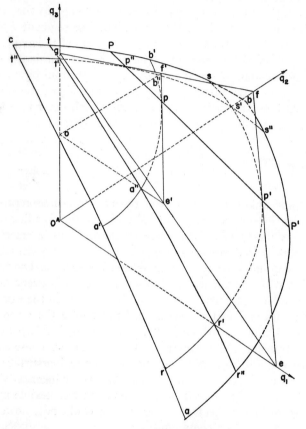

FIGURE IV-3

section within the commodity base planes has been shown. The price plane intersects the q_1, q_3 base plane in $ge'e$, whose slope, $-p_1/p_3$, gives the ratio of q_1's and q_3's prices. Similarly, $gp''f'f$, of slope $-p_2/p_3$, gives the ratio of q_2's and q_3's prices, and $ep'f$, of slope $-p_1/p_2$ gives the ratio of q_1's and q_2's prices.

The maximization of national income requires that the price plane lie tangent to the transformation surface in at least one point, such as p. The position of p determines the economy's relative factor prices, just as in the two-commodity cases. If p falls on an interior point of the transformation surface, as it does in the diagram, then the price plane is tangent to the transformation surface at other points also. The line segment $Pp''pp'P'$ in Figure IV-3 is the locus of all such points of tangency.

The locus of tangency must be a straight line in three-commodity, two-factor cases, moreover. The position of p fixes not only the relative factor prices, ϕ_1/ϕ_2, but also determines the optimal input coefficients F_{kj}' and a_{ij}' which enter into (ii) and (iii)'. There will be only two equations in (ii):

$$\begin{Bmatrix} F_1 \\ F_2 \end{Bmatrix} = F'(I - A')^{-1} \begin{Bmatrix} q_1 \\ q_2 \\ q_3 \end{Bmatrix} \text{ or } \begin{matrix} F_{11}''q_1 + F_{12}''q_2 + F_{13}''q_3 = F_1 \\ F_{21}''q_1 + F_{22}''q_2 + F_{23}''q_3 = F_2 \end{matrix} \quad \text{(ii)}$$

but three unknown q's. Each of the two equations represents a plane in the commodity space and their solution is a line segment which connects all points where the two planes intersect. Since the input coefficients are optimal ones, the line segment, passing through p, must lie on the transformation surface. The transformation surface, moreover, has the same slope in every direction along the line segment of tangency because, with the same input coefficients and factor prices, (iii)' must give the same λ's, or commodity prices, which in turn are proportional to the slope of the transformation function, as shown earlier. These considerations make it apparent that the transformation surface in this example is the section of a cylinder. Whatever its exact shape, it could be entirely covered by a piece of flat but flexible material, like an ordinary sheet of paper, which could not, however, be stretched to form a compound curve.

If another country produces the same three commodities, a price plane of the same slope as that of efg in Figure IV-3 will lie tangent to its transformation surface along another line segment which has the same direction as the line segment $Pp''pp'P'$ in Figure IV-3. The direction of a line in three-space can be represented by the angles which a line parallel to it and passing through the origin makes with each of the three axes. The cosines of the angles α, β, and γ which $Pp''pp'P'$ makes with the q_1, q_2, and q_3 axes are to each other as:[10]

$$\cos \alpha : \cos \beta : \cos \gamma = \begin{vmatrix} F_{12}'' & F_{13}'' \\ F_{22}'' & F_{23}'' \end{vmatrix} : \begin{vmatrix} F_{13}'' & F_{11}'' \\ F_{23}'' & F_{21}'' \end{vmatrix} : \begin{vmatrix} F_{11}'' & F_{12}'' \\ F_{21}'' & F_{22}'' \end{vmatrix}.$$

Another country facing the same relative prices would generate identical F_{kj}'''s and the line of tangency of its price plane and transformation surface would therefore have the same direction.

Thus the three-dimensional transformation surfaces of two countries can be made to lie tangent to each other in a straight-line segment if they can be made to lie tangent in any point lying on the interior of their transformation surfaces. When they do lie tangent in a line, the exact position of any production point along the line segment can change without altering the countries' joint production of either commodity. The changes in production structure that take place along the line of tangency all imply, moreover, exactly the same pattern of trade in factor services, even though they involve different commodity-trade vectors. Because income, relative prices, and income distribution all remain the same at each indeterminate distribution of production between country A and the rest of the world, there is no reason to suppose that r^A, country A's consumption vector, changes with changes in its domestic production structure. Then, since the production vector q^A changes only in such a way as to satisfy (ii) for the same coefficients and factor endowments:

$$F^A = F'^A(I - A'^A)^{-1}q^A,$$

the factoral content of trade, F_t^A, equal to

$$F'^A(I - A'^A)^{-1}t^A = F'^A(I - A'^A)^{-1}r^A - F^A,$$

remains the same for each indeterminate trade pattern associated with a given set of relative prices and input coefficients.

[10] See G. E. F. Sherwood and Angus E. Taylor, *Calculus* (rev. ed., New York, 1942, 1946), pp. 420–422 and 433, ex. 7.

An equilibrium degree of protection is one which just over-
comes a foreign producer's cost advantage in the home market.
If the French, say, can land woolen mittens in the United States
for a dollar a pair, and the domestic production cost is $1.20, the
equilibrium tariff is 20 percent *ad valorem*. This rate, like the
famous scientific tariff rate, places the French and the American
producer on exactly the same footing in the United States. It is
sometimes thought that the scientific, or equilibrium, tariff rate
eliminates trade by eliminating comparative cost differences. But
it must be remembered that, under factor-price equalization, free
trade itself would eliminate comparative (or relative) cost differences and so would bring about the condition the scientific tariff
seeks. For the same reason, the scientific tariff, applied to all
products, does not typically eliminate trade. It may eliminate all
factoral trade, but not necessarily. It necessarily distorts the
pattern of factoral trade, however, by interfering with commodity
trade and factor movements. The interference with trade establishes factor-price disparities between trading partners, and
therefore comparative cost disparities. Equilibrium protection
thus creates the cost disparities which it fully compensates.

Equations (iii)′ show the relationship between a country's
primary-factor prices, $\phi_k{}^A$, and its commodity production costs,
$\lambda_j{}^A$:

$$\lambda^A = [F'^A(I - A'^A)^{-1}]^T \phi^A$$

There is a similar system for the other country, country B. As
the preceding section showed, the specification of any r prices in
any homogeneous economy is sufficient to determine all of its
prices and input coefficients.

Suppose that the authorities in one of the countries, country A,
wish to establish a given set of relative factor prices by disturbing
trade with country B. By properly adjusting taxes, the authorities in country A can always enable a given industry at least to
meet country B's price in its own market. Country A can es-

tablish thereby a set of equilibrium-protection coefficients, h_j^{AB}, in its trade with country B such that

$$\lambda_j^A = h_j^{AB}\lambda_j^B \qquad (j = 1, \ldots, n) \qquad \text{(iv)}$$

for all commodities j and for zero transport costs. If the prices in country B are already determined, equations (iv) yield n price relationships for country A. Unless the coefficients h_j^{AB} were properly chosen, this imposition of $n - 1$ price ratios would violate the $r - 1$ degrees of freedom in country A's economic system. Once they are properly chosen, however, an $n - r$ infinity of outputs, q_j^A, in equations (ii),

$$F^A = F'^A(I - A'^A)^{-1}q^A = F''^A q^A,$$

are possible with the same set of input coefficients, relative prices, and primary-factor endowments. The same thing must also be true of country B, which is also producing n commodities with only r factors. Indeterminacy in the allocation of production between the two countries will result, just as in the free-trade case, if either country can share in the output of a given industry without disturbing the total world output of any commodity.

Indeterminacy under protection would imply a great sensitivity of domestic industries to even small changes in the tariff or other trading conditions affecting the coefficients h_j^{AB}. Under protection, however, the vectors q^A and q^B are not parallel since the coefficients F_{kj}'', on which their direction depends, will not generally be the same in the two countries. Shifts in the output of any industry from one country to the other will therefore affect the total world output of at least r commodities without changing relative prices in either country. This change in total world output could conceivably act on demand so as to change relative prices, however, thereby eliminating the indeterminacy in the production structure.

It is possible to show diagramatically, however, that the indeterminacy remains under fixed protection coefficients regardless of demand conditions and that imports are highly elastic with respect to departures from the equilibrium degree of protection. The straight-line transformation curve $acu'up'b$, or ab for short, in

Figure IV-4 corresponds to the line segment $Pp''pp'P'$ of Figure IV-3. The line segment in Figure IV-3 is straight because the number of commodities which that figure assumes exceeds its number of factors by one. The same holds in Figure IV-4, which assumes two rather than three commodities but only one factor. The line segment $a'prb'$, or $a'b'$ for short, in Figure IV-4 is the

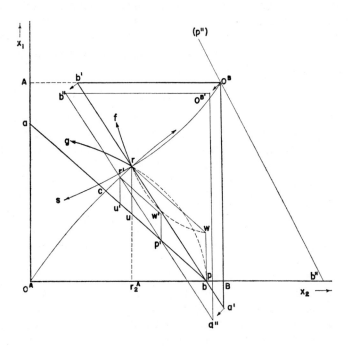

FIGURE IV-4

transformation curve of another country, country B, with its origin at O^B. The difference in the two transformation curves' slopes in Figure IV-4 corresponds, as in the multi-commodity, multi-factoral cases, to differences in relative prices. In the simplified diagram this is made possible only by assuming that production functions differ internationally.

Two devices in the diagram represent demand conditions and can be used to show their lack of effect. The first is the Engel curve. Country A's Engel curve, $O^Acr'r$, connects all the points where country A's market-demand curves are tangent to lines parallel to ab. Country B's Engel curve, O^Brs, starts at O^B and passes through all points at which its market-demand curves are tangent to lines parallel to $a'b'$. The Engel curves of the two countries intersect each other at r, as the figure shows. The second device to represent demand conditions is the offer curve. The offer curves, wrf for country A and prg for country B, are derived in the usual manner from the trading points w and p. Their dotted portions, wr and pr, however, are irrelevant since no country would accept an exchange ratio less favorable than its own internal substitution ratio, equal to the slope of its transformation curve. Thus country A's actual offer curve coincides with the line segment wr, parallel to ab, between w and r, and then follows the curved line out past f. Country B's offer curve follows its transformation curve from p to r and then diverges from it and passes through g.

If country A sets a tariff on imports of x_1 equal to the ratio of the slopes of the two transformation curves, making

$$h_1{}^{AB} = rr_2{}^A/ur_2{}^A,$$

it establishes the equilibrium degree of protection and eliminates its comparative advantage. If production takes place at point p and country A alone levies a tariff, country B will trade from its production point p to its consumption point r, where its terms-of-trade line, $a'b'$, is tangent to its highest attainable market-demand curve. Country A's consumers, however, will trade from w along wr also to r; they produce at p, but in addition receive wp (equal to ru) units of x_1, which their government collects as a tariff on the country's total imports of $rr_2{}^A$ units of x_1.

All offer curves of either country drawn from any point on its transformation curve or on any trading line, like wr, parallel to it, would necessarily cross the country's Engel curve at the same point as the trading line. Thus if country A and country B shared the customs revenue collected in whatever proportion, the world would produce more x_2 and less x_1, and country B's origin, O^B, would move downward to the right. The common consumption point r would then lie between its depicted position and the point

c, and would mark the intersection of the Engel curves of the two countries. Under the equilibrium tariff, any set of offer curves of the two countries will always intersect where the Engel curves cross, and this intersection is therefore an equilibrium consumption-point.

Any production point between p and c would also be an equilibrium one. Let production take place at p' for example. Country B's transformation curve moves downward and to the left in such a way that r slides along country A's Engel curve and settles at r'. The corners of the transformation curve $a'b'$ and its origin O^B move as the arrows indicate. Country A continues to apply the equilibrium tariff so that prices are unchanged and both products are equally profitable in both countries. The new origin, $O^{B'}$, shows that the world output and consumption box, formerly $O^A A O^B B$, has shrunk because of the movement away from desirable specialization. At r', nonetheless, consumers in country B are in equilibrium as before and, moreover, are no worse off. Consumers in country A, though worse off than before, also appear in equilibrium. They trade from w' along $w'r'$, as their government remits to them the $w'p'$ (equal to $r'u'$) units of x_1 it collects on their reduced imports of x_1, until that trading line is tangent to their highest attainable market-demand curve. This occurs where $w'r'$ crosses $O^A cr'r$ at r'.

The equilibrium of country A's consumers in the above example at production points other than p depends on their ignorance of the effects of their purchases on the tariff rebate they receive from the government. In any country, it is reasonable to assume that consumers do ignore this effect, since even were they aware of it, each citizen's share in the rebate from the customs duties he pays is infinitesimal.

Figure IV-4 can also be used to show how sensitive any domestic industry is to its equilibrium degree of protection. Suppose that after production is established at p' country A lowers its tariff by an iota. The domestic x_1 industry would quickly close down. On the other hand, if country A increased her tariff slightly, the production point p would coincide with c in country A and with r in country B, and all trade would disappear. In either situation, the production structure in both countries is perfectly determinate and remains so through further changes in the tariff rate. This example illustrates how indeterminacy in the output of a given industry in a country implies a definite, or determinate, tariff rate. By the same token, determinate domestic output implies no determinate degree of protection.

This dual relationship between the determinacy of production and that of the degree of protection generalizes to multi-factoral, multi-commodity cases. If the number of factors equals or exceeds the number of commodities, the production structure is determinate and any degree of protection which does not create complete specialization equalizes the domestic producers' costs and the import prices they must meet. In Figure IV-1, for example, more than one constant difference in the slopes of *pire* and *puc* will permit both countries to produce and to trade both commodities.

The existence of intermediate goods complicates the discussion of indeterminacy in several ways. In the first place, tariffs or other trade impediments which affect the imports of intermediate goods also affect the production costs of all the goods which use them and so affect their equilibrium degrees of protection. If the tariff on an intermediate product is lowered, the domestic industry may disappear, but its client industries may thereby be able to lower their prices sufficiently to displace competitors abroad. In such a case, not one but several equilibrium tariffs will be upset. In addition, when an industry serving only final demand closes down, it subtracts only one of the industries through which a country competes with the rest of the world. An intermediate industry closing does the same thing, but its products, which are now noncompetitive imports, must be treated as factors primary to the economy which uses but does not produce them. This, in effect, is the definition of a primary factor.

The existence of more than a single trading partner for every country further complicates the analysis of indeterminacy. If, for example, the two countries whose factor endowments are the most extreme relative to each other mutually establish equilibrium degrees of protection and apply most favored treatment to other nations, each one will be the other's sole supplier of goods intensive in its abundant factor or factors which the other has in relatively small amounts. Each country's protection will stop imports of those goods from third countries. This and other peculiarities of the general, m-country case make it necessary to indicate when the identity of a partner country is relevant to the discussion. I shall henceforth use the lower-case letters a $(a = 1, \ldots, m)$ and b $(b = 1, \ldots, m, a \neq b)$ to refer to trading countries in such instances, and in others as well, whenever the assumption of only two countries has no expositional advantage.

The intermediate-commodity input coefficients, $a_{ij}'^a$, corresponding to the industries i which any country, say country a $(a = 1, \ldots, m)$, does not operate, must be placed in its matrix of primary-factor input coefficients, which formerly contained only the elements $F_{kj}'^a$ corresponding to the universally primary factors. Let $A_n'^a$ be the matrix of the noncompetitive-import input coefficients. Then country A's primary-factor input coefficient matrix can be written:

$$\left\{ \begin{matrix} A_n'^a \\ \cdots \\ F'^a \end{matrix} \right\} \quad (a = 1, \ldots, m).$$

Its ordinary input-output matrix, $(I - A_d'^a)$, now contains only the intermediate-input coefficients $a_{ij}'^a$ corresponding to the industries i which country a operates domestically. No intermediate industry i, of course, can appear simultaneously both in the domestic coefficient matrix $A_d'^a$ and in the noncompetitive-import coefficient matrix $A_n'^a$.

Let n_i^a $(i = 1, \ldots, n)$ stand for country a's imports of x_i when it produces none itself. If it does produce x_i, the corresponding competitive imports will be designated by t_i^a, as before. Let n^a be the column vector of the amounts n_i^a. Let $p_{n_i}^a$ be the price which country a's users of x_i pay for n_i^a and let p_n^a be the column vector of these prices. If $p_{n_i}^a$ should ever be as high as the domestic cost at which country a can produce x_i, the corresponding n_i^a will of course be equal to zero.

The prices, p_i^a (where $i = 1, \ldots, n^a$ and n^a is the number of industries country a operates), of all domestically produced goods will now necessarily equal their production costs. Let p^a be the column vector of these domestically determined prices, and assume that $p_{ok}{}^a$ equals $\phi_k{}^a$ so that all factors in country a are employed. Equations (ii) and (iii)' now become:

$$\left\{ \begin{array}{c} n^a \\ \cdots \\ F^a \end{array} \right\} = \left\{ \begin{array}{c} A_n{}'^a \\ \cdots \\ F'^a \end{array} \right\} (I - A_d{}'^a)^{-1} q^a \quad (a = 1, \ldots, m) \quad \text{and} \quad \text{(ii)}$$

$$p^a = \left[\left\{ \begin{array}{c} A_n{}'^a \\ \cdots \\ F'^a \end{array} \right\} (I - A_d{}'^a)^{-1} \right]^T \left\{ \begin{array}{c} p_n{}^a \\ \cdots \\ p_o{}^a \end{array} \right\} \quad (a = 1, \ldots, m). \quad \text{(iii)}'$$

Noncompetitive imports will take place in four types of circumstances. If factor endowments lie outside the equalization region, specialization will occur under free trade, and the products of the industries not operating domestically will be noncompetitive imports. Their prices will depend on their costs in the countries of origin and also upon transport costs and trade restrictions insufficient to establish the respective domestic industries. This type of specialization will cause countries typically to compete in no more than $r - 1$ industries, where r is the number of their common factors, and will render the production structure determinate.

Two types of circumstances can account for competition between two or more trading countries in more than r commodities when their factor prices diverge. Each of these circumstances leads to noncompetitive imports whenever the country in question produces fewer than all n world commodities. If the mapping of factor prices into commodity prices is not univalent, there will be sets of factor prices in two countries which can cause them to produce r or more commodities at the same relative prices. The mapping of factor prices and goods prices must be modified, however, to include as factor prices the prices of the noncompetitive imports in any given trading situation. Thus the mapping function $g(p_o{}^a, p_n{}^a)$ and the matrix F''^a of direct and indirect primary-factor input coefficients must be slightly redefined to include prices and input coefficients for the noncompetitive imports.

The failure of $g(p_o{}^a, p_n{}^a)$ to be globally univalent cannot conceivably cause any two countries to share in the output of many more than r common commodities. Imagine that factor endowments, originally inside the equalization region, move outside it, withdrawing from it more and more. The *local* univalence of $g(p_o{}^a, p_n{}^a)$, which must hold close to the specialization boundaries, will guarantee the initial closing down of all but at most $r - 1$ competing industries, just as in the two-commodity case of Figure III-5. As relative factor prices in the two countries diverge more and more, however, some goods prices will become equalized and will provide a link between the factor prices of the two countries via the mapping $g(p_o{}^a, p_n{}^a)$. If more than r commodity prices are equalized at any point in the factor space, their distribution of production will be partly indeterminate. As factor prices continue to diverge, and additional goods prices are equated, some of those prices formerly equalized will cease to be. At any one time, therefore, it would be extraordinary to find all n goods prices the same when factor prices were different in two countries, if the world produces more than two or three commodities.

Equilibrium protection enables countries to compete in industries which free trade would eliminate in one partner country or the other. It thus counteracts the forces which cause specialization and thus noncompetitive imports. Protection may, for various reasons, fail to compensate exactly for all comparative cost differences, however, and may allow certain foreign industries to overcome their domestic rivals, or vice versa. Nonequilibrium protection must therefore be listed as a cause of specialization.

The calculation of the degree of indeterminacy in the production structures of any two trading partners in either of the above circumstances depends simply on the number of commodities they compete in and on the number of factors they each employ. The degree of indeterminacy will depend on which pair of countries one has in mind, and so it will be convenient to use the symbol D^{ab} ($a = 1, \ldots, m$; $b = 1, \ldots, m$; and $a \neq b$) to denote it and to indicate the relevant pair of countries. If country a is found to produce n^a commodities and country b produces n^b commodities, of which they produce jointly a total of n^{ab} commodities with r factors, then $D^{ab} = n^{ab} - r$, where D^{ab}, by definition, cannot be negative.

The final circumstances which can account for noncompetitive imports is, in a world of protectionism, the main one. One country may lack entirely certain natural resources and other specific factors which its partner possesses. The lack of specific resources causes noncompetitive imports under free trade as well as under protection.

It is possible for the domestic output of some goods to be indeterminate while that of others is determinate. The output of commodities that are the sole users of their specific factors is determinate, since their production costs depend on the intensity with which they use their specific resource as well as on the prices of all allocable factors shared with other domestic industries. Such industries can remain in competition with foreign producers over a range of protection and do not depend therefore on a unique, determinate, degree of equilibrium protection. Many of the industries in Group I fall into this category. But most agricultural industries and all industries in Group II share their primary factors with each other and are sensitive, whenever D^{ab} exceeds zero, to changes in their tariffs or other protectionist instruments.

TRADE RESTRICTIONS AND IMPEDIMENTS

Countries apply protection in many different ways: import, export, production, and consumption taxes and subsidies; multiple exchange rates; quantitative trade, production, and migration restrictions; private cartel arrangements; and the like. In addition, goods and factors encounter real costs in moving from place to place. All of these restrictions and impediments imply protection for groups of producers differentiated according to their products, nationalities, or other political and economic characteristics. Since the common element of protection is discrimination, a single protection coefficient, with superscripts to denote countries or regions and subscripts to denote products, can serve to translate the effects of most types of artificial restriction. A second coefficient with similar superscripts and subscripts can serve to represent the effects of real trade (transport) costs. All protection coefficients cause the ratios between the prices which producers or factor suppliers receive and the prices which their purchasers or employers pay to diverge from unity.

Let $c_{ok}{}^a$ represent the price which country a's suppliers of factor k receive, regardless of where their factors actually work. Let $h_{ok}{}^{aa}$ be the protection coefficient which country a applies to its employers of domestic supplies of factor k. The price they must pay is then:

$$p_{ok}{}^a = h_{ok}{}^{aa}c_{ok}{}^a.$$

Similarly, let $c_i{}^a$ be the price which domestic producers of commodity i in country a receive. The price which domestic users of that product must pay is equal to:

$$p_i{}^a = h_i{}^{aa}c_i{}^a$$

if the product is produced in country a. The coefficient $h_i{}^{aa}$ is the protection coefficient which country a applies to its own producers. The production cost, $c_j{}^a$, of any commodity j which country a produces using domestic factors is then equal to:

$$c_j{}^a = \sum_{k=1}^{r} F_{kj}{}'^a p_{ok}{}^a + \sum_{i=1}^{n} a_{ij}{}'^a p_i{}^a \qquad (j = 1, \ldots, n),$$
$$(a = 1, \ldots, m). \qquad \text{(iii)}'$$

The domestic production cost, $c_j{}^a$, is no longer equal to the Lagrangian undetermined multiplier, $\lambda_j{}^a$, because $p_i{}^a$ is not necessarily equal to $\lambda_i{}^a$. These equalities were derived as the necessary conditions for the maximization of a country's income subject to the constraints of its production functions and factor supplies. Equations (iii) must now be reinterpreted as the conditions which assure each entrepreneur's profit-maximization subject to the market prices he faces:

$$c_j{}^a \partial x_j{}^a / \partial F_{kj}{}^a \leqq p_{ok}{}^a \quad \text{and}$$
$$c_j{}^a \partial x_j{}^a / \partial x_{ij}{}^a \leqq p_i{}^a.$$

Let the protection coefficients which country a applies to country b (through, say, an import tariff) be $h_i{}^{ab}$, or $h_j{}^{ab}$, for commodity i or j and $h_{ok}{}^{ab}$ for factor k. The order of the country superscripts indicates the country which applies the protection and the one which suffers it. Let $u_{ok}{}^{ba}$ be the cost of sending one unit of k factor services from country b to work in country a, and let $u_j{}^{ba}$ be the cost of shipping one unit of commodity j from country b to country a. If two countries, country a and country b, apply equilibrium degrees of protection to commodity j, its cost in country a will bear the following functional relationship to its cost in country b:

$$c_j{}^a = \frac{h_j{}^{ab}c_j{}^b}{h_j{}^{ba}h_j{}^{aa}} + u_j{}^{ba} \qquad (j = 1, \dots, n), (a = 1, \dots, m),$$
$$(b = 1, \dots, m) \qquad \text{(iva)}$$

if country a is the importer. The corresponding relation between factor suppliers' receipts in the two countries is:

$$c_{ok}{}^a = \frac{h_{ok}{}^{ab}c_{ok}{}^b}{h_{ok}{}^{ba}h_{ok}{}^{aa}} + u_{ok}{}^{ba} \qquad (k = 1, \dots, r), (a = 1, \dots, m),$$
$$(b = 1, \dots, m) \qquad \text{(ivb)}$$

where country a is considered to be the country of immigration.

If country a grants some industry i less than its equilibrium degree of protection, it fails to establish any functional relationship between its domestic cost, $c_i{}^a$, and its cost in the relevant countries or country (country b) from which it imports commodity i. Commodity i is then a noncompetitive import and the equation in (iva) corresponding to it must be replaced by:

$$p_{n_i}{}^a = \frac{h_i{}^{ab}c_i{}^b}{h_i{}^{ba}} + u_i{}^{ba} \qquad (i = 1, \dots, n), (a = 1, \dots, m),$$
$$(b = 1, \dots, m).$$

This equation gives the price which country a's consumers, whether they are final consumers or producers of other commodities, must pay for commodity i.

The trade cost terms in equations (iva) and (ivb) are the costs of transport and other trade services, and they depend on the corresponding production functions and input prices. Protection coefficients apply to these costs as to those of any other tradable service and therefore enter into the determination of u_j^{ab} and u_{ok}^{ab} in any particular situation. Even under completely free trade, however, these costs introduce disparities in goods and service prices among different cities, regions, or countries. Their existence would generally break the functional relationships in (iva) for all those goods, such as those belonging to Group II and many belonging to Group I, which share their primary factors with other goods. Most such industries would fail to receive equilibrium degrees of protection and countries would trade in fewer of them than they use primary factors. This is because the existence of transport costs would cause factor prices to diverge in two regions which did not have identical relative factor endowments. The divergence of factor prices would make the production costs of most commodities diverge as well, but to a degree that would depend on their relative factor intensities. Goods of extreme factor proportions would therefore be the most likely to diverge sufficiently in comparative costs to overcome shipping charges.

The divergence of relative factor prices causes movable factors, like labor and capital, to move if they encounter no excessive migration restrictions. For this reason, the prices of labor and capital tend to be fairly uniform within an integrated market area and so, then, do the local production costs of the broad range of manufactured, or Group II, commodities. The prices of immovable factors and the costs of the goods they produce remain disparate, however. Hence primary commodities, like raw materials, are far more important in interregional trade than are secondary products, when compared to the relative importance of the two groups in total output. Protection, which hampers trade in the products of the allocable factors more than trade in those of specific resources, causes the same imbalance to appear in trade among countries having different relative prices of labor and capital.

VARIETIES OF PROTECTION AND ECONOMIC WELFARE

Some combinations of the sectoral protection coefficients, the h_i^{ab}, set by country a can be expected to achieve the production structure and relative prices which its customs authorities desire at less cost to society than other combinations. The first section of this chapter has shown that, in a two-commodity, two-factor example, internal taxes could achieve the same point on the transformation curve as a set of tariffs, but that it could do so at a lower social cost. The example also assumed, however, that there were no intermediate goods.

Intermediate goods cloud the problem because they destroy the neat distinction between consumer and producer upon which rests the case for the desirability of production subsidies and taxes. They also make it necessary to distinguish among alternative methods of paying production subsidies and levying internal taxes. Although other possibilities exist, it is useful and not too complicated to distinguish between taxes and subsidies applying to the total market cost of commodities and those which are levied on or paid to the value-adding activity, on the one hand, and, on the other, excises and subsidies which treat the same commodity differently according to whether or not it is earmarked for final or intermediate use.

The first question is whether or not internal interventions can achieve the same set of relative commodity prices for a given set of relative factor prices as can tariffs alone or tariffs and export subsidies. Suppose that the authorities make no distinction themselves between final and intermediate uses and wish to pick a set of h_i^{aa}'s as nearly equivalent in effect as possible to a given set of h_i^{ab}'s. The typical equation in (iii)$'$ is now:

$$\frac{p_j^a}{h_i^{aa}} = \sum_{k=1}^{r} F_{kj}'^a p_{ok}^a + \sum_{i=1}^{n} a_{ij}'^a p_i^a \qquad (a = 1, \ldots, m),$$
$$(i = 1, \ldots, n), (j = 1, \ldots, n).$$

Solving this set of simultaneous equations for commodity prices in terms of primary-factor prices yields the system:

$$p^a = [F'^a (\text{diag } h^{aa^{-1}} - A'^a)^{-1}]^T p_o^a.$$

With the h_i^{aa}'s considered as known, equations (i)$'$ and (iii) still contain enough restrictions to determine all n prices from the $r - 1$ relative factor prices. If some intermediate goods are primary factors to country a, their prices may be placed in the vector of independent variables along with the $p_{ok}{}^a$, as before. Because they can set as many $h_i{}^{aa}$'s as there are commodity prices equal to those of some other country, country a's authorities can always duplicate the effect on the prices, $p_j{}^a$, of any given set of equilibrium-protection coefficients, $h_i{}^{ab}$, applying to the two countries for fixed relative factor prices.

Discriminatory taxation or subsidization of value added by industry has the same flexibility. Let the coefficient $v_j{}^a$ be equal to one plus the tax rate on the income which sector j in country a generates. The typical equation in (iii)$'$ can now be written:

$$c_j{}^a = \sum_{i=1}^{n} a_{ij}{}'^a p_i{}^a + v_j{}^a \sum_{k=1}^{r} F_{kj}{}'^a p_{ok}{}^a \qquad (k = 1, \ldots, r),$$
$$(a = 1, \ldots, m).$$

If $p_j{}^a = c_j{}^a$ applies in the absence of any excise taxes or subsidies and if industry j operates in country a, the system of equations in (iii)$'$ is:

$$c^a = [(I - A'^a)^{-1}]^T \operatorname{diag} v^a F'^{aT} p_o{}^a.$$

The authorities can arrive at any desired set of relative commodity prices from any given set of relative factor prices by using value-added production subsidies and taxes, just as they can by using the former type. They act on different components of total cost, however, and so can be expected to lead to different input proportions. Suppose that the $F_{kj}{}'$ and $a_{ij}{}'$ were constant at all relative prices. The authorities could then find a set of $v_j{}^a$'s identical in effect to a given set of $h_i{}^{aa}$'s:

$$v_j{}^a = \left(h_j{}^{aa} c_j{}^a - \sum_{i=1}^{n} a_{ij}{}' p_i{}^a \right) \Big/ \sum_{k=1}^{r} F_{kj}{}' p_{ok}{}^a.$$

The value-added protection coefficients would have to diverge the most from unity for those commodities which had relatively low primary-factor costs. The sectors producing them would therefore have the greatest incentive to substitute intermediate for primary factors, if input coefficients are variable.

Thus the three types of protection considered so far — protection through trade intervention, discriminatory excises, and value-added taxes and subsidies — are not perfect substitutes for one another. Trade intervention is generally considered protection par excellence, largely because it must be discriminatory. Excise taxes or subsidies on the total cost of production could be made neutral with respect to relative factor shares, but they would inevitably discriminate accidentally according to the cost structure of industries. Only value-added taxes or subsidies could be made truly neutral, and they are therefore useful as a referent when one speaks of neutral fiscal policies. Equal *ad valorem* value-added taxes imply the equality of all the $v_j{}^a$'s and the absence of any discrimination or protection. The matrix diag v^a is then a scalar matrix and its position in system (iii)' does not matter. A given set of relative factor prices will yield the same *relative* goods prices no matter what the single tax rate:

$$c^a = \text{diag } v^a [F'^a (I - A'^a)^{-1}]^T p_o{}^a.$$

Such a tax is equivalent to taxing by the same percentage each factor supplied, that is, to make all $h_{ok}{}^{aa}$'s the same, and does not cause substitution among inputs because it does not change relative prices.

Because discriminatory internal taxes and subsidies affect input proportions and thus the optimality of equations (iii), they prevent a country from producing on its transformation locus. If the $v_j{}^a$'s and $h_i{}^{aa}$'s are considered as given, equations (iii) still permit one to derive the locus along which the country will transform factor-service inputs and commodities into one another. The new, inferior, locus will be flat in the $n - r$ hyperspace and so the analysis of structural indeterminacy remains the same. But the case for the superiority of production subsidies over trade intervention is lost. Trade intervention lowers consumer welfare by imposing different final prices between separated markets; yet each country still trades from the surface of its optimum transformation locus. In some situations, one of the above three types of protection will be better than either of the others, but it would be difficult to determine which one.

Some combination of at least two of these protectionist policies would presumably be the best in any particular situation. The way to design the best policy is to consider what corresponds to discriminatory subsidization or taxation in the cases admitting no intermediate commodities. It is necessary to establish a set of protection coefficients that enables producers, acting according to the maximizing conditions of (iii), to equate marginal private and social costs. Thus $p_i{}^a$ must be the same as $c_i{}^a$ for all commodities which country a produces. The way to accomplish this is to discriminate between final and intermediate consumers, as through a retail tax. Let $s_i{}^a$ be equal to one plus the rate of the domestic retail tax or subsidy, and let $m_i{}^a = s_i{}^a p_i{}^a = s_i{}^a c_i{}^a$ be the retail price of commodity i in country a. The price which producers in country a pay for commodity i is equal to:

$$\frac{h_i{}^{ab} c_i{}^b}{h_i{}^{ba}} + u_i{}^{ba}$$

if country a imports x_i from country b. Suppose that transport costs can be ignored. Consumers in country a will then face the same prices as those in country b if $h_i{}^{bb} = 1$ and if $s_i{}^a = h_i{}^{ba}/h_i{}^{ab}$. Country a must therefore levy tariffs and pay trade subsidies if it wishes to minimize the distortions of discriminatory internal taxation and subvention. The tariffs and trade subsidies should apply, however, only to consumers who use the products in question for production, and not to final consumers. Then the productive system can operate on its maximum efficiency locus, and final consumers can maximize their utility with respect to world commodity prices.

WORLD GENERAL EQUILIBRIUM UNDER PROTECTION

The preceding three sections have skirted the determination through trade of the actual prices of any given country and have concentrated instead only on certain price and cost relationships which must hold whatever the actual prices. When protection coefficients are given, the world price system depends upon the demand and supply conditions of *each* country linked in trade with the rest.

Each individual is assumed to substitute one commodity for others or for leisure until further substitutions within his income possibilities no longer increase his total satisfaction. His final commodity demands and factor supplies depend only upon the relative prices he faces. The final demands and supplies of individuals facing common sets of relative prices can be aggregated to yield the amounts pertaining to each country. Let r_i^a be country a's final demand of commodity i. Then

$$r_i^a = D_i^a(m_1^a, \ldots, m_n^a; c_{o1}^a, \ldots, c_{or}^a) \qquad (i = 1, \ldots, n),$$
$$(a = 1, \ldots, m). \qquad \text{(va)}$$

Residents of country a may supply factors to other countries as well as to their own. Let S_k^a be the total amount of factor k which the residents of country a supply. This amount depends upon the prices that suppliers in country a receive, as well as upon the local prices they must pay for final goods:

$$S_k^a = S_k^a(m_1^a, \ldots, m_n^a; c_{o1}^a, \ldots, c_{or}^a) \qquad (k = 1, \ldots, r),$$
$$(a = 1, \ldots, m). \qquad \text{(vb)}$$

Governments are assumed to distribute their tariff or other protection revenue to their own citizens or to governments or citizens of foreign countries. If a government's protection revenue is negative, it is assumed to collect the deficit from its citizens in the form of nondiscriminatory taxes. Each citizen's income thus comes partly from his factor earnings and partly from government transfers, and he spends what he receives, but no more. These assumptions guarantee that each country's payments will balance.

It may be convenient at this point to streamline somewhat and to gather in one place the equations of the homogeneous economy of each country:

$$\psi_j(F_{1j}'^a, \ldots, F_{rj}'^a; a_{1j}'^a, \ldots, a_{nj}'^a) = 1 \quad \text{and}$$

$$q_j^a = x_j^a - \sum_{i=1}^{n} a_{ji}'^a x_i^a, \qquad (j = 1, \ldots, n), (a = 1, \ldots, m). \quad \text{(i)}'$$

$$F_k^a = \sum_{j=1}^{n} F_{kj}'^a x_j^a \qquad (k = 1, \ldots, r), (a = 1, \ldots, m). \quad \text{(ii)}$$

$$p_{ok}^a \geqq c_j^a \partial \psi_j(F_{1j}'^a, \ldots, F_{rj}'^a; a_{1j}'^a, \ldots, a_{nj}'^a)/\partial F_{kj}'^a \quad \text{and}$$
$$p_i^a \geqq c_j^a \partial \psi_j(F_{1j}'^a, \ldots, F_{rj}'^a; a_{1j}'^a, \ldots, a_{nj}'^a)/\partial a_{ij}'^a$$
$$(k = 1, \ldots, r), (i = 1, \ldots, n), (j = 1, \ldots, n),$$
$$(a = 1, \ldots, m). \qquad \text{(iii)}$$

$$c_i{}^a = C_i{}^{ab}(c_i{}^b, u_i{}^{ab}) \quad \text{or} \quad p_{ni}{}^a = \frac{h_i{}^{ab}c_i{}^b}{h_i{}^{ba}} + u_i{}^{ab}$$

$$(i = 1, \ldots, n), (a = 1, \ldots, m), (b = 1, \ldots, m). \tag{iva}$$

$$c_{ok}{}^a = C_{ok}{}^{ab}(c_{ok}{}^b, u_{ok}{}^{ab})$$
$$(k = 1, \ldots, r), (a = 1, \ldots, m), (b = 1, \ldots, m). \tag{ivb}$$

$$m_i{}^a = s_i{}^a p_i{}^a \qquad (i = 1, \ldots, n), (a = 1, \ldots, m). \tag{ivc}$$

$$p_i{}^a = h_i{}^{aa} c_i{}^a \qquad (i = 1, \ldots, n), (a = 1, \ldots, m). \tag{ivd}$$

$$p_{ok}{}^a = h_{ok}{}^{aa} c_{ok}{}^a \qquad (k = 1, \ldots, r), (a = 1, \ldots, m). \tag{ive}$$

$$r_i{}^a = D_i{}^a(m_1{}^a, \ldots, m_n{}^a; c_{o1}{}^a, \ldots, c_{or}{}^a)$$
$$(i = 1, \ldots, n), (a = 1, \ldots, m). \tag{va}$$

$$S_k{}^a = S_k{}^a(m_1{}^a, \ldots, m_n{}^a; c_{o1}{}^a, \ldots, c_{or}{}^a)$$
$$(k = 1, \ldots, r), (a = 1, \ldots, m). \tag{vb}$$

The functions $C_i{}^{ab}$ and $C_{ok}{}^{ab}$ are only shorthand ways of writing the more complicated functions in (iva) and (ivb) on pages 145 and 155.

None of the system's equations depends on any absolute price, and so it can determine only price ratios. Each price level can be known only by specifying any price in any country:

$$p_1{}^1 = 1. \tag{vi}$$

Balance equations stating that all factor services supplied and commodities produced are completely consumed complete the world general-equilibrium system:

$$\sum_{a=1}^{m} S_k{}^a = \sum_{a=1}^{m} F_k{}^a \qquad (k = 1, \ldots, r) \quad \text{and} \tag{viia}$$

$$\sum_{a=1}^{m} q_i{}^a = \sum_{a=1}^{m} r_i{}^a \qquad (i = 1, \ldots, n). \tag{viib}$$

To be determinate, a general-equilibrium system must contain just as many independent equations as it has unknowns. The above system has a maximum of $2n$ gross and net commodity outputs and $rn + n^2$ input coefficients to determine for each country producing all the commodities. In addition, it must determine $2r$ domestic factor supplies and demands and n domestic commodity demands for each country. Prices of goods and factors do not have to be determined expressly by price concept and country because the various protection coefficients in functions (iva) through (ive) are all known. Those functions permit the expression of every country's prices in terms of those of any other country or group of countries. The system has only to determine one basic set of $r + n$ prices covering all commodities and factors for the world as a whole. If each country produces all commodities, there is a maximum of $(3n + rn + n^2 + 2r)m$ equations in (i)′, (ii), (iii), and (v), and $(1 + r + n)$ equations in (vi) and (vii). Not all of these equations are independent, however. Any single equation in the system could be ignored and the rest of the system would supply the missing information. In addition, as was seen earlier, the relations in (iii)′, because of Euler's theorem, constitute a set of unsuspected dependencies among equations (i)′ and (iii) in each country. The system thus has just enough equations to determine all *national* prices, input coefficients, demands, and supplies as well as the world output of each commodity. It cannot, in general, determine the exact allocation of production among countries.

PROTECTION AND TRADE STRUCTURE

The Heckscher–Ohlin theory of international trade can now be generalized to show that protection and relative factor endowments play similar logical and quantitative roles in determining trade flows. The link between protection and trade flows is through factor prices — in other words, through the economic effectiveness rather than the physical amounts of factors.

Differences in input prices, including those of primary factors, the relevance of more than two trading regions or countries, and the possibility of specialization when factor endowments lie outside the equalization region and when national industries fail to receive equilibrium protection make it necessary to alter the trade formulations of Chapter Three. System (3) of that chapter must now read:

$$t^a = r^a - (I - A_d'^a)\left\{\begin{array}{c} A_n'^a \\ \cdots \\ F'^a \end{array}\right\}^{-1}\left\{\begin{array}{c} n^a \\ \cdots \\ F^a \end{array}\right\} \quad (a = 1, \ldots, m). \quad (1)$$

System (1) gives country a's real competitive trade flows in terms of its consumption and net-output vectors, taken as known from the solution of the general-equilibrium system of the preceding section. The input coefficients in the matrices F'^a and A'^a, the noncompetitive imports in the vector n^a, and country a's factor supplies in the vector F^a are considered to be known from that solution. Assume for convenience that only customs protection applies, so that all protection coefficients h_i^{aa} and s_i^a are equal to unity and $p^a = c^a$. Multiplying system (1) by country a's consumer prices, also known from the solution of the world system, gives the value of country a's competitive trade flows:

$$\text{diag } p^a t^a = \text{diag } p^a r^a - \text{diag } p^a (I - A_d'^a) \left\{ \begin{array}{c} A_n'^a \\ \cdots \\ F'^a \end{array} \right\}^{-1} \left\{ \begin{array}{c} n^a \\ \cdots \\ F^a \end{array} \right\}.$$

Since by definition

$$(I - A_d'^a) = \text{diag } p^{a^{-1}} (I - A_d^a) \text{ diag } c^a, \quad (A_n'^a)^{-1}$$
$$= \text{diag } c^{a^{-1}} (A_n^a)^{-1} \text{ diag } p_n^a, \quad \text{and} \quad F'^{a^{-1}} = \text{diag } c^{a^{-1}} f^{a^{-1}} \text{ diag } p_o^a,$$

the system

$$\text{diag } p^a t^a = \text{diag } p^a r^a - (I - A_d^a) \left\{ \begin{array}{c} A_n^a \\ \cdots \\ f^a \end{array} \right\}^{-}$$

$$\times \left\{ \begin{array}{cc} \text{diag } p_n^a \cdot 0 \\ \cdots\cdots\cdots\cdots\cdots \\ 0 \cdot \text{diag } p_o^a \end{array} \right\} \left\{ \begin{array}{c} n^a \\ \cdots \\ F^a \end{array} \right\} \quad (a = 1, \ldots, m) \quad (2)$$

gives the value of country a's competitive trade flows in terms of its factor prices, including those of its noncompetitive imports, as well as of the amounts of its factor endowments and noncompetitive imports. The factor and noncompetitive-import bills, equal to $p_{ok}^a F_k^a$ and to $p_{ni}^a n_i^a$, rather than the corresponding physical quantities, explain competitive trade flows.

MEASURING THE EFFECTS OF PROTECTION

Protection allows domestic industries to compete with foreign industries and it changes relative commodity and factor prices. Since production structure is indeterminant whenever a large number of sectors compete with foreigners, the sectoral effects of protection are not important economically. Protection significantly affects world economic efficiency and the relative shares of factors in each country. The former effect is difficult to measure and is necessarily smaller than the latter. Since relative factor shares determine trade flows under protection, it is theoretically possible to judge the effects of protection on factor shares through a knowledge of trade flows and factor endowments.

Leontief's test of relative factor endowments provides a method for measuring the effects of protection on relative factor shares. It can measure the difference between actual factor prices and those which would obtain under factor-price equalization. It cannot, however, indicate how much of the divergence between domestic and foreign relative factor prices would persist under free trade if it failed to equalize factor prices.

Because system (2), which shows that factor incomes affect trade and vice versa, is merely a balance equation, it can be used to measure the effects of protection only under specified assumptions regarding changes in the input coefficients, $f_{kj}{}^a$ and $a_{ij}{}^a$, with respect to changes in relative prices. It is also necessary to know or assume the corresponding changes in consumption amounts in the vector r^a. The common assumption that physical input coefficients remain the same under all relative prices is unrealistic. Chapter Six shows that commercial policy causes even the intermediate-commodity input coefficients $a_{ij}{}'$ to vary significantly. It is necessary, as the only practical alternative, to assume that the value coefficients remain constant. This assumption asserts that all input-substitution elasticities are equal to unity and that production functions are of the following linear-exponential type:

$$\psi_j(F_{1j}{}', \ldots, F_{rj}{}'; a_{1j}{}', \ldots, a_{nj}{}') = \prod_{k=1}^{r} F_{kj}{}'^{f_{ki}} \prod_{i=1}^{n} a_{ij}{}'^{a_{ij}}$$

$$= 1 \qquad (j = 1, \ldots, n)$$

where

$$\sum_{k=1}^{r} f_{kj} + \sum_{i=1}^{n} a_{ij} = 1.$$

The partial derivatives of this function with respect to the input coefficients are

$$\partial \psi_j / \partial F_{kj}' = f_{kj}/F_{kj}' \quad \text{and} \quad \partial \psi_j / \partial a_{ij}' = a_{ij}/a_{ij}'.$$

Therefore, by virtue of (iii),

$$f_{kj} = p_{ok}{}^a F_{kj}'^a / c_j{}^a \quad \text{and} \quad a_{ij} = p_i{}^a a_{ij}'^a / c_j{}^a \quad (k = 1, \ldots, r),$$
$$(i = 1, \ldots, n), (j = 1, \ldots, n), (a = 1, \ldots, m).$$

The exponents of the production functions thus turn out to be equal to the input coefficients in value terms, which are therefore the same at every set of relative prices and so in every country.

It is most convenient to assume that demand functions are also linear-exponential and that countries therefore spend a constant share of their incomes on each product, despite changes or differences in their relative prices. Call this constant share R_i:

$$R_i = p_i{}^a r_i{}^a / Y^a \quad (i = 1, \ldots, n), (a = 1, \ldots, m)$$

where

$$Y^a = \sum_{i=1}^{n} p_i{}^a r_i{}^a = \sum_{k=1}^{r} p_{ok}{}^a F_k{}^a + \sum_{i=1}^{n} p_i{}^a t_i{}^a + \sum_{i=1}^{n} p_{n_i}{}^a n_i{}^a.$$

The lack of a country superscript indicates that R_i is assumed to be the same constant in every country. Let R be the column vector of elements R_i. Under these assumptions, country a's competitive trade flows depend as follows upon its primary-factor endowments and the value of its noncompetitive intermediate imports:

$$\text{diag } p^a t^a = \text{diag } Y^a R$$
$$- (I - A_d) \left\{ \begin{array}{c} A_n \\ \cdots \\ f'^a \end{array} \right\}^{-1} \left\{ \begin{array}{c} \text{diag } p_n{}^a n^a \\ \cdots \cdots \cdots \\ F^a \end{array} \right\}. \tag{3}$$

In system (3), diag Y^a is the scalar matrix of consumer income in country a. The elasticity of substitution assumptions make it possible to neglect the country superscripts for the matrices A_d

and A_n of intermediate-commodity input coefficients. The matrix f'^a, equal to diag $p_o{}^a f$, varies with changes in relative factor prices and does so in a simple way when f is assumed invariant. Its typical element, $f_{kj}{}'^a$, is the amount of factor k that each dollar's worth of commodity j directly employs. This is fortunately the primary-factor input coefficient which Leontief used in his measurement. It permits the approximate measurement of the effects of commercial policy.

The basic Leontief test consists of premultiplying system (1) by

$$\left\{ \begin{matrix} A_n{}'^a \\ \cdots\cdots \\ F'^a \end{matrix} \right\} (I - A_d{}'^a)^{-1}$$

to obtain

$$\left\{ \begin{matrix} A_n{}'^a \\ \cdots\cdots \\ F'^a \end{matrix} \right\} (I - A_d{}'^a)^{-1} \iota^a$$

$$= \left\{ \begin{matrix} A_n{}'^a \\ \cdots\cdots \\ F'^a \end{matrix} \right\} (I - A_d{}'^a)^{-1} r^a - \left\{ \begin{matrix} n^a \\ \cdots\cdots \\ F^a \end{matrix} \right\}.$$

This expression gives the factor contents of country a's trade and domestic-consumption vectors, but only as measured by its own sets of input coefficients. By substitution, it can be converted into a form employing the same input coefficients which Leontief used:

$$\left\{ \begin{matrix} A_n \\ \cdots\cdots \\ f'^a \end{matrix} \right\} (I - A_d)^{-1} \text{diag } p^a \iota^a$$

$$= \left\{ \begin{matrix} A_n \\ \cdots\cdots \\ f'^a \end{matrix} \right\} (I - A_d)^{-1} \text{diag } Y^a R - \left\{ \begin{matrix} \text{diag } p_n{}^a n^a \\ \cdots\cdots\cdots\cdots \\ F^a \end{matrix} \right\}. \quad (4)$$

This formulation of the Leontief test could be obtained also by considering system (3) merely as a set of trade balance equations and premultiplying it by

$$\left\{ \begin{array}{c} A_n \\ \cdots \\ f'^a \end{array} \right\} (I - A_d)^{-1}.$$

The same assumptions regarding tastes and input substitutability as those made in deriving system (3) make it possible to consider the matrices A_n and A_d and the vector R of system (4) as constant so that only the matrix f'^a introduces country a's peculiar input coefficients.

System (4) consists of $n - n^a + r$ balance equations, each of which gives the trade balance in its respective noncompetitive-import or primary-factor service. The equations are independent so that the balance, in the services of any noncompetitive import, say, contained in country a's competitive trade does not affect the measurement of traded services of capital and labor. The trade balances of the primary-factor services which competitive trade contains are the last r equations of (4) and can be written:

$$F_t^a = F_r^a - F^a.$$

Leontief used the equations in this system corresponding to labor and capital, and he therefore correctly discovered that the United States imports capital services and exports labor services in its competitive trade. The Leontief test, however, cannot account for the factor services, in particular those of labor and capital, which noncompetitive imports contain and which may cause it to misrepresent the relative factor endowments of the United States and the rest of the world. The test would certainly fail badly if free trade and extreme factor endowments caused a country to specialize in, say, the capital-intensive sectors of agriculture and manufacturing, thereby making unobservable the labor and capital services entering through the noncompetitive but labor-intensive imports. America's noncompetitive imports are almost entirely commodities containing specific natural resources which it lacks, however, and there is no reason to suppose them to contain an abnormal amount of either labor or capital.

Although one can safely disregard the influence of noncompetitive imports on Leontief's results and although system (4) accurately reflects the labor and capital content of a country's trade, Leontief's results nonetheless fail to show that the United States has less capital per worker than the rest of the world. The matrix f'^a makes $F_r{}^a$, the factor content of America's final consumption, a biased estimate of the relative factor endowments of the rest of the world. It is biased even though country a's, or America's, tastes are not factor-biased at any level of income. To estimate world factor endowments and therefore to judge correctly any country's relative endowments, it is necessary both to know how the world as an integrated economy with a common set of relative prices would produce that country's final demand and to know its final demand vector under factor-price equalization.

The special assumptions regarding elasticities of substitution permit one to guess what the input coefficients would be under factor-price equalization. Let $p_{ok}{}^*$ be the price which factor k would receive if the factor endowments of every country lay within the world equalization region and if trade were free of all restrictions. Let

$$g_k{}^a = p_{ok}{}^a / p_{ok}{}^* \qquad (k = 1, \ldots, r), (a = 1, \ldots, m)$$

be the ratio between the actual price of factor k in country a and that factor's price under equalization. The matrix of such coefficients will be equal to:

$$\text{diag } g^a = \text{diag } p_o{}^a \text{ diag } p_o{}^{*-1} \qquad (a = 1, \ldots, m).$$

Let

$$f'^* = \text{diag } g^a f'^a \qquad (a = 1, \ldots, m)$$

be the matrix of physical primary-factor inputs per dollar's worth of output under factor-price equalization. Further, let

$$Y^* = \sum_{k=1}^{r} F_k{}^a p_{ok}{}^*$$

and let diag Y^* be the scalar matrix of country a's income under equalization. Then the column vector,

$$F_r{}^* = f'^* (I - A)^{-1} \text{ diag } Y^* R,$$

gives, under the special assumptions of system (3), the amounts of factor services which the world would devote to country a's final demand under factor-price equalization.

Because tastes in country a are assumed not to be factor-biased, the vector $F_r{}^*$ is proportional to world factor endowments:

$$f'^*(I - A)^{-1} \operatorname{diag} w^{-1} \operatorname{diag} Y^*R = F^W.$$

Therefore,

$$\operatorname{diag} w^{-1}F_r{}^* = F^W$$

where w is the ratio between country a's and the world's incomes under equalization, and diag w is the scalar matrix of that ratio. Country a's true factor-service trade vector, $F_t{}^*$, is consequently equal to the difference between the vector $F_r{}^*$, which measures world relative factor endowments, and the vector F^a of its own factor supplies:

$$F_t{}^* = F_r{}^* - F^a \qquad (a = 1, \ldots, m).$$

If country a's original factor endowments lie outside the equalization region, so that factor-price equalization requires placing some of its factors in other countries or placing other countries' factors in country a, the vector $F_t{}^*$ will consist in part of factor services traded directly rather than through the intermediary of commodity trade.

The comparison of $F_r{}^a$, the false estimate of the world's relative factor endowments, with $F_r{}^*$, the correct measure under the assumptions of system (3), indicates by how much the divergence between country a's actual factor prices and its prices under equalization disturbs the Leontief test. Let the scalar y indicate the ratio of country a's income under factor-price equalization to its actual income so that

$$Y^* = yY^a \qquad (a = 1, \ldots, m).$$

The false estimate is then equal to

$$F_r{}^a = f'^a(I - A)^{-1} \operatorname{diag} Y^aR,$$

and the correct one to

$$\begin{aligned} F_r{}^* &= f'^*(I - A)^{-1} \operatorname{diag} y \operatorname{diag} Y^aR \\ &= \operatorname{diag} y \operatorname{diag} g^af'^a(I - A)^{-1} \operatorname{diag} Y^aR \qquad (a = 1, \ldots, m). \end{aligned}$$

By substitution, therefore,

$$F_r^* = \operatorname{diag} y \operatorname{diag} g^a F_r^a \qquad (a = 1, \dots, m). \qquad (5)$$

The scalar y reflects the gain in efficiency that factor-price equalization would bring about. It also reflects the absolute level of prices in country a, which depends only upon the particular combination of protection coefficients so that its value is determinate in any given case and F_r^* can theoretically be calculated (see the numerical example in the following section). Since diag y is only a scalar matrix, however, the matrix diag g continues to show how the distortion of relative factor prices can upset the calculation of endowments.

Protection, then, amounts to a new explanation of the Leontief paradox, which in turn offers a powerful method for measuring the effects of protection. As Chapter Three shows, the only failing of Leontief's calculation, as a test for relative factor endowments under free trade, was the unavoidable one of using a single country's input-output and primary-factor input coefficient matrices as substitutes for those of the world as a whole. This made it necessary to neglect noncompetitive imports, which form a large proportion of total imports and which could explain the Leontief paradox if they were labor-intensive products. The ratio of noncompetitive to total imports, however, clearly depends on the degree of protection applied. The high United States ratio of competitive Group I imports to total competitive imports also reflects the degree of protection, as does the lack of specialization in capital-intensive Group II products. Protection is therefore the most plausible of the theoretically and empirically possible explanations of the Leontief paradox. It requires no special assumptions in order to hold, and at the same time it explains the very characteristics of United States imports that are potentially the most dangerous to Leontief's method. It also explains other characteristics which do not accord with actual American relative factor endowments; for instance, under free trade, a large number of Group II products would appear as noncompetitive imports.

Measuring exactly the effects of protection on country a's factor returns theoretically requires, then, not only the special

172 · THEORY OF TRADE AND PROTECTION

assumptions of system (3) but also knowledge of actual world factor endowments, F^W, and the elements in the matrix $f'^a(I - A)^{-1}$ corresponding to the amounts of each of country a's factors which the industries it does not operate would use, directly and indirectly, per dollar's worth of their output under country a's relative goods and factor prices.

Suppose that the required information is available. Then

$$g^a = \operatorname{diag} y^{-1} \operatorname{diag} F_r{}^{a-1} F_r{}^*$$
$$= \operatorname{diag} y^{-1} \operatorname{diag} F_r{}^{a-1} \operatorname{diag} wF^W \qquad (a = 1, \ldots, m).$$

If one lets
$$\operatorname{diag} z = \operatorname{diag} w \operatorname{diag} y^{-1},$$
then
$$g^a = \operatorname{diag} z \operatorname{diag} F_r{}^{a-1} F^W \qquad (a = 1, \ldots, m). \qquad (6)$$

Since diag z is a scalar matrix, its value would not have to be known to determine the ratios of the disparities, $g_k{}^a$, in the vector g^a. Thus, without knowing world income under factor-price equalization, one could determine the ratio of the price of labor to that of capital in country a under protection to the ratio of their prices under equalization.

There is no reason not to go ahead and make the further assumptions necessary for such a determination. Obviously the result will be only a guess, and so it is best to separate assumed magnitudes from known ones in order to let each reader substitute his own notions of the unknown magnitudes and thus form his own judgment. The column numbers written above the following ratio serve to identify the figures in its numerator and denominator:

$$\frac{g_1{}^a}{g_2{}^a} = \frac{\overset{1}{z} \; \overset{2}{F_1{}^W} \; (\overset{3}{\$328{,}519{,}190{,}000} - \overset{4}{\$42{,}542{,}929{,}152} + \overset{5}{\$19{,}091{,}182{,}262} + \overset{6}{\$32{,}467{,}406{,}115})}{z \; F_2{}^W \; (\quad 47{,}273{,}526 \quad - \quad 3{,}040{,}689 \quad + \quad 1{,}049{,}894 \quad + \quad 1{,}785{,}501 \quad)}.$$

The constant z in column 1 cancels out when one is looking only for the ratio of the factor-price disparities. Its value is necessary, however, if one wishes to know the effect of protection and international factor immobility upon the real incomes of labor and capital in the United States and abroad. Under column 2 are the total world supplies of F_1 (labor) and F_2 (capital) — I shall make guesses for these shortly. Column 3 contains, in the numerator, the United States's capital stock, in dollars at 1947 prices, and in the denominator, its supply of man-years. Both figures are taken from Appendix Table II-A. The numerator figure in column 4 is equal to the amount of capital whose services the United States exported, according to Leontief's calculation, and that in column 5 to the amount whose services it imported through competitive imports. The denominator figures in the same columns give the amounts of labor whose services the United States exported and imported, respectively.[11] The figures in the numerator and denominator under column 6 are guesses of the amounts of capital and labor whose services the United States imported in 1947 through noncompetitive imports, which were in turn taken as equal in value to the difference between the value of total exports and that of competitive imports. This difference was equal to $10,502.7 million, which is large compared to the $6,175.7 million of competitive imports. The guess was made simply on the assumption that the ratio of capital to labor services in noncompetitive imports was equal to that ratio in competitive imports. The ratio of the numerator to the denominator is thus the same under both columns 5 and 6.

Under that special assumption, and with a standing for the United States, the ratio of price disparities is equal to:

$$\frac{g_1{}^a}{g_2{}^a} = \frac{F_1{}^W F_{r_1}{}^a}{F_2{}^W F_{r_2}{}^a} = \frac{F_1{}^W}{F_2{}^W} \times \$7,171.18/\text{man-year}.$$

The figure $7,171.18 is the implicit estimate Leontief made of the amount of capital employing each man-year of labor in the world as a whole. The only remaining step is to make an estimate of the actual ratio of capital to labor in the world as a whole. The United States has approximately 6 percent of the world's popu-

[11] Total exports in 1947 were $16,678.4 million and competitive imports $6,175.7 million (Wassily Leontief, "Domestic Production and Foreign Trade," *Economia internazionale*, 7:16 [February 1954], notes e and f). The figures were multiplied by the following coefficients of direct-plus-indirect capital and labor which each million dollars of total exports and of competitive imports contained (*ibid.*, p. 24):

	Exports	Imports
Capital (dollars, in 1947 prices)	2,550,780	3,091,339
Labor (man-years)	182.313	170.004

lation. If one assumes that the supply of man-years bears the same proportion to total population in the world as a whole as in the United States, F_1^W is equal to 784,470,533 man-years. Estimating the world capital supply requires the boldest guess of all. I feel that it is reasonable to suppose that the United States has at least a quarter of the world's total capital stock. This figure seems to agree with the United States's large share of total world income and its small population. It implies that the whole world has $1,675.11 and the world excluding the United States $1,256.33 of capital, in 1947 prices, per man-year; these figures certainly do not seem unreasonably low. The reader is warned, however, that he must make his own guesses or, preferably, his own estimates. My guesses amount to asserting that the ratio of g_1^a to g_2^a for the United States is equal to 4.28.

This ratio is obviously sensitive to the estimate of world capital and labor supplies. It is insensitive to whatever mistake comes from the estimate of the amount of capital and labor services in noncompetitive imports in column 6 of the ratio. Ten million dollars' worth of goods, even if produced with nothing but labor, could hardly employ at American wages more than 2,500,000 man-years, of which 1,785,501 are already counted in the estimate. On the other hand, if they contain almost purely capital, then at American interest rates it is hard to see how they could have brought in more than about $200 billion worth. This great capital intensity would, of course, imply an even higher ratio of g_1^a to g_2^a. The basic reason why the ratio is high as soon as one admits that the rest of the world has considerably less capital per worker than the United States is that total exports are small relative to national income. This makes the difference between the entries in column 4 and those in columns 5 and 6 necessarily small with respect to those in column 3, which give the country's total domestic supply of the factors. This in turn implies that foreign trade would be a vastly greater percentage of American national income if trade were free.

Now it is time to turn back to the special assumptions which system (3) made and which underlie the determination of the ratio of g_1^a to g_2^a. Those assumptions were that the elasticities of substitution of goods for one another in final usage and of inputs in production are equal to one, and that the preference and production functions are everywhere identical. The identity of production functions, however, is unessential; systematic differences among countries in general productive efficiency affect only the scalar z and not the ratios of the $g_k{}^a$'s. Tastes, on the other hand, are certainly not identical because preference functions are not homeothetic: relative preferences for certain types of goods increase with higher levels of per capita income. To the extent that agriculture is capital-intensive, that manufactures and services are labor-intensive, and that the United States is wealthy, this special assumption depresses the estimate of the ratio of $g_1{}^a$ to $g_2{}^a$ for the United States.[12]

The assumption that production functions are approximately linear-exponential has a certain amount of empirical justification. It is fairly widely accepted as the explanation of the temporal stability of factor shares in national income, a stability, moreover, which seems to be even more evident in individual manufacturing industries than in the economy as a whole.[13] Chenery and Watanabe have found that input-output tables of countries vary less in value than in underlying physical magnitudes, so that the matrices $A_d{}^a$ are approximately constant.[14] A recent study of the elasticity of substitution of capital for labor found that it varies from industry to industry. The median elasticity of substitution, however, seems to be close, and perhaps even equal, to one.[15]

The special assumptions of system (3), therefore, would seem unable to temper the conclusion that American and foreign protection and the international immobility of labor and capital

[12] Cf. Appendix Table II-A.

[13] Melvin W. Reder, "Alternative Theories of Labor's Share," *The Allocation of Economic Resources*, ed. Moses Abramovitz and others (Stanford, 1959), pp. 199–200, n. 51.

[14] Hollis B. Chenery and Tsunehiko Watanabe, "International Comparisons of the Structure of Production," *Econometrica*, 26:503–504 and 503, n. 14 (October 1958).

[15] The median elasticity of substitution for a cross-section sample of twelve Japanese and American manufacturing industries was .93. An alternative test indicated, however, an elasticity slightly greater than unity. See K. J. Arrow, H. B. Chenery, B. S. Minhas, and R. M. Solow, "Capital-Labor Substitution and Economic Efficiency," *Review of Economics and Statistics*, 43:239, 245–246 (August 1961).

raise the real earnings of labor in this country, depress them in the rest of the world, that they do the opposite to the real earnings of capital, and that the effects are considerable. The next chapter will show that the commercial policies of the United States and of certain of its trading partners strongly support this conclusion.

A NUMERICAL EXAMPLE

Before examining actual commercial policies, it may be useful to illustrate by means of a numerical example the quantitative relationships among tariff rates, relative factor prices, and national income. The numerical example may also make clearer several of the difficult points in the two preceding sections by giving them concrete reference.

To serve the latter purpose, it is best to keep the example itself as simple as possible. Suppose that there are only two countries, A and B, and that A alone interferes with trade. Assume that B is so large relative to A that A's commercial policy has no effect on B's prices. Let there be three sectors producing three commodities according to the following linear-exponential production functions:

$$x_3 = F_{13}{}^{f_{13}}F_{23}{}^{f_{23}}F_{33}{}^{f_{33}}x_{13}{}^{a_{13}}x_{23}{}^{a_{23}}x_{33}{}^{a_{33}}$$
$$= F_{13}{}^{.5}F_{23}{}^{.3}F_{33}{}^{.2}x_{13}{}^{0}x_{23}{}^{0}x_{33}{}^{0};$$
$$x_2 = F_{12}{}^{f_{12}}F_{22}{}^{f_{22}}F_{32}{}^{f_{32}}x_{12}{}^{a_{12}}x_{22}{}^{a_{22}}x_{32}{}^{a_{32}}$$
$$= F_{12}{}^{.37}F_{22}{}^{.13}F_{32}{}^{0}x_{12}{}^{0}x_{22}{}^{0}x_{32}{}^{.5};$$
$$x_1 = F_{11}{}^{f_{11}}F_{21}{}^{f_{21}}F_{31}{}^{f_{31}}x_{11}{}^{a_{11}}x_{21}{}^{a_{21}}x_{31}{}^{a_{31}}$$
$$= F_{11}{}^{.328}F_{21}{}^{.072}F_{31}{}^{0}x_{11}{}^{0}x_{21}{}^{.60}x_{31}{}^{0}. \tag{i}$$

Commodity 3 is a raw material, the specific resource of which is F_3, and it goes directly and entirely to sector 2, which produces a semimanufacture, x_2. This product in turn goes to sector 1, which produces |what will be assumed to be the only final commodity, x_1. Thus R_1 is equal to one and R_2 and R_3 are both equal to zero. Since the ratios of the exponents for capital and labor bear the following relationship:

$$.3/.5 > .13/.37 > .072/.328,$$

the activity of mining the raw material, x_3, is taken as being the most capital-labor intensive and that of finishing x_2 to make the final commodity, x_1, is taken as being the least.

Let country B, the rest of the world, possess the three factors in the proportions: $F_1^W : F_2^W : F_3^W = 35 : 12 : 3$. Its actual endowments are as much greater than these numbers as is necessary to make country A's actual endowments insignificant by comparison. Factor units can just as well be defined, as it will be convenient to do, so that the price of each factor in the integrated economy of country B is equal to one. Let country A's actual factor endowments be:

$$\begin{Bmatrix} F_1^A \\ F_2^A \\ F_3^A \end{Bmatrix} = \begin{Bmatrix} 23.7544 \\ 24.0000 \\ 4.0000 \end{Bmatrix}.$$

If country A's factors were all employed at world factor prices under factor-price equalization, the shares of labor, capital, and land in national income would be .4590, .4637, and .0773, respectively. The corresponding shares in country B are .70, .24, and .06, so that country A is seen to be quite labor-poor, quite capital-rich, and fairly land-rich.

The matrix f is equal to

$$f = \begin{Bmatrix} .328 & .37 & .5 \\ .072 & .13 & .3 \\ .0 & .0 & .2 \end{Bmatrix}$$

and its inverse to

$$f^{-1} = \begin{Bmatrix} 8.125 & -23.125 & 14.375 \\ -4.500 & 20.500 & -19.500 \\ 0 & 0 & 5.000 \end{Bmatrix}.$$

This matrix can be used to determine how many dollars' worth of each product country A would produce under free trade and whether or not it will specialize. If it does not specialize under free trade, its gross output of each commodity will be greater than zero, and its factor prices will be the same as those of the rest of the world. The gross-output vector, in value terms, is equal to

$$\text{diag } p^A x^A = f^{-1} \text{ diag } p_o^A F^A.$$

If the world factor-price matrix, which has been made to equal the identity matrix, is substituted for country A's factor-price matrix, however, its output of x_1 would be negative. This indicates that A's given factor endowments lie outside the equalization region and that it would therefore specialize under free trade. Its customs authorities can avoid specialization and protect sector 1 against the other sectors only by raising, through commercial policy, $g_1{}^A$ relative to $g_2{}^A$ and $g_3{}^A$. These $g_k{}^A$'s will in turn affect its commodity prices and determine the degrees of protection that each industry requires.

Let the authorities initially choose protection coefficients such that country A's factors receive the following money wages:

$$\begin{Bmatrix} p_{o1}{}^A \\ p_{o2}{}^A \\ p_{o3}{}^A \end{Bmatrix} = \begin{Bmatrix} 1.63146 \\ .50 \\ .25 \end{Bmatrix}.$$

They are thus prepared to raise the wage of labor relative to that of capital by somewhat more than three times, and to that of land by somewhat more than six times. Assume that they plan to do so by means of tariffs and trade subsidies rather than by means of production subsidies and taxes, and that transport costs are all zero. The vector of factor incomes, which determines a country's production and trade structure, is now equal in country A to:

$$\begin{Bmatrix} p_{o1}{}^A F_1{}^A \\ p_{o2}{}^A F_2{}^A \\ p_{o3}{}^A F_3{}^A \end{Bmatrix} = \begin{Bmatrix} 38.7544 \\ 12.0000 \\ 1.0000 \end{Bmatrix}.$$

Since the relative shares of the three factors in country A's national income are now .7488, .2319, and .0193, country B will export to A, net, capital and land services and will import from A labor services.

Country A's production vector, in value terms, is equal to $f^{-1} \text{diag } p_o{}^A F^A$ or to:

$$\begin{Bmatrix} p_1{}^A x_1{}^A \\ p_2{}^A x_2{}^A \\ p_3{}^A x_3{}^A \end{Bmatrix} = \begin{Bmatrix} 51.7544 \\ 52.1053 \\ 5.0000 \end{Bmatrix}.$$

Its net-output vector in value terms, diag $p^A q^A$, is equal to $(I - A)$ diag $p^A x^A$ or to:

$$\begin{Bmatrix} p_1^A q_1^A \\ p_2^A q_2^A \\ p_3^A q_3^A \end{Bmatrix} = \begin{Bmatrix} 1 & 0 & 0 \\ -.6 & 1 & 0 \\ 0 & -.5 & 1 \end{Bmatrix} \begin{Bmatrix} 51.7544 \\ 52.1053 \\ 5.0000 \end{Bmatrix} = \begin{Bmatrix} 51.7544 \\ 21.0526 \\ -21.0526 \end{Bmatrix}.$$

Its consumption vector, diag $p^A r^A$, under the special assumption about demand conditions will be equal to:

$$\begin{Bmatrix} p_1^A r_1^A \\ p_2^A r_2^A \\ p_3^A r_3^A \end{Bmatrix} = \begin{Bmatrix} Y^A \\ 0 \\ 0 \end{Bmatrix}$$

where Y^A is country A's money income. In order to find country A's trade flows it is necessary to find world prices (equal, in this example, to p_i^B) and A's prices of each commodity. These are needed to determine that value for country A's income at world market prices which balances its payments.

Relative factor prices in both countries are known beforehand. Equations (i)′ and (iii) therefore can be solved for the input coefficients, F_{kj}' and a_{ij}', and for the goods prices in both countries. The equations in (ii) can then be solved for the actual amounts of the outputs in country A. Part of the work of finding the outputs has already been accomplished in finding the value of country A's outputs of the three commodities. It will accordingly be simpler to begin with the gross-output vector, diag $p^A x^A$. Since

$$p_j^A = p_{ok}^A F_{kj}'^A / f_{kj} \qquad (j = 1, \ldots, 3), (k = 1, \ldots, 3),$$

then

$$p_j^A x_j^A = p_{ok}^A F_{kj}^A / f_{kj},$$

and these equations can be solved directly for all the factor allocations.

The output and price of x_3^A can also be found directly: $p_3^A x_{32}^A$ is known, and dividing it by p_3^A indicates the physical amount, x_{32}^A. The price and output of the product x_2 in country A can then be determined, as well as those of x_1. Similarly, the input coefficients and prices of country B's commodities can be found. Its outputs cannot be determined since B's absolute factor endowments have not been specified. The results are as follows:

$$F'^A = \begin{Bmatrix} 1.2807 & .9815 & .6747 \\ .9173 & 1.1260 & 1.3210 \\ 0 & 0 & 1.7613 \end{Bmatrix};$$

$$A'^A = \begin{Bmatrix} 0 & 0 & 0 \\ .8826 & 0 & 0 \\ 0 & .9835 & 0 \end{Bmatrix};$$

$$F'^B = \begin{Bmatrix} 1.9032 & 1.6491 & 1.4001 \\ .4178 & .5794 & .8401 \\ 0 & 0 & .5600 \end{Bmatrix};$$

$$A'^B = \begin{Bmatrix} 0 & 0 & 0 \\ .7811 & 0 & 0 \\ 0 & .7959 & 0 \end{Bmatrix};$$

$$\begin{Bmatrix} x_1^A \\ x_2^A \\ x_3^A \end{Bmatrix} = \begin{Bmatrix} 8.1245 \\ 12.0317 \\ 2.3711 \end{Bmatrix};$$

$$\begin{Bmatrix} p_1^A \\ p_2^A \\ p_3^A \end{Bmatrix} = \begin{Bmatrix} \$6.3702 \\ \$4.3307 \\ \$2.2016 \end{Bmatrix}; \begin{Bmatrix} p_1^B \\ p_2^B \\ p_3^B \end{Bmatrix} = \begin{Bmatrix} \$5.8024 \\ \$4.4571 \\ \$2.8001 \end{Bmatrix}; \begin{Bmatrix} h_1^{AB} \\ h_2^{AB} \\ h_3^{AB} \end{Bmatrix} = \begin{Bmatrix} 1.0979 \\ .9716 \\ .7863 \end{Bmatrix}.$$

Country A's exports of x_2 and imports of x_3 are accordingly, at world prices:

$$p_2^B t_2^A = \$-21.6674;$$
$$p_3^B t_3^A = \$\ \ 26.7757.$$

In these commodities A has an import deficit of \$5.1083 at world prices, which it must make up by exporting an amount of x_1 worth \$5.6081 at its own price of that commodity. Subtracting this from $p_1^A x_1^A$ gives its national income at its own market prices:

$$Y^A = \$46.14627.$$

This completes the determination of country A's trade flows. It exports x_1 under an export subsidy of 9.78 percent and x_2 under an export tax of 2.8 percent of their world prices. It imports the raw material, x_3, with an import subsidy of 21.374 percent.

Country A's factors earn \$51.7544 but are able to purchase an amount of x_1, at A's price, worth only \$46.1463. The difference is equal to the total amount of trade subsidies the government pays minus the amount it receives from the export tariff, or \$5.6081. The government must collect this balance from its subjects in the form of nondiscriminatory internal taxes.

Now suppose that someone applies the Leontief test to country A's trade. He first obtains the vectors:

$$f'^A(I - A)^{-1} \operatorname{diag} p^A t^A = \operatorname{diag} p_o{}^{A^{-1}} f(I - A)^{-1} \operatorname{diag} p^A t^A$$

$$= \left\{ \begin{matrix} F_{t_1}{}^A \\ F_{t_2}{}^A \\ F_{t_3}{}^A \end{matrix} \right\} = \left\{ \begin{matrix} -3.9547 \\ -1.8498 \\ 7.0751 \end{matrix} \right\} = F_t{}^A$$

and

$$f'^A(I - A)^{-1} \operatorname{diag} p^A r^A = \left\{ \begin{matrix} F_{r_1}{}^A \\ F_{r_2}{}^A \\ F_{r_3}{}^A \end{matrix} \right\} = \left\{ \begin{matrix} 19.7997 \\ 22.1502 \\ 11.0751 \end{matrix} \right\} = F_r{}^A.$$

The vector $F_t{}^A$ shows that country A seemingly exports capital services as well as labor services, despite the lower share of its income than of country B's going to capital. This anomaly can arise in marginal cases if a factor-service balance nearly equals zero because a country's imports and exports at its own domestic prices do not balance, even though its trade balances at world prices. The above formulation thus includes some disturbance resulting from the government account. The disturbance disappears, however, if one measures country A's factor-trade balance by measuring that of country B, which follows a neutral commercial policy:

$$f'^B(I - A)^{-1} \operatorname{diag} p^B t^B = f(I - A)^{-1} \operatorname{diag} p^B t^B$$

$$= F_t{}^B = \left\{ \begin{matrix} 3.6217 \\ -.7398 \\ -2.8819 \end{matrix} \right\}.$$

This account shows that country A indeed imports capital services.

The special assumptions and the altered Leontief test formulation of the preceding section make it possible to calculate country

A's factor-service trade under factor-price equalization. The first step is to calculate the vector F_r^* which gives country A's consumption of primary-factor services under equalization and which thereby indicates the relative factor endowments of the world as a whole:

$$F_r^* = f(I - A)^{-1} \operatorname{diag} Y^*R.$$

Factor-price equalization would cause each of country A's factors to earn one dollar per unit. Its national income would then be $51.7544 and its consumption of the three factor services would be:

$$\begin{Bmatrix} F_{r_1}^* \\ F_{r_2}^* \\ F_{r_3}^* \end{Bmatrix} = \begin{Bmatrix} 36.228080 \\ 12.421056 \\ 3.105264 \end{Bmatrix}.$$

Comparing this vector with country A's actual factor-endowment vector shows that it is indeed capital-rich and labor-poor. The elements in the vector stand in the relative proportions $35:12:3$, which were those the numerical problem assigned to the factor endowments of country B and therefore of the whole world.

Country A's actual consumption, valued at the prices which would obtain under factor-price equalization, is worth but $42.0331 instead of $46.1463. The difference between these two figures reflects not only the loss of efficiency under protection, but also the alteration in country A's absolute price level. Protection generally alters the price level as well as relative prices. The loss of efficiency can be measured by taking the ratio of Y^* to country A's actual income, measured at the prices which would obtain under factor-price equalization. This ratio is equal to 1.23.

The suppliers of the separate production factors fare quite differently under protection. Protection raises the real income of suppliers of F_1^A from $23.7544 to $31.4749, at the same final commodity price, p_1^B, or by a factor of 1.325. They lower the incomes of suppliers of F_2^A and F_3^A by factors of .40608 and .20304, respectively. These coefficients are the real returns to each unit of the factors.

It is important to notice that the change in relative factor prices exceeds in magnitude the change in relative goods prices. If $h_3{}^{AB}$ were set equal to one and the other protection coefficients as well as the $g_k{}^A$'s changed in the same proportion as $h_3{}^{AB}$, then $h_2{}^{AB}$ would be equal only to 1.2358 and $h_1{}^{AB}$ to 1.3963. The raw material, x_3, would be imported without subsidy or tariff while exports of x_2 received a subsidy of 23.58 percent and those of x_1 one of 39.63 percent. These relative protection coefficients are much smaller than the relative factor-price changes and indicate that seemingly low tariffs have a large effect on functional income distribution and on resource allocation.

Factor-price changes will always change commodity prices in lesser proportion if production functions are homogeneous of degree one and have continuous first partial derivatives. The effect of a given factor-price change on each commodity price will depend, moreover, on the share of that factor in the total value of the commodity. If commodities vary in factoral cost composition in any particular equilibrium, therefore, changes in relative factor prices will change relative commodity prices, but to a lesser extent. Let the vector π_o equal $\log p_o$, where p_o is the column vector of the factor prices. Let the vector π equal $\log p = \log g(e^{\pi \cdot}) = \theta(\pi_o)$ where p is the vector of commodity prices and the function g is the general mapping of factor prices into commodity prices. Then:

$$\frac{\partial \log g_j(p_{ok})}{\partial \log p_{ok}} = \frac{p_{ok}}{g_j(p_{ok})} \frac{\partial g_j(p_{ok})}{\partial p_{ok}} = \frac{p_{ok}}{p_j} F_{kj}{}'' = f_{kj}{}''$$

$$(k = 1, \ldots, r), (j = 1, \ldots, n).$$

The Jacobian matrix, $\theta'(\pi_o)$ of the equation system $\pi = \theta(\pi_o)$, is therefore related to that of the mapping $p = g(p_o)$ and to the matrix F'' of system (iii)' as follows:

$$\theta'(\pi_o) = \operatorname{diag} p^{-1} g'(p_o) \operatorname{diag} p_o = \operatorname{diag} p^{-1} F''^T \operatorname{diag} p_o = f''^T$$

where f'' is the $r \times n$ matrix of coefficients $f_{kj}{}''$. These coefficients are simply the total share of direct and indirect factor k in commodity j so that

$$f'' = f(I - A)^{-1}.$$

This derivation shows that the wage-bill coefficients, $f_{kj}{}''$, are equal to the corresponding elasticities of commodity prices with respect to factor prices: f_{kj}'' is at once the proportion of the value of commodity j going to its ultimate suppliers of factor k and the percentage change in its price in response to a one percent change in the price of factor k.[16]

Now, the elements in any column of matrix f'' must add up to unity because, by Euler's theorem, the factor shares must exhaust the value of each product. Therefore f_{kj}'' is always less than unity.

The matrix f'' of factor shares in the numerical example is equal to

$$f(I - A)^{-1} = \begin{Bmatrix} .70 & .62 & .50 \\ .24 & .28 & .30 \\ .06 & .10 & .20 \end{Bmatrix}.$$

Factor 2, for example, receives 24 percent of the price of commodity 1. If the price of factor 2 rises by 1 percent and all other factor prices remain constant, the price of commodity 1 rises by .24 percent. In practice, commodities can be ranked according to the shares of any particular factor. The commodities in the example have been ranked according to their labor intensity, commodity 1 being the most labor-intensive. The factor shares thus provide an unambiguous way of speaking of factor intensity when more than two factors exist. If factor-intensity crossovers are not too common or important, a country's tariff rates should be correlated with the factor shares corresponding to the factors which it protects and negatively correlated with those corresponding to the factors against which it discriminates. The next chapter uses this method to show that the United States discriminates in favor of labor and against natural resources.

The numerical example suggests a third measure of the degree of protection. When countries restrict imports of manufactured and processed commodities but allow raw materials to enter relatively freely, they raise the domestic price of manufactures and therefore the prices of labor and capital with respect to the

---

[16] The derivation has been taken from Chipman, pp. 4 and 5, and adapted to the case involving intermediate commodities.

prices of natural resources and domestic, as well as imported, raw materials. This price distortion should cause a substitution of raw materials for labor and capital in manufacturing industries. Each unit of the final commodity, x_1, in the numerical example, for instance, consumes directly and indirectly .868 units of the raw material, x_3, in protectionist country A, but only .6217 units in free-trading country B. Chapter Six measures the effect of this raw-material substitution in three comparable countries and shows that it is considerable.

INDETERMINACY AND THE METHOD OF PROTECTION

The duality between the indeterminacy of output and the determinancy of the respective protection coefficients, and vice versa, helps to explain the method of protection that is used in particular circumstances. Since any protection applied to intermediate products lowers the protection of their consumer industries, intermediate products typically enjoy less protection. This is especially true of industries producing raw materials: because such industries are the sole users of their specific resources, they will produce at some level even without protection. Indeterminacy applies most, therefore, to the industries belonging to Group II and depending only on the broad generic factors, labor and capital, in any country. These industries are extremely sensitive to the degree of protection.

If a Group II product is unimportant in other production processes and if a tariff protects its industry, that tariff rate is likely to exceed its equilibrium level and effectively to eliminate imports. Unnecessarily high tariffs not only give countries a bargaining advantage at no real cost in tariff negotiations, but they avoid the considerable trouble necessary to find the exact rate which protects the domestic industry. For the same reason, countries often prefer import quotas for intermediate Group II products. This obviates the need to calculate the exact tariff, yet permits some imports. Quotas eliminate the need to adjust the tariff to changes in economic conditions and the danger that any industry enjoying them will suffer from sudden increases in imports. The widespread use of trade quotas, production restrictions, and excessively high import duties greatly reduces, and perhaps eliminates, the indeterminacy in the international allocation of production.

THE COMMERCIAL POLICIES OF FIVE INDUSTRIAL COUNTRIES

THE best material for the study of commercial policy would be complete information regarding foreign and domestic prices and costs. Prices and costs reflect all trade impediments and in turn determine the profitability of industries and the returns to primary factors in each country or region. Comprehensive cost and price data are generally unavailable, however, and one is forced to rely on published customs tariffs, quota restrictions, and the like. The tariff rate either faithfully indicates the price disparity that it causes or else eliminates all imports and indicates surplus protection. It is therefore the best practical source for determining a country's commercial policy. The structure of the tariff also parallels that of other restrictions, such as quotas and administrative measures, which are much more difficult to evaluate.

THE UNITED STATES

The United States, like every country, protects manufacturing and processing industries at the expense of raw materials:

for the most part, crude foodstuffs and raw or partly processed materials are admissible either duty free or at low tariff rates, while manufactured goods, including manufactured foods and beverages, fall mainly within the middle and higher duty brackets. Among the industrial materials, there is a general — though not entirely consistent — tendency for the cruder forms of a given material to carry lower rates than the partly or considerably processed forms.[1]

Since labor is the United States's scarcest factor and since, as the Leontief test shows, its commercial policy protects labor, it is reasonable to suspect tariffs on labor-intensive products to be the highest at any given stage of processing or manufacture:

[1] U.S. Congress, Subcommittee on Foreign Trade Policy of the House Committee on Ways and Means, *Foreign Trade Policy* (Compendium of Papers), 85th Congress, 2nd session (Washington, 1957), p. 213.

Among finished manufactures, however, the same tendency toward correlation of tariff rates with the degree of physical processing between farm or mine and final product is not observable. Instead, the height of the duty tends, as a general rule, to vary roughly with the ratio of the direct labor costs to total costs in the industry performing the final stages of fabrication. Rates applicable to the complex products of our principal mass production manufacturing industries are distinctly more moderate, on the whole, than those on goods produced by labor-intensive industries, particularly where the production process is characterized by skilled artisanship, rather than advanced engineering techniques.[2]

The two influences which seem to explain the structure of the American tariff theoretically merge into a single explanation based on the relative factor intensities of commodities and on the factors which American policy favors and disfavors. If, for instance, high tariffs are correlated with high direct-plus-indirect labor cost coefficients, and vice versa, this would indicate that tariffs generally favor labor. Since capital and labor, in the long run, are the only allocable factors used in all industries, protection of labor necessarily implies discrimination against capital. By the same token, a negative correlation between tariffs and direct-plus-indirect natural-resource cost coefficients for each sector would indicate discrimination against natural resources.

Two circumstances rule out a direct application of this general approach. First, land-use coefficients, in value terms, for the various types of natural-resource inputs are not available, even though they are measurable. Second, direct labor and capital cost coefficients are available for a large number of American manufacturing and other industries, but the corresponding direct-plus-indirect coefficients can be calculated only according to the less comprehensive industrial classification of the United States input-output table.

Despite the lack of natural-resource coefficients and a more detailed input-output table, one can obtain sufficiently accurate correlations of tariff rates with the direct-plus-indirect land and labor coefficients. The correlation between tariffs and land use requires only that one speak of raw materials in an unambiguous way, as he can if the input-output matrix is triangular. Perfect triangularity means that all elements above (or below) the diagonal of a matrix are zero. If the input-output matrix has this property, one can identify raw-material sectors as those which sell their output to other sectors but buy only from the suppliers of primary factors. Processed raw materials and other semi-finished products can be identified in the same scheme, since each sector typically has a unique position in the industrial hierarchy spanning primary and final commodities. Since each material receives further services of labor and capital as it passes toward final consumption, its relative natural-resource content diminishes. It follows that the direct-plus-indirect primary-factor coefficients of industries low in the industrial hierarchy will necessarily be close to their corresponding direct coefficients.

The necessity of aggregating sectors to make tables of practical size obscures the intrinsic triangularity of the economy. This is especially true when sectors are classified according to the major materials they process, without regard to the stage of manufacture. Some methods of aggregation nonetheless preserve the triangularity with more success than others do. The French input-output table, for instance, classifies sectors according to both the stage of manufacture and the material processed, and it is therefore one of the most triangular of all input-output tables. On the other hand, many condensed versions of the United States table, as well as those of other nations, unnecessarily obliterate the triangularity of their economies.

Despite unfavorable classification schemes, however, every input-output table is quite triangular.[3] Chenery and Watanabe have identified and measured the triangularity of the production structures of several countries by combining their interindustry flows into a composite table.[4] For Italy, Japan, and the United States, they computed the ratio, u_j, of the value of each sector's total nonhousehold inputs to that of its total output. They also calculated the ratio, w_i, of the value of each sector's sales to other industries compared to the value of its total sales.[5] Thus, industries low in the industrial hierarchy should have low u_j and high

[3] See Robert Dorfman, Paul A. Samuelson, and Robert M. Solow, *Linear Programming and Economic Analysis* (New York, 1958), pp. 255, 264.
[4] Hollis B. Chenery and Tsunehiko Watanabe, "International Comparisons of the Structure of Production," *Econometrica*, 26:487–521 (October 1958).
[5] Chenery and Watanabe, p. 492.

w_i coefficients. These two measures of industrial position give rise to the four-way classification which Table 8 shows. The

TABLE 8. *Types of Productive Sectors*

Final			Intermediate		
III. Final manufactures			**II. Intermediate manufactures**		
	w	u		w	u
Apparel	.12	.69	Iron and steel	.78	.66
Shipbuilding	.14	.58	Paper and products	.78	.57
Leather and products	.37	.66	Petroleum products	.68	.65
Processed foods	.15	.61	Nonferrous metals	.81	.61
Grain-mill products	.42	.89	Chemicals	.69	.60
Transport equipment	.20	.60	Coal products	.67	.63
Machinery	.28	.51	Rubber products	.48	.51
Lumber and wood products	.38	.61	Textiles	.57	.69
Nonmetallic mineral products	.30	.47	Printing and publishing	.46	.49
Industry, n.e.c.	.20	.43			
IV. Final primary production			**I. Intermediate primary production**		
	w	u		w	u
A. Commodities			Agriculture and forestry	.72	.31
Fishing	.36	.24	Coal mining	.87	.23
B. Services			Metal mining	.93	.21
Transport	.26	.31	Petroleum and natural gas	.97	.15
Trade	.17	.16	Nonmetallic minerals	.52	.17
Services	.34	.19	Electric power	.59	.27

Source: Hollis B. Chenery and Tsunehiko Watanabe, "International Comparisons of the Structure of Production," *Econometrica*, 26:493 (October 1958).

so-called final sectors in that table have low w_i coefficients, while the primary sectors have low u_j coefficients. The distinction among the sectors, in particular among the three industrial groups, in Table 8 is clear despite the combination of products and materials in several of them, for few sectors lie close to the mean value of u_j.[6]

The goods in group I, which corresponds to sector 3 in the numerical example of the preceding chapter, are the most land-intensive, while those in group III, which corresponds to sector 1 in the numerical example, are the least. Further, these group I

[6] Chenery and Watanabe, pp. 492–493.

commodities, as Appendix Table II-A reveals, use large amounts of direct capital in proportion to direct labor (about $17,000 per man-year when Leontief's data are adapted to the classification of Table 8), while those in group II use smaller amounts (about $7,700), and those in group III use the least of all (about $4,000).

The goods in group I are subject to very low duties in the United States. Crude foodstuffs, which are primarily tropical products, pay only a 1 percent duty on the average and many of them enter duty-free. Many of the most important ores, such as nickel, iron, antimony, tin, and cobalt, are duty-free. Other ore duties, even those on lead and zinc, are moderate and often suspended. Copper, though nominally duty-free, has been subject to a discriminatory excise tax since 1932.[7] Dutiable imports of agricultural crude materials, other than foodstuffs, pay an average rate of 18 percent. Apparel wool, with its excessively high duty, accounts almost entirely, however, for this high average. Dutiable items, moreover, represent only slightly more than a quarter of the total value of agricultural crude-material imports.[8] Duties collected are only about 6 percent of the value of these imports. The other crude materials of group I, as well as the semifinished materials of group II, are also subject to low duty rates, with few exceptions. The average rate for dutiable items in these two groups is 6 percent *ad valorem*, but since half are duty-free, the average for all commodities in both groups is only 3 percent.[9]

Within the group III category, processed foods, including primarily sugar, alcoholic beverages, processed meat, and dairy products, are nearly all dutiable and they pay, on the average, a tariff of 12 percent.[10] Among the other products in this group, four fifths of them are dutiable, at an average rate of 20 percent.[11] Average tariff rates, particularly in a heterogeneous category such as manufactures, are poor measures of the degree of protection. Since few rates on manufactures fall short of the max-

[7] Don D. Humphrey, *American Imports* (New York, 1955), pp. 299–312.
[8] *Foreign Trade Policy*, p. 214.
[9] *Foreign Trade Policy*, pp. 213–214.
[10] *Foreign Trade Policy*, p. 214.
[11] *Foreign Trade Policy*, p. 214.

imum rates applied to items in the lower groups, it is safe to conclude that manufactures are without doubt the most highly protected broad category of commodities.

Since manufactured commodities are, on the average, highly labor-intensive, it appears that the high wages in the United States both require and explain the high average duties on this group. Some manufactures are, nonetheless, more labor-intensive than others, and a few are exceedingly capital-intensive. To what extent, then, do differences in factor intensity explain the considerable dispersion of the manufactured goods' tariff rates about their average level? Beatrice N. Vaccara has correlated tariff rates with the direct labor-cost and labor-use coefficients of 311 separate manufacturing industries in the United States, covering practically the whole manufacturing sector.[12] In addition to the higher degree of protection for manufactures than for the other important sectors, she found significant correlation between both labor-use and labor-cost coefficients and the degree of protection.[13] She found also that protection effectively prevents all imports of competitive manufactured commodities.[14]

The only exception one might take to Vaccara's method concerns her unavoidable use of direct, rather than direct-plus-indirect, labor coefficients. Most manufacturing sectors purchase the bulk of their intermediate inputs from other manufacturing (or semimanufacturing) sectors, rather than from the raw-material-producing sectors.[15] Thus the factor contents of the more basic sectors have little effect on those of the manufactured products. The factor content of whatever semifinished product a manufacturing sector might purchase in relatively large quantities will, however, affect its own factor content significantly.

---

[12] Beatrice N. Vaccara, *Employment and Output in Protected Manufacturing Industries* (Washington, 1960).

[13] Vaccara, *passim*, and pp. 7, 22, 23, 28–29, 50–78.

[14] Competitive imports were less than 1 percent of the value of shipments of 168 out of 302 industries for which Vaccara computed the ratio of imports to domestic shipments; they were 5 percent or more for only 58 industries. But the domestic shipments of those 58 industries were only 9 percent of the total shipments of the industries she analyzed (pp. 23–24).

[15] According to the Department of Labor interindustry table, 75 percent of the materials and fuels which the manufacturing section uses consists of manufactured products. Vaccara, p. 14, n. 4.

As a result, the labor intensity of the manufacturing stage of production may be more than offset by the capital intensity of its intermediate inputs, especially if the final manufacturing stage adds relatively little value to the product.

The actual correlation between the direct labor coefficients and the corresponding direct-plus-indirect labor coefficients of the United States's manufacturing industries is 0.886.[16] This high correlation completely vindicates Vaccara's method. Indeed, it would undoubtedly be higher still were it possible to make the calculation for her 311 sectors, rather than for the 143 manufacturing sectors contained in Leontief's data.

The strong correlation between protection and factor intensity is further and final evidence that factor-intensity crossovers play no significant role in determining production structures and trade flows. If they did, the necessity to protect many capital-intensive United States industries against low-paid foreign labor substituting for capital would have eroded the correlation. The consistency of Vaccara's results with those of Leontief and Tarshis effectively disposes of the bugbear of factor-intensity crossovers.

The commercial policy of the United States, even without taking into account foreign restrictions against its exports, fits exactly the explanation in Chapter Four of the Leontief paradox. One might wonder why, if protection has largely eliminated manufactured imports, recent tariff reductions have not led to large increases in them. Until recently, however, the American tariff has included many rates that were well above their respective equilibrium degrees of protection. These can be lowered without encouraging imports. Also, many other methods of restricting trade operate both in the United States and abroad with varying degrees of subtlety.

Three studies indicate that, when the degree of protection falls below its equilibrium level, imports increase quite rapidly. The first of these studies, by L. B. Krause, analyses the effects of the tariff reductions negotiated at Torquay in 1951.[17] It shows that

[16] Correlation of columns 1 and 3, sectors 21–164, of Wassily W. Leontief, "Factor Proportions and the Structure of American Trade," *Review of Economics and Statistics*, 38:403–407 (November 1956).

[17] "United States Imports and the Tariff," *American Economic Review*, 49:542–551, Papers and Proceedings (May 1959).

the reductions did little to increase overall imports, but that reductions of 30 percent or more in duties on a few commodities, particularly those which had received high rates, led to large increases in imports. In the second study, M. E. Kreinin examines the effects of the 1955 and 1956 negotiations under the General Agreement on Tariffs and Trade on United States import volumes and prices. He finds that the 2.7 percent decrease in American import prices which the 1955 negotiations achieved caused a 40 percent increase in imports of the affected commodities. The less extensive 1956 reductions lowered import prices only 1 percent between 1956 and 1959; yet, because of the tariff reductions, imports of the affected commodities increased 12 percent over that period.[18] Finally, J. Wemelsfelder finds that the German tariff reductions of 1956 and 1957, which reduced import prices of industrial products by 10 to 12 percent, caused an increase of 100 percent in imports by 1960.[19] Notice that all of these studies look only at short-term increases in imports. Kreinin found that foreign supply prices rose as a result of the tariff reductions much more than United States import prices of the same goods fell. Time enough had not elapsed by 1959, therefore, for foreign countries to shift resources to the newly favorable export lines. Krause's and Kreinin's studies indicate that from now on United States tariff reductions can be expected to lead to large increases in imports unless, of course, direct production subsidies and taxes and other devices intervene to maintain the former production structure. All of the studies indicate, in corroboration of the analysis in Chapter Four, that imports are highly sensitive to reductions in the tariff once excessive protection has been eliminated.

JAPAN

Since the United States employs more capital per worker than any other country, it obviously employs more than the rest of the world as a whole. It is thus natural that its tariff, in addition

[18] "Effect of Tariff Changes on the Prices and Volume of Imports," *American Economic Review*, 51:314–320 (June 1961).

[19] "The Short Term Effect of the Lowering of Import Duties in Germany," *Economic Journal*, 70:97–98 (March 1960).

to allowing land services to enter freely, should discriminate against imports of labor services. Although Japan is the most labor-rich of all of the major industrial countries, it is impossible now to say whether it has more or less capital per man than the rest of the world. Japan's foreign trade reflects its intermediate capital-labor endowment. More than 70 percent of its exports of capital-intensive or fairly capital-intensive manufactured products, such as railway rolling stock, chemical fertilizers, rayon yarn, textile machinery and parts, staple fiber yarn and fabrics, cement, enameled iron ware, cotton and woolen yarn, iron and steel, aluminum, copper, and so on, go to low-income countries. Over 70 percent of such relatively labor-intensive commodities as ships, raw silk, blouses, plywood, cultured pearls, silk fabrics, fish and shell fish (canned or bottled), fish and whale oil, toys, linens, cameras, radios, and the like, go to high-income, and therefore capital-rich, countries.[20] In 1958, each of these two markets was taking about 50 percent of Japan's exports, although in prewar years the share of the low-income market was considerably higher. Tatemoto and Ichimura have published a Leontief test of Japanese trade which finds that Japan exported capital services and imported labor services in 1951. This finding has an easy explanation:

These paradoxical findings occur at least partly because Japan's place in the world economy is midway between the advanced and underdeveloped countries. In consequence, she may be expected to have a comparative advantage in labor-intensive goods when trading with the former and in capital-intensive goods when trading with the latter. If this conjecture is not far from reality, there would be a tendency in Japanese foreign trade for labor-intensive exports to go to advanced and capital-intensive exports to underdeveloped countries. Since about 25 percent of Japanese exports went to advanced and 75 percent to underdeveloped countries in 1951, it is not surprising to find that on balance Japan appears as a "capital-abundant" country in comparison with the rest of the world.[21]

To test this hypothesis, the authors isolated Japan's trade with the United States from that with its other trading partners and

[20] Saburo Okita, "Post-War Structure of Japan's Foreign Trade," *Economia internazionale*, 13:96–97 (February 1960).
[21] Masahiro Tatemoto and Shinichi Ichimura, "Factor Proportions and Foreign Trade: The Case of Japan," *Review of Economics and Statistics*, 41:445 (November 1959).

performed a separate Leontief test for the two resulting regions. They find that Japanese exports to the United States were indeed more labor-intensive than its exports to other countries and that United States exports to Japan were more capital-intensive than competitive imports from that country.[22]

The dualism of the trade structure of any country which, like Japan, is neither capital-rich nor capital-poor compared to the rest of the world makes difficult any attempt to determine which of these two general factors its commercial policy protects. In addition, Japan, like many other countries, relies more on non-tariff forms of protection than the United States does. Quantitative import controls have been common as well as discriminatory internal taxes and subsidies, including subsidized loans and the like, and export subsidies. This compounds the difficulty but, at the same time, if a country does not have an extreme labor-capital endowment ratio, the enquiry is less essential: the truth may be that the country favors one of the general factors no more than the other. Such countries, by protecting manufacturing and processing activities generally, will automatically protect whichever general factor needs protection vis-à-vis a particular trading partner.

The Japanese tariff presents the same correspondence between high duty rates and high stages of manufacture as the American tariff does. Indeed, in this respect, the Japanese tariff is much simpler to study because it has been more rationalized according to precisely that principle, probably because labor protection does not have to interfere. Its duty rates, moreover, are almost entirely *ad valorem*, rather than specific. But most imports, until recently at least, require licenses. The government, in assigning licenses, has given first priority to importers of foods and basic raw materials, with second priority to importers of machinery and industrial equipment needed to expand and modernize plants, especially those which can contribute directly to export expansion.[23] Any raw-material duty is drawn back if the finished product is exported within two years. Certain items, mainly essential

---

[22] Tatemoto and Ichimura, pp. 445–446.
[23] U.S. Department of Commerce, *Investment in Japan* (Washington, 1956), p. 57.

machinery, crude petroleum, synthetic tanning materials, dyes, and iron and steel, may be imported duty-free for specified periods.

Table 9 tabulates Japanese *ad valorem* duty rates, according to Chenery's and Watanabe's four-way classification, to illustrate the correspondence between rates and the degree of fabrication. The scheme of aggregation in the table is not ideal for such a purpose, since it classifies several sectors, such as "lumber and wood products," according to the materials they process rather than their stage in the hierarchy. The section of intermediate primary products, or raw materials, consequently, does not really contain all raw materials, but actually only those which are common to several sectors as defined in the table. For this reason, Table 10 presents separately several important production chains. It is clear that if one had an input-output table for Japan sufficiently detailed to distinguish such production chains, the average deviation in duty rates of many of the sectors in Table 9 would diminish.[24] Tables 9 and 10 show clearly that Japanese duties are closely related to the degree of fabrication of the goods they protect. The average deviation, like the arithmetic average duty, is low for the intermediate primary commodities and shows the low degree of protection they enjoy. Table 10 shows this tendency in greater detail for certain production chains.

It is curious to observe that Japan reserves some of its highest duties for precisely those commodities in which other industrial countries most fear Japanese competition. The Japanese tariff has been completely rewritten since the war, so it seems unlikely that it contains purely accidental or historical protection. The high duties on these export commodities may, however, stem from a desire to obtain bargaining authority in prospective tariff negotiations or from a fear of potential imports from such places as Hong Kong, India, and Pakistan. If the tariffs support export

---

[24] The average deviation from the mean is the simplest measure of dispersion. It is the average of the absolute differences of each member of a group from the group mean. If this measure is equal to zero, the arithmetic average of duties serves perfectly as the group *ad valorem* tariff. A low average deviation is an indication that the arithmetic average duty rate is a reasonable substitute for an average computed by means of an ideal set of weights.

TABLE 9. *Classification of Sectors by Average Import Tariff, Japan, 1960*

Sector	Eliminated items	Range of import duties	Number of items[a]	Import duty Arithmetic average	Import duty Average deviation from mean
I. Intermediate primary production					
Metal mining	2[b]	0 %	7	0 %	0
Petroleum	–	5	1	5	0
Coal mining	–	0	1	0	0
Agriculture and Forestry	2[c]	0–20	122	4.4	4.9
Nonmetallic mineral	–	0–10	31	1.6	2.7
Scrap (of all commodities)	–[d]	0–10	16	0.9	2.8
			178		
II. Intermediate manufactures					
Coal products	2[e]	10–20	2	15.0	10.0
Iron and steel	–	0–20	57	15.1	1.4
Textiles	14[f]	0–30	86	13.3	5.3
Paper and products	1[g]	10–20	32	13.6	3.5
Petroleum products		5–30	6	17.6	4.5
Chemicals	9[h]	0–30	156	15.0	6.5
Leather and products (excl. apparel)	8[i]	10–35	14	20.0	7.8
Nonfarm metal products	7[j]	0–20	43	15.2	5.3
Rubber products (excl. apparel)	2[k]	15–20	2	17.5	2.5
			398		
III. Final manufactures					
Grain-mill products	3[l]	25 %	5	25.0	0
Lumber and wood products	2[m]	0–20	9	7.6	5.9
Machinery	–	10–40	93	19.5	5.0
Apparel (incl. rubber and leather)	5[n]	20–30	22	25.9	3.2
Transport equipment (excl. ships)	–	15–40	144	22.5	7.9
Printing and publishing	5[o]	30–50	6	33.3	5.5
Nonmetallic metal products	7[p]	5–25	45	13.9	5.1
Shipbuilding	–	15	1	15.0	0
Industry, n.e.c.	–[q]	0–50	41	21.8	11.0
Processed foods	6[r]	0–40	59	23.5	10.2
Textiles (final consumption)	–	10–30	15	22.7	7.8
			310		
IV. Final primary production					
Fishing	3[s]	0–10	6	1.7	1.7

TABLE 9 (*notes*)

[a] All told, 39 items are not included in the above categories because of their unusual nature, particularly by-products and goods combined with precious metals, feathers, coral, and ivory.
[b] Bismuth with a duty of 5% and mercury with a duty of 10% are the only exceptions to a zero duty.
[c] Feathers and down for ornament (40%) and rare roots (40%).
[d] Includes scrap metals, waste paper, used sacks, rags, scrap textiles.
[e] By-products; cokes (0%) and coal tar (5%).
[f] Combined with precious stones, furs, shells, or ivory (50%) and 12 textile products that were clearly final consumption goods.
[g] Metallic foil of precious metal (40%).
[h] Methyl and ethyl alcohol (50%), cosmetics (40–50%), saccharin (35%), and alcoholic medicinal preparations (35%).
[i] Tanned furskins (40%) and leather products, combined with furs, shells, feathers, and precious stones (50%).
[j] Combined with precious stones (50%), coated with precious metals (30%).
[k] Dental rubber (5%).
[l] By-products; fodder and feed, wheat bran, rice bran (all 0%).
[m] Rare tropical woods (40%), combined with precious stones (50%).
[n] Combined with precious stones, ivory, coral, feathers, and fur (50%).
[o] Books, magazines, art works, currency, drawings, etc. (all 0%).
[p] Shards, microscope glass, glass cullets (all 0%), combined with precious stones (35–50%).
[q] Eight very high items (40–50%) pulled the average upwards.
[r] Tobacco (335%) and alcoholic beverages (50%).
[s] Sponges (10%) and coral (20%).
Source: Compiled by Richard Robinson from *Japan Trade Guide, 1960* (Tokyo: Jiji Press, 1960).

subsidies, one would expect Japanese prices to exceed foreign ones; whereas if either of the other two explanations holds, Japanese prices should be lower.

Existing price comparisons seem to support the latter reasoning. Tarshis found that labor-intensive products are cheap in Japan when compared with their counterparts in the United States, the United Kingdom, and the Soviet Union. Other studies indicate that labor-intensive commodities may be comparatively cheap in Japan even in comparison with other countries. A study of Komiya and Watanabe gives direct evidence, at any rate, that finished goods in general are relatively cheap there, especially as compared with those of the United States: "From an international point of view, prices of Japanese final consumption goods are much lower than prices of raw materials and intermediate goods, and this price differential may make an important contribution to her processing trade system. From another viewpoint, this differential means that the price of goods in Japan might decrease relatively in company with increasing labor input."[25] Table 11 gives what, according to them, is the most

[25] Tsunehiko Watanabe and Ryutaro Komiya, "Findings from Price Comparisons, Principally Japan vs. the United States," *Weltwirtschaftliches Archiv*, 81.2:85–96 (1958).

TABLE 10. *Average Import Tariff by Stage of Production in the Main Production Chains, Japan, 1960*

Coal and products			Chemicals	
Coal and coal tar	0%		Unrefined natural chemicals	0%
Cokes	5		Vegetable and animal oils	10
Coal-tar distillates	20		Explosives	10
Iron and steel			Industrial chemicals	15
Ore and scrap	0		Paints	15
Pig iron	10		Fireworks and ammunition	20
Ingots	12.5		Inks	20
Bars, sheets, rails, wire	15		Drugs, pharmaceuticals	20
Pipe, wire rope	15		Matches	25
Textiles and apparel			Artificial perfumes	25
Raw cotton, silk coccoons,			Dyes	25
raw wool	0		Soaps	25
Cotton, linen, hemp yarn	5–7.5		Antibiotics	25
Cotton, linen fabrics	10–15		Cosmetics	45
Cotton clothing	20		Leather and products	
Jute and wool yarn	10		Roller leather	10
Wool fabrics	20		Industrial belting	10
Wool clothing	25		Dyed leather	20
Wool pile fabrics	30		Tanned skins	30
Silk yarn	15		Shoes	30
Silk thread	20		Leather gloves	30
Silk fabric	15		Leather belts	30
Silk pile fabric	30		Rubber and products	
Tablecloths, curtains,			Raw rubber	
carpets, cushions	30		(natural and synthetic)	0
Embroidered clothing	30		Rubber manufactures	15
Petroleum and products			Vulcanized rubber	20
Petroleum, crude	10		Lumber and wood products	
Grease	18		Logs and lumber	0–5
Lubricating oil	22.5		Firewood	0
Light refined products	20		Matchsticks	0
Heavy refined products	30		Charcoal	10
			Shooks	15
			Wood manufactures	20

Source: See Table 9.

representative pattern of this differential. The comparisons in that table are with the United States, but the authors found in comparing export prices of various countries that Japanese manufactured goods also appeared to be relatively cheaper than those of, say, Hong Kong.[26]

[26] Watanabe and Komiya, p. 87, table 5; and p. 91, table 9.

TABLE 11. *Export-Price Pattern of Japanese Finished Goods*

Production chain	Yen price per dollar's worth in U.S.	Ratio to official exchange rate
Textiles		
Raw cotton	408.1	1.14
Cotton yard (no. 20)	253.8	0.71
Cotton fabric	280.4	0.78
Hose, cotton	182.6	0.51
Dress shirt, cotton	161.7	0.45
Steel products		
Pig iron	498.9	1.39
Wire rod	440.5	1.22
Steel plate	454.4	1.26
Wire	393.4	1.09
Nails	329.4	0.94

Source: Tsunehiko Watanabe and Ryutaro Komiya, "Findings from Price Comparisons, Principally Japan vs. the United States," *Weltwirtschaftliches Archiv*, 81.2:86 (1958).

There is reason to believe, therefore, that the tariffs on capital-intensive semimanufactures maintain a significant differential between Japanese costs and the most advantageous foreign import prices, whereas the tariffs on finished manufactures are ineffective in raising domestic Japanese prices.

THE UNITED KINGDOM, WEST GERMANY, AND FRANCE

Germany, the United Kingdom, and France are much wealthier than Japan and yet they are considerably poorer than the United States. In comparison with the world at large, they must be considered as relatively well endowed with capital. Their commercial policies probably protect labor, just as does that of the United States. Their intermediate capital endowments are reflected in the structure of their tariffs on manufactures. In contrast to United States duties, few European ones are very high and few are very low; they tend to cluster around an average which, nonetheless, varies from country to country. Lower duties suffice to forestall labor-intensive imports because European labor is cheaper than American labor, but their duties on capital-intensive imports, coming mainly from the United States, cannot be as low as the American ones and still provide protection. Because the question of whether their tariffs protect labor or capital is less critical than the same question for the United States, I decided to use French, British, and West German commercial policy to illustrate the other important aspect of industrial countries' protection: their discrimination in favor of raw-material imports. The similar endowments, cultures, economies, and trading opportunities of these three countries, combined with their different levels of protectionism, make a comparative study possible.

The ratio of the prices of manufactures to those of raw materials will be the highest in the country which protects manufactures the most, relative to raw materials. This price divergence should lead to a substitution of raw-material inputs for capital and especially labor, which protection of manufactures renders expensive. The numerical example at the end of Chapter Four shows how this works. It will be recalled that, under the assumption of the Cobb-Douglas production functions used there, the protected final-commodity sector in country A used, directly and indirectly, more raw materials per unit of output than the corresponding unprotected sector in country B. In addition, the ratio between the two rates of utilization was equal to the ratio of the protection coefficient of the final manufacture to that of the raw material in the country applying protection. Figure V-1 illustrates graphically the same basic proposition. The isoquants, Q_1, Q_2, Q_3, Q_4, Q_5, and Q_6 represent different levels of output for the manufacturing industries in a country. The inputs of raw materials, and of labor and capital, which the diagram lumps together, determine the country's output of manufactures. Thus $O_M c_1$ units of labor-capital combine with $O_M r_1$ units of raw materials to produce Q_4 units of manufactures. The curve $O_R p_2' p_1' R$ is a production function for raw materials; its elevation gives the domestic output of raw materials as a function of the amount of labor-capital, reading from right to left, which they use. The length of the horizontal axis shows the total supply of labor-capital; it is assumed that whatever labor-capital does not work in manufacture works in producing raw materials, so that if

$O_M c_1$ units are employed by the former, $O_R c_1$ units are employed by the second activity.

The relative prices of raw materials and of the other factors determine their relative amounts employed to produce a unit of

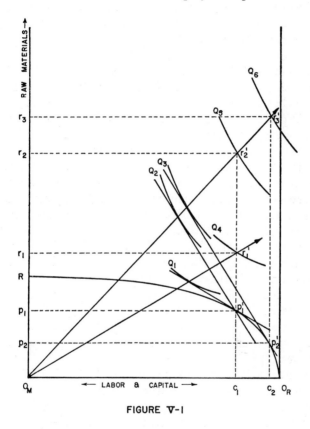

FIGURE V-I

manufactures. The slopes of the lines tangent to the isoquants represent these price ratios. The slope of the tangent to Q_1, tangent also to $O_R p_2' p_1' R$ at the point p_1', indicates the free-trade price ratio between raw materials and labor-capital. The point of tangency uniquely determines the amount of raw materials produced. At this price ratio, $O_R c_1$ units of labor-capital will be used to produce $O_M p_1$ units of raw materials. The country uses the remaining $O_M c_1$ units of labor-capital to produce manufactures. The slope of the ray $O_M r_1'$ gives the ratio of raw materials to labor-capital used in producing manufactures at their free-trade price ratio. This shows that $O_M c_1$ units of labor-capital should work with $O_M r_1$ units of raw materials to produce Q_4 units of manufactures. Since only $O_M p_1$ units of raw materials are produced domestically, imports of $p_1 r_1$ units are required to overcome the domestic deficit.[27]

If the domestic price of manufactures rises relative to that of raw materials, the slope of the price-ratio line will become steeper. Suppose that the slope of the tangent to Q_2 represents this new domestic price ratio. The amount of raw materials cooperating with a unit of labor-capital will now increase, as shown by the new ray $O_M r_2' r_3'$. The country will continue to produce $O_M p_1$ units of raw materials only if the government directly subsidizes raw-material producers. If it does not, the equation of marginal revenue and marginal cost will, under perfect competition, induce a shift of the allocable labor-capital away from raw materials into manufacturing. At the price ratio which the slope of the tangent to Q_2 through p_1' gives, p_2' becomes the new raw-material production point and $O_M c_2$ units of labor-capital will produce Q_6 units of manufactures. The domestic raw-material deficit has, of course, increased, and the country must import at least $r_2 p_1$ units of raw materials even if it maintains, by means of a direct subsidy, the free-trade production of raw materials. The country will import $r_3 p_2$ units of raw materials if no subsidies are paid to raw-material producers.

The increased demand for raw materials, arising from lower domestic production and greater domestic requirements, will immediately cause an increased demand for imports. Exports of manufactures to pay for these imports might not follow so rapidly, especially if the original reason for the increased price

[27] They must be paid for, of course, by exports of manufactures. In the two-commodity model of Figure V-1, the only form of protection appropriate would be an export subsidy on manufactures. Or one could imagine that the isoquants Q represent an aggregate production function for many different types of manufactures, some of which the country will normally export and some of which it will normally import. In that case, import restrictions could effectively raise the domestic price of manufactured goods.

of labor-capital relative to raw materials is simply wage, and other cost, inflation. Domestic inflation, accompanied by balance-of-payments difficulties, is an important cause, or rather justification, of trade restrictions. Authorities hesitate to impose the same restrictions upon raw materials as upon other imports, since they mistakenly feel it will only raise costs more. This reasoning, which the following discussion will document, aggravates the effect illustrated in Figure V-1.

It is generally accepted that France is the most protectionist of the three countries. Thus its policies should cause the price of finished goods to exceed that of raw materials by a greater amount than in either of the other countries, and France should use more raw materials in producing a given item. The first task, then, is to reveal the extent of French protectionism by comparing it with that of the United Kingdom and Germany. The next chapter measures the raw-material substitution effect resulting from this protection.

The task would be easier if it were possible simply to make direct intercountry price comparisons at each stage in the industrial hierarchy. The excellent price study by Gilbert and Kravis, while showing that French prices are generally higher than those of the other countries examined, unfortunately does not distinguish different stages of manufacturing,[28] and so could not be adapted to this scheme. Since adequate price comparisons are lacking, it is necessary to study the actual instruments of commercial policy and to try to judge their effects upon prices. If tariffs were the only instrument, and if they did not eliminate all imports of some commodities, this task should not be too difficult. Unfortunately, tariffs have not been the only means of

[28] Milton Gilbert and Irving B. Kravis, *An International Comparison of National Products and the Purchasing Power of Currencies* (Paris, 1954); and *Comparative National Products and Price Levels* (Paris, 1958). Another Organization for European Economic Cooperation study of comparative prices also proved inadequate because of its scant coverage. See OEEC, Economic Committee, "Price Disparity Study: Report on Limited Study of Price Disparity Data, Note," EC (58) 1, scale 2, January 13, 1958 (Paris, 1958), p. 19 (mimeographed). See also *Rapport général de la commission créée pour l'étude des disparités entre les prix français et étrangers* [The Nathan Report] (Paris, 1954); and "Les Comparaisons internationales de prix," *Etudes et conjonctures*, no. 2 (February 1959).

restricting imports. Licensing requirements and their attendant import quotas, together with currency restrictions in some instances, have dominated in several European countries for varying periods.[29] If importers request licenses for fewer imports than the authorities allow, the quota obviously has no effect at all on domestic prices. If the article is covered by a tariff, however, it always establishes a minimum price disparity. It is therefore best to begin with a simple comparison of the tariffs applied by the three countries. Later it will be necessary to examine import quotas, especially in France, since that country has used this type of control most often.[30]

The effect of recent trade restrictions is of primary interest. Nevertheless, the levels of protection that have been applied in the past are probably still significant, and it may be useful therefore to review briefly the recent tariff history of the three countries.

The British tariff achieved its present structure in the twelve-year period following the First World War. In 1921, the Safeguarding of Industries Act was passed in behalf of certain so-called key industries, mainly precision instruments and a fairly wide

[29] Their use in France extends back to the 1930s.

[30] The argument that countries imposing heavy restrictions on imports of fabricated products use more raw materials, *ceteris paribus*, than low-tariff countries assumes, of course, that price disparities for finished products, and therefore for labor and capital versus raw materials, do in fact exist. Where the number of commodities is greater than the number of factors, if relative factor endowments lie within the equalization region, tariffs placed on some but not all industrial products might only make the distribution of world production determinate, or more nearly so. But there is little danger that the import restrictions and export subsidies discussed here fail to affect internal prices. They can fail only if no imports of protected commodities take place; otherwise, the tariff, or other restriction, necessarily raises their prices. Since France allowed no manufactured goods to enter without a tariff and yet imports took place, its tariffs and other restrictions must have raised the prices of imported goods, of import-competing domestic goods, and therefore of factors as well. The studies mentioned in note 28 indicate that before the devaluation of December 1958, French prices were higher than the world prices of many manufactured goods, and Table 14 shows that relatively high prices of manufactured goods reflected the high labor prices in France. Moreover, the duties actually collected by the French government on imports of manufactures were very nearly the same percentage of the value of those imports, by tariff sections, as were the average *ad valorem* tariff duties for the sections.

cross-section of chemicals. The rate established for these industries was $33\frac{1}{3}$ percent. But the formal termination of British free
trade is generally dated from the passage of the Import Duties
Act of 1932. By establishing a general revenue duty of 10 percent,
the tariff was purported not to be protectionist. Nevertheless,
most raw materials were exempted from the duty, while the rate
for manufactures was 20 and that for luxuries $33\frac{1}{3}$ percent. In
addition, the McKenna Act established a rate of $33\frac{1}{3}$ percent on
imports of motor cars, clocks and watches, and musical instruments. The Ottawa agreements of 1932 reduced the revenue and
McKenna duties on products of the British Commonwealth and
exempted commonwealth products from all other duties of the
Import Duties Act. A few duties were subsequently raised, some
to as high as 50 percent (photographic equipment, some instruments), but duties on manufactures still cluster around 20 percent, and those on luxury items are still $33\frac{1}{3}$ percent. By far the
most common tariff for semimanufactures is 10 percent, and
practically all raw materials are admitted duty-free.[31]

Germany established a new tariff schedule during 1950 and
1951. Its previous tariff was specific, dating back to the beginning
of the century. Henry C. Wallich holds that although the new
tariff, which established *ad valorem* rates, was difficult to compare
with the old, it was more protective than its predecessor, even
in the latter's prime.[32] The salient feature of prewar German trade
policy was probably the set of measures which Schacht established, in order to supply Germany more cheaply with raw
materials, and the autarchic policies designed to lessen Germany's
dependence on imported raw materials.

If the rates of the new German tariff were higher than those
they replaced, they did not last long.[33] By an ordinance of

[31] See Political and Economic Planning, *Tariffs and Trade in Western Europe*
(London, 1959). This extremely useful source gives the tariffs of the Western
European countries according to the Brussels Classification and therefore permits,
for the first time, comparisons among the tariff rates of different countries according
to an identical reporting scheme.
[32] *Mainsprings of the German Revival* (New Haven, 1955), p. 258.
[33] The new rates, it should be remarked, were prepared in anticipation of the
Torquay conference of the General Agreement on Tariffs and Trade. They were
probably deliberately set rather high in order to give room for bargaining, but
the concessions that Germany made at Torquay were insufficient to bring the

June 29, 1956, duties which lay between 0 and 17 percent on industrial products were reduced by 20 percent, and those between 16 and 25 percent were lowered by 25 percent. All duties exceeding 28 percent on industrial products were lowered to 21 percent. On August 15, 1957, most duties on industrial products were reduced by another 25 percent. Consequently, the highest present rate on industrial products is no more than 16.75 percent.[34] None of these reductions applied to agricultural products.

French commercial policy presents, as it has for some time, a considerably less enlightened picture. The report of the French Commission on Price Disparities concludes, in tones common to such reports in many countries: "The French market, except for short periods, has largely been isolated from foreign markets for the past twenty years . . . The economic cloistering has, in effect, permitted our country to develop, purely on the basis of internal exigencies, practices or policies which could not fail to have consequences on the structure of national costs."[35]

A detailed comparison of the postwar French tariff with those of Germany and Great Britain for the period 1950–1955 shows that it was undoubtedly higher, in its protective incidence, than that of the former, but no higher than that of the latter. Few German tariffs exceeded the French tariffs on the same item.[36] The exceptions were almost entirely in the agricultural sector; indeed, agriculture itself constituted the one broad area in which German protection was at least as high as French and British. The German rates on chemicals exceeded the French only in

---

rates down to the desired level. See Wallich, p. 258. For the rates, see General Agreement on Tariffs and Trade, *Consolidated Schedules of Tariff Concessions* (Geneva, 1952), vol. 5.

[34] The short list of exceptions is given in Great Britain's *Board of Trade Journal*, March 28, 1958, p. 773. It is regrettable that this reduction had to be rescinded to bring the external tariffs of the OEEC countries in line in 1962.

[35] Report of the "Commission créée pour l'étude des disparités entre les prix français et étrangers," quoted in Warren C. Baum, *The French Economy and the State* (Princeton, 1958), pp. 267–268.

[36] Political and Economic Planning, *Tariffs and Trade in Western Europe*, *passim*.

isolated instances.[37] The German duties exceeded the French on about half of the items under "rubber," but were only about 1 percent higher, excepting only nonvulcanized rubber sheets and sheeting. Several wood and cork products were more highly protected by the Germans than by the French, probably because of their close association with agriculture. None of these items was of any great relative importance, however. In the category "paper and board," the Germans protected only cigarette paper (a government monopoly in France and therefore automatically protected from foreign competition), straw paper, and cardboard and related products. Until 1956, the Germans applied slightly higher rates on woolen and animal-hair yarns not for retail sale, and also on woven woolen and fine animal-hair fabrics containing artificial fibers. Among nonmetallic mineral products, the Germans protected only glass mirrors more heavily than the French did. German and French protection of iron and steel products seems to have been roughly the same. For several semifinished products, the French rates were little more than half the German.[38] Within this category, however, the French rates either exceeded or equaled the German on all other products. For the large class of finished manufactures, the German duties equaled or exceeded the French only in negligible instances, and in very few cases were the two sets even approximately the same.[39]

Therefore, German rates for industrial products, even under the comparatively high German tariff of 1950 through 1955, were almost all lower than the corresponding French rates. The

[37] Namely, certain alcohols, monomeric vinyl acetate, aluminium oxide and sulphate, some carbon blacks, some glycerols and alkaloids, potassium chloride (a chemical raw material), basic slag, sweeteners, perfume base, some minor cosmetics, raw casein, artificial graphite, refined tall oil, abietic acid, wood tar, phenol formaldehyde resins and urea formaldehyde, penicillin, and proprietary medicines. Corrections have been made for the German tariff reductions of June 1956.

[38] Specifically, blooms, billets and slabs of steel, except alloyed, forged sheet bars, and tinplate bars of unalloyed steel.

[39] Those products for which the German tariffs were higher are entirely comprised under the headings of iron and steel bolts, spark-ignition parts, typesetting machinery and parts, calculating machines, lamp globes, leather gloves, footwear with leather or rubber soles containing more than 5 percent of silk or manmade fibers, photographic film, matches, mother-of-pearl buttons, and finished wood pipes.

exceptions, such as they were, occurred mainly in the broad group of semimanufactures. On the other hand, the Germans placed higher tariffs on raw materials, although the difference was so slight as to make this a negligible point.[40]

Some convenience of presentation is gained, and some accuracy and information lost, in constructing statistical measures to compare tariffs. Raymond Bertrand has made comparable averages of the tariff rates of France and the other original Common Market countries. In one study, he shows that the French duties on manufactures do not vary greatly, within any tariff section, from the arithmetic average duty for that section.[41] He could have further reduced the average dispersion of the duties by choosing categories that follow the stage of manufacture more strictly than the French customs nomenclature does. This is true especially of those sections for which, like section VIII (skins, leathers, pelts, and their products), or section IX (wood, charcoal, cork, rush and straw products), the principle of classification is the material worked.[42]

In another study, Bertrand compares the tariff levels of the Common Market countries. His summary of the results for France and Germany is reproduced in Table 12, and it shows that France protects manufactures more than Germany does. Some of the data provided in the table require further comment. First, as Bertrand states, the purely fiscal intentions behind most of the duties are hard to separate from their protective ones.[43] For instance, the high German duties on mineral fuels should certainly be reduced, since they consist mainly of high consumption taxes on petroleum. It was estimated that the degree of

[40] A scattering of duties on basic wood and pulp products, unrefined palm and cottonseed oil, and edible lard and oleo stearine constitute the sole instances in which the German exceeded the French rate, and these were among the negligible instances in which duties in either country were different from zero.

[41] Raymond Bertrand, "Analyse du tarif douanier français par industries," *Cahiers de l'Institut de Science Economique Appliquée*, Series R — Etudes et matériaux pour le Marché Commun, 61:13, special issue (November 1957).

[42] See Ministère des Finances et des Affaires Economiques, *Tarifs des droits de douane d'importation et d'exportation* (Paris, January 1, 1959). Bertrand gives an example of the effect of eliminating raw materials from the textile chapters ("Analyse du tarif douanier français," p. 12).

[43] Raymond Bertrand, "Comparaison du niveau des tarifs douaniers des pays du Marché Commun," *Cahiers de ISEA*, 64:8, special issue (February 1958).

TABLE 12. *German and French Tariff Levels, 1953–1955*
(in percent *ad valorem*)

Item	Germany	France	Standard International Trade Classification section numbers
All tariffs (1,910 items)			
Arithmetic average	15.5	18.1	
First quartile	6.0	10.0	
Median	12.0	17.0	
Third quartile	19.0	23.0	
I. Food, drink, and tobacco (366 items)			0, 1
Arithmetic average	24.8	23.0	
First quartile	9.0	10.0	
Median	18.0	19.0	
Third quartile	25.0	29.0	
II. Raw materials, other than mineral fuels (232 items)			2, 4
Arithmetic average	6.4	8.1	
First quartile	0	0	
Median	2.0	0	
Third quartile	11.0	15.0	
III. Mineral fuels and related materials (29 items)			3
Arithmetic average	49.7	6.8	
First quartile	—	3.0	
Median	56.0	5.0	
Third quartile	—	8.0	
IV. Chemicals (401 items)			5
Arithmetic average	13.3	19.5	
First quartile	8.0	13.0	
Median	14.0	21.0	
Third quartile	20.0	25.0	
V. Manufactured products (882 items)			6, 7, 8, 9
Arithmetic average	13.5	18.5	
First quartile	7.0	15.0	
Median	12.0	19.0	
Third quartile	19.0	20.0	

Source: Raymond Bertrand, "Comparison du niveau des tarifs douaniers des pays du Marché Commun," *ISEA Cahiers*, 64:17–18 (February 1958).

refinery protection, that is, the duty borne by imported but not by home-refined products, was in Germany 6 percent and in France 8 percent in 1957.[44] The relevant German degree of refinery protection in 1953–1955 was therefore about the same as the French. Second, certain relatively high French rates in the

[44] Political and Economic Planning, *Tariffs and Trade in Western Europe*, p. 8.

raw-material category are levied on materials which have actually undergone some degree of fabrication, refinement, or processing.[45] Third, while the *ad valorem* duty actually collected on imports of manufactures was practically identical to the arithmetic averages of the listed duties for these goods, the paid duty on imports of raw materials was a negligible percentage of their listed value. The average duty for natural and synthetic rubber, for example, was 15 percent, while the duty actually paid represented no more than 0.2 percent of the value of rubber imports in 1956.[46] Finally, between 1952 and 1958 the French augmented the duties on most goods except raw materials by what was termed a Special Temporary Import Tax. Its typical rate for manufactures was 10 percent. Both its incidence and its application will be treated more thoroughly below.

QUANTITATIVE RESTRICTIONS

Collected tariffs provide an index of the minimum protective incidence which the commercial policy of a country applies to products. This section will show that the conclusions already drawn are not confounded by more direct restrictions upon imports. Quantitative restrictions are imposed to protect given industries, to insulate an inflationist country from the rest of the world, and to eliminate indeterminacy. In Europe the second and third of these motives were probably responsible for the introduction of import quotas, while in the United States the first has been more important. Nonetheless, the application of European quotas has followed the same principle as that of tariffs: quotas are instruments of prejudice in favor of raw materials and against practically all other imports. In addition, France's use of quotas was more restrictive than Britain's or Germany's. Because it is difficult to measure accurately the extent to which an import quota protects a domestic product, it is most convenient to illustrate these points historically. During

---

[45] See sections III, V, II, chapters 12, 13, and 14, of the French Customs Tariff in *Tarifs des droits de douane d'importation et d'exportation*.

[46] Bertrand, "Analyse du tarif douanier français," pp. 17–23.

the alternate liberalization and deliberalization of trade in France between 1950 and 1958, raw materials were consistently the last to be hindered by, and the first category to be freed from, an unequal imposition of quantitative restrictions.

The combination of United States aid, the effects of four recent devaluations, the temporary absence of German and Japanese competition, and other countries' liberalization of import restrictions all contributed to a favorable balance of payments for France by the year 1950. The country was able, therefore, to comply with the Code of Liberalization of the Organization for European Economic Cooperation (OEEC), and by May 1951 it had set free of quantitative restrictions 75 percent of its 1948 imports from other European countries. Moreover, France liberated 65 percent of private imports of manufactures, instead of the 60 percent required by the OEEC.

It would seem from this that France's liberalization measures at that time were as important as those of its partners. But it should be pointed out that, aside from a few finished textiles, no finished consumer goods appeared on the French list.[47] Further, the percentage of imports liberated, the measure used by the OEEC, is inaccurate and ambiguous. This measure could be reasonably reliable, even for comparison with years not too much later than the base year, only on the assumption that trade was free in the year used as a base. But this was not true of 1948. If a country had stifled imports of a certain good in that year, it would receive little credit, according to the OEEC criterion of liberalization, for removing this restriction. As a result, there was little incentive to do so. It is difficult to say that one country exploited this weakness more than another. But, both France and Great Britain (which then extensively employed a system of state trading) received much smaller percentages of their total imports from the OEEC countries than did the other members of the organization.[48] Imports of the other OEEC countries,

[47] For the complete list of goods freed by France by May 1951, see OEEC, Comité des Echanges, "Libération des échanges, consolidation et étape des 75%, France," TC-51-12/05 (Paris, May 7, 1951; mimeographed).

[48] William Diebold, *Trade and Payments in Western Europe* (New York, 1952). pp. 182–183.

2I4 · THEORY OF TRADE AND PROTECTION

notably Germany and Denmark, increased during 1950 as a result of their liberalization measures,[49] but those of France remained the same. France was accused of practicing hidden, or administrative, protectionism, and circumstantial evidence, at least, supports the accusation. The actual administration of import licenses was left to the technical committees of the Economic Council, and these advisory bodies were staffed largely by members of the trade associations.[50]

Germany, meanwhile, was unable to reach 75 percent liberalization by 1951 and, in December 1950, was forced to suspend liberalization measures for one year. It had experienced a rapid increase in consumer demand in 1950 and at the same time was beginning to feel severely the price effects of the Korean War boom in imported raw materials. French exports, on the other hand, increased during 1950, while imports remained low. But the relative position of the two countries was soon to be reversed. Prices steadily rose in France after the devaluation in 1949. French and English importers had reacted more slowly than the Germans to the rise in raw-material prices and found themselves obliged to replenish their stocks a few months later, at much higher prices. The great demand in France for raw materials was increased by a rapid rise in industrial production, especially at the end of 1951 and the beginning of 1952. The combination of these forces induced a payments crisis which obliged the French to suspend all liberalization measures a month after the Germans resumed them.[51] The Germans have not resorted to further quantitative restrictions since that time.

Although the French required a license on every import, they did not restrict imports of the main raw materials. In partial

[49] Diebold, p. 187.
[50] Baum, p. 251. The newspaper *Neue Zürchner Zeitung* called these various trade associations "citadels of protectionism" (quoted in Diebold, p. 201).
[51] The French suspension came on February 4, 1952. It is worth observing that the German liberalization list of January 1, 1952, contained many manufactures: the major textiles and apparel items were liberated along with leather goods, all types of machinery and road vehicles, electrical appliances, clocks, watches, cameras, and the like. The German list of January 1, 1952, resembles very closely the French list of goods for which licenses were still required in January 1960. For the complete lists, see *Board of Trade Journal*, February 9 and 16, 1952, and January 8 and 15, 1960.

compensation for their repudiation of liberalization, the French submitted to the OEEC every six months an import program for the semester. This program always listed "incompressible imports," whose level presumably could not be reduced and in accordance with which licenses on other products had to be issued so as not to exceed the total import capacity of the economy. Most of the important raw materials — coal, textile materials, petroleum, paper pulp, chemical raw materials, and ores — appeared on the list. Between 1948 and 1954, imports were reduced most severely on a wide range of textiles, chemicals, and paper products.[52]

Largely because of a reduction in the rate of industrial expansion, the French balance of payments began slowly to improve toward the end of 1953, and France cautiously liberated a few imports. Between September 25 and December 2, 1953, quotas were lifted on agricultural goods whose imports were valued at 2,044,698,000 francs per month in 1948; on raw materials whose imports were 16,560,041,000 francs per month; and on manufactures whose imports were 4,710,110,000 francs per month.[53] All but an insignificant amount of the liberated manufactured imports consisted of semimanufactures close to the raw-material stage (coal tar was the most important item), basic chemical materials, medicines, and certain machine tools.[54]

The import program which France submitted for the semester beginning on April 30, 1954, provides the means for evaluating the degree of restrictiveness remaining on manufactured imports. The OEEC required that France set forth its quotas on goods freed at the time France had achieved 75 percent liberalization. Quotas for manufactured goods whose imports were 32,891,000,000 francs per month in 1948, allowed imports of only 13,860,000,000 francs worth of those goods per month in 1954.

[52] For the complete list and the levels of imports, see OEEC, C(53)245, January 4, 1954, addendum, scale I; C(54)124, May 4, 1954, p. 5; and C(54)281, March 31, 1954, annex I (all mimeographed).
[53] The main raw materials on this list had not appeared in the list of incompressible imports. These were natural rubber, some metal ores, raw skins and hides, raw silk, and also refractory bricks, copper, aluminum, and tin which are really semimanufactures, although not so classified by the liberalization lists.
[54] OEEC, C(53)245.

During 1954, the OEEC twice requested that France reattain the 75 percent stage of liberalization. By the end of 1954, the liberalization percentages in the three categories, agricultural products, raw materials, and manufactures, stood respectively at 56.3, 82.0, and 49.8. More than half of the trade liberated after 1948 consisted of raw materials.[55] By this time all raw materials of any importance had been freed of quotas. Finished manufactures, except certain types of machinery, were still on the quota lists. Imports of manufactures in late 1954 were less than half of their value in May 1951, the time of the 75 percent liberalization.[56]

TABLE 13. *Percentages of French Dollar Imports Liberated by January 1959* (in millions of French francs)

Category	Total imports	Imports on government account	Imports on private account	Products liberated	Percentage of liberalization
Food and feeding stuffs	16,015	12,600	3,415	185	0.54
Raw materials	66,434	5,724	60,710	50,560	83.28
Manufactured goods	64,631	9,450	55,181	9,502	17.22
Total	147,080	27,774	119,306	60,247	50.50

Source: OEEC, Joint Trade and Intra-European Payments Committee, "Relaxation of Quantitative Restrictions on Imports of Goods and Restrictions on Invisible Transactions and Transfers in Relation to the Dollar Area: France," TP(59)5/05, June 4, 1959, scale 2, p. ii. This source also gives a complete list of the dollar products liberated as of January 1959 (pp. 1–46). The list compiles the products freed by the "Notice to Importers," *Journal officiel*, December 18 and 31, 1958, January 13, 1959, and February 7, 1959.

By April 1955, France finally reachieved 75 percent liberalization of its imports from the other members of the OEEC. The percentages for the three categories distinguished by the OEEC,

[55] OEEC, Conseil, "Libération des échanges, France" C(54)308, November 24, 1954, scale I, p. 35 (mimeographed).

[56] The list is given in OEEC, "The French Import Program for 1st October, 1954–31st March, 1955," C(54)281, esp. p. 5. The OEEC obliged France to increase its planned imports of cotton textiles and to allow those imports to equal 40 percent of those of the new reference period. See also OEEC, C(54)297, 1954, p. 4 (mimeographed). Certain steel products, liberated under the first import program in 1954, were again restricted in order to compensate for an exempted increase in fuel requirements. See *Journal officiel de la république française, Lois et décrets*, October 20, 1954, pp. 9864–9865; hereafter cited *J.O.*

agricultural products, raw materials, and manufactures, were respectively 61.6, 93.6, and 61.2. The majority of manufactures liberated consisted of various types of semimanufactured, and other producer, goods. Some finished consumer goods also appeared on the list.[57] Imports from the dollar area were not freed until later; in December 1959, only 4 percent of such imports were free of licensing requirements. Table 13 shows for each OEEC sector the percentage of 1953 dollar imports which France liberated by 1959.

THE SPECIAL TEMPORARY IMPORT TAX (FRANCE)

There is strong reason to suppose that the above liberalization measures had little effect. As each new stage was reached in France's restoration of 75 percent liberalization, she consistently applied a new special tax to most of the items set free. It is entirely possible that the new measures not only compensated for the relaxation of the old, but actually exceeded them in their restrictive effects.

The special import tax on liberated items appeared first in April 1954, when France reached 53 percent liberalization.[58] According to the French delegation to the OEEC, the purpose of the special tax was to help eliminate disparities between foreign and French prices and to help finance the reconversion of certain industries damaged by liberalization.[59] However, Edgar Faure, then Minister of Finance, argued that the precarious balance of payments required such a measure if France were to meet its obligations under the OEEC agreements. Although the rate varied with the type of product, Faure claimed that the tax was

[57] For the complete list of goods freed from quantitative restrictions as of April, 1955, see OEEC, "Measures of Liberalisation of Trade Taken by France," C(55)79, May 6, 1955, annex, scale 1 (mimeographed).

[58] The tax was established by Decree No. 54–438 of April 17, 1954, reported in J.O., April 18, 1954, pp. 3789–3795. The following decrees modified the text: Decree of October 19, 1954 (reported in J.O., October 20, 1954, pp. 9863–9864); December 22, 1954 (J.O., December 23, 1954, p. 12046); January 10, 1955 (J.O., January 11, 1955, p. 470); March 31, 1955 (J.O., April 1, 1955, p. 3232); June 22, 1955 (J.O., June 23, 1955, p. 6243).

[59] Letter from the French Delegation to Secretary General Marjolin; OEEC, TFD/TD 625 and C(54)111, 1954 (mimeographed).

not discriminatory: "If the rate of this tax has been differentiated, this is not in order to give additional protection to certain branches of the economy, for the maximum is in effect the general rate. However, we have been able to reduce it in certain cases to 10 percent, or even to avoid it altogether in order to prevent a dangerous impact on the domestic price level or a displacement of traditional trading channels."[60]

Actually the tax was discriminatory in a double sense. Appendix IV shows that its rates varied according to the stage of manufacture, with raw materials generally exempted. Coal tar, among the selected raw materials with zero tariffs, was the only one which had to pay the special import tax. For goods with nonzero tariff rates, the supplementary import tax was, by and large, closely related to the level of the tariff. This tax thereby raised by as much as 35 or 45 percent the total import duty on the semimanufactures, and the few finished manufactures, that were liberated.[61]

The second type of discrimination was regional and arose from a curious accident. The liberalization measures applied, of course, only to trade with other members of the OEEC; until recently only 4 percent of 1948 trade from the dollar area, for example, enjoyed the same freedom. But under the General Agreement on Tariffs and Trade (GATT), a member country could not place an import duty on a product unless it applied the duty equally to all countries signatory to the agreement. Therefore, France could not apply the special tax just to the liberated trade with other OEEC countries, but was obliged to apply it to imports from any GATT country.

France's Special Temporary Import Tax understandably became an object of concern to both the OEEC and the GATT. If the balance of payments could justify such a measure, it is doubtful that the various institutions and agreements that are now supposed to work for the ultimate freeing of trade will ever

[60] Declaration of Faure to the Council of Ministers of the OEEC, C(54)139, May 5, 1954 (mimeographed). My English translation.

[61] In addition to Appendix IV, see OEEC, TFD/TD 606, May 14, 1954 (mimeographed), which gives the list of goods liberated by May 1954, their tariff rates, and their rates under the new tax.

achieve any lasting results. The OEEC showed less understanding of the nature of the tax, and less fortitude in opposing it, than did the GATT. Fearing that France would abandon its commitments entirely, the OEEC was willing to settle for the illusion of trade liberalization. It simply conducted hearings on the effect of the tax and invited member countries to submit reports indicating the extent to which their exports had suffered.[62] In addition, the OEEC recommended that France relinquish the tax as soon as its payments should permit.[63] France responded by pointing out that its imports had increased at roughly the same time that liberalization was resumed — therefore the tax could not be restrictive.[64]

The GATT reacted more strongly to France's tax. It also examined the tax and declared France guilty of increasing the incidence of customs charges above the maximum rates set forth in Article II of the agreement and found, moreover, that the tax "introduces, in respect of the products affected, an increase in the incidence of the preference in excess of the maximum margins

[62] Various OEEC countries submitted such reports. It is not clear how they were able to separate the additional influence of the tax from that of the ordinary customs duty on products which, until that time, had been subject to quotas. The injured exports were mainly manufactured goods, with a few agricultural products. The goods which were mentioned most frequently included photographic films, rubber products, leather goods, textile machinery and spare parts, machine tools, large motors, generators and transformers, wool yarn, wool blankets, cotton thread, men's and boys' clothing, aluminum and copper semimanufactures, certain basic chemicals, and calculating machines. No raw materials were mentioned. See OEEC, Steering Board for Trade, "List of Goods Freed by France since May, 1954, for Which Member Countries Fear that the Special Temporary Tax May Represent a Considerable Obstacle to Exports: Special Temporary Tax Applied by France," SBC(55)34, May 24, 1955, annex IV; C(55)184, 1955, annexes III, IV, V; TFD/TD 626; TP(54)19, October 27, 1954; SBC(55)27, 1955, table 1; and TFD/TD 742, 1955 (all mimeographed). Italy seems to have suffered most from the tax.

[63] OEEC, TFD/TD 626.

[64] The Steering Board for Trade of the OEEC was not mislead by this argument. It remonstrated that the counterpart of the 10 percent increase in imports of 1954 over those of 1953 was an 8 or 9 percent increase in industrial production for the same period, and that 1953 was a year of particularly heavy import restrictions. See OEEC, Comité de Direction des Echanges, SBC(55)34. The OEEC also observed that imports of those goods subject to the highest tax increased less than did those of goods subject to the lower rates. See "Importations en provenance des pays membres et des leurs T.O.M.," C(55)40, February 18, 1955, annex II, p. 9 (mimeographed).

permissible under Article I."[65] The GATT expressed regret that France had applied the tax without consulting the contracting parties, and it authorized any country adversely affected to take compensating action. The contracting parties also asked the French government to "take steps to reduce the present degree of discrimination against the trade of the contracting parties whose exports are subject to the tax and to which the liberalization measures taken by the French government did not apply."[66]

EXPORT SUBSIDIES

Great Britain, West Germany, and France, along with most other countries, remit all domestic indirect taxes on goods that are exported. This practice is nondiscriminatory as long as the excises represent the same proportion of value added for each sector. To the extent that indirect taxes are usually a higher proportion of value added on consumption goods, their remission is equivalent to an export subsidy on such items. For instance, the purchase tax in Great Britain stimulates the exportation, and discourages the domestic consumption, of consumer goods. Germany remits its main tax, the turnover tax, as well as its less important indirect taxes. In addition, it allows a deduction from taxable income of an amount equal to 3 percent of export sales.[67] French exporters did not pay the turnover tax, which was also their country's main tax until 1954, nor do they now pay the 20 percent value-added tax replacing it. These tax reimbursements in Germany and France tend to encourage exports generally, without encouraging exports of one group of products more than those of another.

On the other hand, reimbursements to French exporters for direct labor taxes undoubtedly encourage exports of labor-

[65] OEEC, "Decision Taken by the Contracting Parties to the General Agreement on Tariffs and Trade on 17 January, 1955," SBC(55), January 17, 1955, annexes (mimeographed).

[66] OEEC, "Decision Taken by the Contracting Parties," SBC(55).

[67] Wallich, pp. 248–249.

intensive goods.[68] At the same time that the French government decided to reimburse social charges and the wage tax, it set up a system of direct export subsidies.[69] These two measures, constituting the export program, discriminated among products, as did the Special Temporary Import Tax. All finished and the vast majority of partly finished manufactured exports were reimbursed not only for their social and fiscal charges, but received in addition the full direct export subsidy of 8.72 percent of the price of the good.[70] Steel and iron, and some other semimanufactures, received the reimbursements plus a direct subsidy of 5.45 percent (unless they came under the European Coal and Steel Community agreements). The great majority of raw-material producers received no reimbursements under this system, although certain raw-material exporters were allowed the two reimbursements without direct subsidy.[71]

[68] The practice of reimbursing the 5 percent wage tax and the heavy social-insurance charges (equal to about 40 percent of total workers' compensation) began in March 1951. The decrees instituting, and later modifying, the export program are the following: Arrêté, February 6, 1952 (see the *J.O.* of February 8, 1952); Arrêté, January 31, 1953 (*Moniteur officiel du commerce et de l'industrie* — hereafter cited *M.O.* — no. 1542, February 5, 1953, p. 360); Arrêté, February 7, 1953 (*M.O.*, no. 1543, February 12, 1953, p. 417); Note No. 1457, "Constitution des dossiers" (*M.O.*, no. 1549, March 26, 1953, p. 830); Décision No. 1526, "Codification de la réglementation douanière" (*M.O.*, no. 1585, December 3, 1953, p. 3090); "Liste des services départementaux des enquêtes économiques" (*M.O.*, no. 1585, p. 3095); Arrêté rectifié, June 16, 1954 (*M.O.*, no. 1614, June 24, 1954, p. 1821); Arrêté, June 18, 1954 (*M.O.*, no. 1614, June 24, 1954, p. 1821); Arrêté, July 31, 1954 (*M.O.*, no. 1620, August 5, 1954, p. 2237); Avis, July 31, 1954 (*M.O.*, no. 1620, p. 2238); Décision, August 3, 1954 (*M.O.*, no. 1621, August 12, 1954, p. 2299). See A. Solomonidis, *Guide pratique de l'exportateur français* (Paris, 1955), p. 36; also "Quelques données sur le remboursement des charges sociales et fiscales aux exportateurs," *Bulletin hebdomadaire de statistique de l'INSEE*, November 5, 1955.

[69] The references for the export-subsidy program are the same as those given in the preceding note. In addition, see "Etude sur l'aide à l'exportation," *M.O.*, no. 1608, May 13, 1954, p. 1324; Maurice Byé, "L'Aide à l'exportation," *J.O.*, *Avis et rapports du Conseil Economique*, February 14, 1953, pp. 203–204; "Le Problème des échanges extérieurs," *J.O.*, *Avis et rapports*, March 21, 1952, pp. 39–45; and "L'Aide de l'état à l'exportation," *Statistiques et études financières*, no. 84, supplement (December 1955).

[70] This, of course, would be a much higher percentage of the value added per unit by the exporting enterprises.

[71] For a complete list of products and their various export advantages under the program, see Solomonidis, pp. 37–69. By a decree of September 14, 1954

The deterioration of the balance of payments, which began with the increase of industrial production in 1956, caused the French government to raise direct export subsidies to 20 percent under the "20 percent operation" of August 1957. That measure required importers to pay a tax of 20 percent on all imports other than raw materials, and it paid exporters a premium of the same amount. The 20 percent operation, therefore, was merely a rationalization of the Special Temporary Import Tax and the export-aid program it replaced.

THE PRICES OF DOMESTIC RAW MATERIALS

Because they have allowed foreign competition, Great Britain, West Germany, and France have introduced policies to keep certain key domestic raw-material industries from declining. In each country, coal mining is the main raw-material industry to receive significant protection. In France, Germany, and the other European Coal and Steel Community countries, the price of coal is set equal to its average, rather than its marginal, cost of production, which leads to a substantially lower price. In addition, since the war, the French have invested a vast amount of capital in their coal mines under the modernization and equipment plans. This capital has been supplied at much less than the market rate of interest, and sometimes free, and so has brought down the average cost of production. In most cases, however, domestic production of raw materials has been allowed to decline (or to expand less than it otherwise would have done) in all three countries.

(*J.O.*, September 18, 1954), the direct subsidies of 8.72 percent were reduced to 7.50 percent, and those of 5.45 percent to 4.20 percent, effective January 1, 1955. Eleven months later these rates were lowered to 5 and 2.5 percent, respectively. Most goods were then accorded the rate of 5 percent, which was generalized to all products in April 1956. Subsidies on agricultural products were largely specific, but it appears that their *ad valorem* equivalents were very high. G. Marcy has estimated them at 35 percent for 1956. See his "Libération progressive des échanges et aide à l'exportation en France depuis 1959," *Balances extérieures et problème monétaire, 1919–1959, Cahiers de ISEA*, Series P, no. 2, special number. See also Jean Weiller and André Néel, "Commerce extérieur," *Revue d'économie politique* (July–October 1956), pp. 758ff; *J.O., Avis et rapports*, March 25, 1957, p. 339; and Solomonidis, p. 37.

French coal subsidies were made flexible to ensure that users of domestic and imported coal always paid the same price. In those rare cases when the price of imported coal exceeded that of domestic, an import subsidy was paid.[72] Another version of this same policy was applied to raw materials other than coal.[73] The purpose of this "parafiscal" system of taxes and subsidies was to equalize domestic and foreign prices.

INFLATION AND CHANGES IN THE RELATIVE COSTS OF LABOR AND RAW MATERIALS (FRANCE)

Between the devaluations of 1949 and of December 1958, French prices increasingly rose above those of its main trading partners. Many forces cooperated to bring this about: colonial involvements, welfare programs, other government expenditures leading to a chronically unbalanced budget, rapidly increasing private consumption, and pressure for higher pay. Wages were inflexibly tied to the cost-of-living index under the system known as the Salaire Minimum Interprofessionelle Guarantié, and they rose in step with rises in the price level.[74]

Table 14 indicates the extent to which the inflation in 1950–1951 carried French wages beyond wages in some of the other European countries. It has been estimated that by 1953 French labor costs were 10 percent higher than British, 3 percent higher than Belgian, 6.4 percent higher than German, 28 percent higher than Italian, and 56 percent higher than Dutch wages.[75] These figures were obtained simply by comparing wage rates and social charges converted into francs at the official exchange rates, and not to comparative costs of equal-efficiency labor units. If such a comparison could be made, it would doubtless lessen the difference between, say, the costs of an efficiency unit of labor in

[72] The subsidy on imported coal amounted to 18 billion francs in 1953, for instance. See Baum, pp. 125–126.

[73] The main raw materials involved were nickel, superphosphates, nitrates, sulphur, and sulphuric acid, paper pulp, oils and greases, and crude petroleum.

[74] For a description of how this system functioned, or rather malfunctioned, see François Perroux, "The Obliteration of the Economic Function of Wages and Structural Inflation," in International Economic Association, *Round Table on Wage Determination* (Seeligsberg, September 4–14, 1954), p. 4 (mimeographed).

[75] *Rapport général de la commission créée pour l'étude des disparités*, p. 15.

TABLE 14. *Effects of Inflation in France and Other Countries, 1950–1952*

Country	Percentage rise between June 1950 and the third quarter of 1952		Percentage rise of wages between June 1950 and the first quarter of 1952
	Wholesale prices	Cost of living	
France	37.9	36.3	52.1
Great Britain	26.7	20.3	16.4
Germany	33.8	11.3	23.6
Italy	11.3	15.5	14.4
Switzerland	12.2	8.1	5.4
Belgium	18.4	12.2	18.1

Source: Louis Rosenstock-Franck, "Prix français et prix étrangers," *Cahiers d'information économique*, 5:9 (September–October 1953).

France and Italy, but would increase that disparity between British and French units.

Table 15 shows the change in relative prices of labor and raw materials in France since 1950. It can be seen from the last column of that table that, except during the Korean War boom in raw materials, wages have risen steadily at a rate much greater than that of raw-material prices. Prices of imported raw materials

TABLE 15. *Relative Price Increases of Raw Materials and Labor in France, 1950–1958*

Year	Price index for imported raw materials	Wholesale price index for raw materials	Wage index	Index of wages divided by wholesale prices of raw materials
1950	100.0	100.0	100	100
1951	145.5	141.8	125	88
1952	108.7	140.5	145	103
1953	99.7	135.0	148	110
1954	98.1	132.3	157	120
1955	97.3	132.9	166	125
1956	97.8	139.0	181	130
1957	104.1	147.7	198	134
1958	102.7	154.8	215	139

Note: "Raw materials" includes coal.

Source: Computed from data in *Annuaire statistique, 1957* (Paris, 1957), pp. 54, 69; and *Annuaire statistique, 1959*, p. 294 and p. 323, table 5.

have risen, over the period, much less than those of domestically produced materials, as one would expect since the latter contain French primary factors whose cost rose with inflation. But the competition from foreign raw materials, imported free of tariffs or other restrictions, must have kept down the prices of French raw materials.

The price indices of imported raw materials and those of wholesale domestic raw materials can be combined by means of the quantity weights computed in Chapter Six, Table 22, to obtain a composite index. Table 16 gives an index of the ratio of wages to

TABLE 16. *Index of Wages Divided by Raw-Material Prices, France, 1950–1958*

Year	Index
1950	100.0
1951	86.4
1952	124.4
1953	135.8
1954	148.3
1955	157.3
1956	168.1
1957	163.9
1958	186.6

raw-material prices derived from these indices, and the rise shown there is dramatic. In any such comparison, however, the choice of the base year has an effect on the magnitude and, in some cases, even the direction of the result. If 1949 had been used instead of 1950, the rise in wages relative to raw-material prices would have been slightly less and, had 1951 been chosen, the relative rise would have been precipitously greater. The base year 1950 probably represents as good a compromise as any other, especially since it stands at the beginning of a period in which France's policy was clearly more restrictive than Germany's and Great Britain's. The index reflects, then, the increasingly severe effect of French commercial policies on the prices of manufactures, and therefore of labor, relative to those of raw materials.

RAW-MATERIAL USAGE IN WEST GERMANY, THE UNITED KINGDOM, AND FRANCE, 1950–1955

PROTECTION, by raising the prices of finished products more than those of their raw-material inputs, causes substitution of raw materials for other factors of production. The raw-material input coefficients, a_{ij}', where the subscripts i run over the commodities considered as raw materials, will accordingly be highest in the countries whose policies most raise the price of x_j relative to that of x_i. To the extent that one country applies more protection generally than another, its aggregate raw-material usage for a given structure of production should be larger than that of the other. The simplest way in which to study this *raw-material substitution effect* of protection would be to compute the vector

$$x^a = (I - A'^a)^{-1}(r^a - t^a)$$

to find the actual usage in country a of those commodities x_i^a that are raw materials and to compare it with those coming from the computation:

$$x = (I - A'^b)^{-1}(r^a - t^a).$$

The input-coefficient matrix of a second country, country b, has been substituted for that of the first country in this computation in order to determine how much of each input country a would use, directly and indirectly, under country b's coefficients. The x_i's corresponding to raw materials could then be weighted by the common import prices of raw materials facing the two countries, or by their average if they differed slightly, in order to obtain a single measure of comparative usage.

This method requires more data than are available. The input coefficients, in physical amounts, it needs would require not only conventional input-output tables in value terms for each country in the comparison, but also the consumer and producer price of each commodity to convert those tables to physical units. Only France, among the countries to be compared, has an adequate input-output table. A comparison of raw-material usage using this method is ruled out, therefore.

The alternative method used is not too different, however. The total raw-material consumption of each of the three countries was found by adding imports to domestic production minus exports, all in common 1950 prices. This consumption was expressed as a proportion of value added in industry, also in common 1950 prices.[1] Finally, for France and Germany, the countries showing the largest difference in raw-material consumption, a correction was made for possible significant differences in industrial structure. This took care only of the direct raw-material consumption effect but, since that difference was so slight, accounting for the indirect effects was unnecessary.

INDUSTRIAL PRODUCTION

I have adopted H. H. Liesner's definition of industrial production, which includes construction, gas, water, electricity, handcrafts, and manufactures, but not agriculture, food and tobacco processing, mining, or services. He first calculated the value added in each industry in the United Kingdom and West Germany for 1950. From this, and from published production indices, he obtained the value added for succeeding years.[2] The earliest reliable estimate of French production is that of 1952, and production indices use that year, rather than 1950, for their base. It was necessary, therefore, to estimate industrial value added for 1952, to calculate the value added for 1950–1955 in 1952 prices, and then to deflate the whole series to 1950 prices.

The value added by French industry, gross of depreciation and at factor cost, was 3,922 billion francs in 1952.[3] The French data include mining, other than coal mining, in manufacturing output,

---

[1] This part of the study is quite close in method and detail to H. H. Liesner's *The Import Dependence of Britain and Western Germany: A Comparative Study* (Princeton, 1957), to which I am greatly indebted.

[2] Liesner, pp. 80–83.

[3] Ministère des Finances, *Rapport sur les comptes de la nation*, II: *Méthodes* (Paris, 1955), pp. 224–227, tables 1, 4, 5, and 6, columns headed "Revenue intérieur net" and "amortissements."

so its value-added had to be subtracted from the above figure. Separate figures for mining are not published, so its weight in the production index prepared by the Institut National de Statistiques et Etudes Economiques (INSEE) was used as an estimate of its value added.[4] This calculation gave a figure of 110 billion francs for value added by mining. Total industrial production, by Liesner's definition, was 3,812 billion francs in 1952, at 1952 prices.

The figures for the other years between 1950 and 1955 were obtained by constructing an index from the INSEE's production index. This new index consists of twelve subindices for manufacturing, gas, water, electricity, and construction, weighted according to their importance in 1952 industrial production. The resulting figures were converted, by means of wholesale price indices, to obtain French industrial value added for comparison with that of Britain and West Germany. The best available French industrial-price index,[5] however, is imperfect for the present purposes. It is based mainly on semimanufactures, the prices of which have risen more slowly than those of finished products. This is partly because the prices of semimanufactures are more sensitive to the prices of raw materials, which rose less rapidly than industrial prices generally. It is also partly because the government has directly controlled the prices of certain important semimanufactures.[6] A true index of the prices of industrial inputs other than raw materials would rise more rapidly than the index used. (The index of wages, for example, supports this conclusion.) As a result, the estimate of the value added by manufacturing in France in 1950 and in the years following is probably too high. The subindices for gas, water, electricity, and construction do not incur this difficulty.

The final step — that of comparing French industrial production with that of West Germany and of Great Britain — requires that the 1950 prices of the factors adding value in industry be comparable in all three countries. It would be

[4] INSEE, "Indices de la production industrielle," *Etudes statistiques*, 3:107ff (Paris, July–September, 1958).

[5] INSEE, *Annuaire statistique de la France, 1958* (Paris, 1959), p. 290.

[6] See John Sheahan, "Problems and Possibilities of Industrial Price Control: Postwar French Experience," *American Economic Review*, 41:346ff (June 1961).

dangerously simple to use the official exchange rates and to convert all figures into, say, United States dollars. The French franc in 1950 was overvalued with respect to the British pound, and Liesner found that the German mark of that year was also somewhat overvalued with respect to the pound. Gilbert's and Kravis' calculations suggest that the French franc of 1950 must be depreciated by about 9.63 percent for industrial goods to bring it to purchasing-power parity with the British pound.[7] If this was the average disparity between British and French industrial prices, and since industrial prices include those of raw materials, the industrial *value-added disparity* was somewhat larger. Therefore, once again, the estimate of French value added by industry vis-à-vis that of the other countries is probably too high. The results of the above computations are shown, along with Liesner's, in Table 17.

TABLE 17. *Value Added by Industry in West Germany, Great Britain, and France*

(in millions of 1950 U.S. dollars)

Year	West Germany		Great Britain		France	
	Value added	Index	Value added	Index	Value added	Index
1950	7,200	100.0	13,400	100.0	6,099	100.0
1951	8,500	118.0	13,900	104.0	7,001	114.8
1952	9,000	125.0	13,400	100.0	7,018	115.1
1953	10,000	139.0	14,300	107.0	7,085	116.2
1954	11,100	154.0	15,500	116.0	7,774	127.5
1955	12,900	179.0	16,400	122.0	8,464	138.8

Source: H. H. Liesner, *The Import Dependence of Britain and Western Germany: A Comparative Study* (Princeton, 1957), p. 43; and the sources given in the text.

A comparison of the index of French industrial production given in Table 17 with that of the INSEE,[8] which has roughly the same coverage, shows that the INSEE index rises less rapidly. Therefore, it appears that if the series of industrial

[7] Milton Gilbert and Irving B. Kravis, *An International Comparison of National Products and the Purchasing Power of Currencies* (Paris, 1954), esp. tables 10 and 11.

[8] INSEE, *Initiation à la comptabilité nationale* (Paris, 1957), p. 45, indices for "industries de transformation" and "construction."

production presented in Table 17 suffers from bias, that bias probably exaggerates the actual rate of growth.

DOMESTIC RAW-MATERIAL PRODUCTION

Now it is necessary to confront the above figures, which refer to the inputs of primary factors, with figures relating to the raw materials used in manufacturing. These inputs are equal to domestic raw-material production, plus net imports, plus depletion of raw-material stocks, in any given year. The first job is to estimate domestic production. The estimate for any country

TABLE 18. *British, West German, and French Production of Raw Materials*
(in millions of dollars at 1950 prices)

Year	Country	(1) Wood & timber	(2) Paper pulp	(3) Textile materials	(4) Ores & metals	(5) Crude petroleum	(6) Coal	(7) Skins & hides	(8) Total
1950	Germany	230.7	76.3	12.0	62.0	24.4	1,302.1	33.0	1,740.5
	Britain	84.4	1.6	60.0	54.0	0	1,962.8	41.0	2,203.8
	France	174.8	16.6	23.7	142.8	2.2	610.6	64.3	1,035.0
1951	Germany	247.3	86.7	10.0	70.0	30.0	1,411.0	36.0	1,891.0
	Britain	75.2	2.8	62.0	62.0	0	2,022.6	42.0	2,266.6
	France	212.3	37.7	28.1	168.0	6.5	643.0	61.8	1,157.4
1952	Germany	241.3	73.7	9.0	78.0	38.2	1,455.1	37.0	1,932.3
	Britain	67.5	2.5	65.0	69.0	0	2,054.7	38.0	2,296.7
	France	205.0	37.0	28.1	192.9	8.7	664.1	65.0	1,200.8
1953	Germany	214.3	71.7	9.0	76.0	57.5	1,467.6	43.0	1,939.1
	Britain	64.8	3.2	69.0	67.0	0	2,034.2	38.0	2,276.2
	France	295.0	30.7	31.0	200.1	8.7	639.9	65.2	1,270.6
1954	Germany	220.9	94.1	8.0	74.0	58.0	1,511.6	45.0	2,011.6
	Britain	56.8	3.2	72.0	67.0	0	2,033.3	47.0	2,279.3
	France	311.5	38.6	31.0	206.9	10.9	659.1	69.5	1,327.5
1955	Germany	271.8	90.2	7.0	80.0	68.5	1,546.5	42.0	2,106.0
	Britain	52.8	3.2	70.0	69.0	18.8	2,011.0	44.0	2,268.8
	France	350.4	42.1	32.6	236.9	15.3	672.7	72.3	1,422.3

Source: The entries in columns 1–5 and 7 for West Germany and Great Britain are from Liesner, p. 52. Pulpwood was transferred from the category "wood" to that of "paper pulp," and a separate category was created for crude petroleum. The entries for France in the same columns were calculated from Appendix Table V-A and Liesner's prices (*ibid.*, tables 8 and 9, pp. 50 and 52). The prices used to derive column 7, "skins and hides," from column 9 of Appendix Table V-A are the average import values for skins and hides reported in OEEC, Statistical Bulletins, *Foreign Trade*, series 3 (Paris, quarterly). The figure for coal has been derived by weighting production of hard and soft coal by the appropriate prices, derived in Appendix V. Total coal production, including that going directly to households, was used. See the sources for Tables V-B, V-D, and V-E.

will correspond to a point somewhere between p_1 and p_2 in Figure V-1.

The physical output of most raw materials produced by France between 1950 and 1955 is shown in Table V-A in Appendix V. Difficulties arose in attaching values to the physical magnitudes in order to render them comparable with Liesner's estimates for Britain and Germany. For all categories but hides and skins, which he omitted, and coal, for which his estimates were apparently inaccurate, his prices, calculated from OEEC statistics on British and German trade, proved adequate. It would have been incorrect, without knowing the proper deflators, to use French domestic or import prices.

A good deal of care was required in attaching the proper prices to coal, both because of its great importance as a raw material and because of the variations in its quality among the three countries. Section 1 in Appendix V lays out the methods and sources used. Table 18, which compares the raw-material production of the three countries, gives the results.

IMPORTS AND EXPORTS OF INDUSTRIAL MATERIALS

Table V-G in Appendix V gives German, British, and French imports of raw materials for 1950–1955, at current prices, according to the categories used to classify domestic production of those materials. To imports of raw materials, it is evident that those of semimanufactures close to the raw-material stage must be added, since they are near-substitutes for raw materials. Appendix Table V-H gives the imports, by the same material categories, of more nearly finished commodities. The totals of these two tables, reported in Appendix Table V-I, are equal to imports of industrial materials, at current (each year's) prices.

Industrial materials already contain value added by industry, and, because of this, an imprecision threatens to corrupt the analysis. Appendix Table V-J shows, however, that the percentage of semimanufactures in the French-imported industrial materials was much lower than that for the German or British. Moreover, the low percentage of semimanufactures in French imports of industrial materials was no accident, but was clearly the result of the restrictive French policies. Table 19 gives im-

TABLE 19. *British, West German, and French Imports of Industrial Materials*
(in millions of dollars at 1950 prices)

Year	Country	(1) Oils & greases	(2) Rubber	(3) Wood & timber	(4) Pulp & paper	(5) Textile materials	(6) Ores & metals	(7) Crude petroleum	(8) Coal	(9) Skins & hides	(10) Chemicals	(11) Other	(12) Total
1950	Germany	222.9	56.8	49.5	43.8	516.0	187.9	41.3	41.6	80.9	46.2	179.9	1,466.8
	Britain	354.6	144.3	284.0	201.4	1,095.2	595.4	207.9	—	142.1	141.9	331.6	3,498.4
	France	153.4	60.7	30.1	58.9	517.1	166.1	299.0	153.9	58.3	83.1	124.1	1,704.7
1951	Germany	216.1	58.2	55.9	60.0	373.3	238.3	68.1	75.9	69.0	53.6	146.1	1,414.5
	Britain	356.5	204.5	437.0	267.1	1,014.5	629.0	368.3	18.8	179.0	231.1	358.2	4,064.0
	France	240.2	77.9	37.7	77.6	492.8	207.1	351.0	212.8	66.7	94.0	125.7	1,983.5
1952	Germany	162.5	63.6	85.3	49.0	424.2	339.9	75.6	107.5	75.1	60.7	189.5	1,632.9
	Britain	324.2	123.5	273.3	200.3	888.9	791.8	495.6	5.3	152.3	146.2	261.0	3,662.4
	France	174.8	78.5	37.4	62.5	459.5	248.7	433.8	221.9	76.5	110.6	102.4	2,006.6
1953	Germany	228.9	80.2	92.1	64.3	528.6	385.0	96.6	132.1	76.6	70.5	224.6	1,979.5
	Britain	312.4	149.8	342.6	220.2	1,073.5	680.0	530.5	5.6	137.5	143.8	313.0	3,908.9
	France	197.7	74.6	29.4	60.7	534.1	218.4	477.7	164.7	65.2	86.8	115.4	2,024.7
1954	Germany	267.6	97.7	128.9	88.5	581.5	541.8	126.7	77.7	76.0	102.8	267.6	2,356.8
	Britain	306.9	172.6	379.4	290.4	1,006.0	683.7	570.0	45.2	134.8	186.0	337.3	4,112.3
	France	240.7	86.8	29.1	78.1	551.8	264.0	527.2	168.4	65.2	108.0	136.6	2,255.9
1955	Germany	287.3	113.6	165.1	108.3	658.6	762.6	150.4	145.3	101.1	122.8	325.4	2,940.5
	Britain	299.3	208.6	443.2	346.9	990.0	903.1	576.6	173.6	133.3	202.8	336.9	4,614.3
	France	262.1	100.2	53.1	98.3	537.4	367.9	544.3	200.2	73.5	190.3	175.0	2,602.3

Source: The entries in columns 1–7 and 10–11 for Britain and West Germany are from Liesner, p. 84. British coal imports in 1950 prices were obtained by deflating the data in Table V–G in Appendix V, column 8, by an index constructed to take account of actual tonnages. Tonnage figures are given in OEEC, *Foreign Trade*. German coal imports at 1950 prices were calculated from data published in Statistische Bundesamt, *Der Aussenhandel der Bundesrepublik Deutschland*, I: *Zusammenfassende Übersichten* (Wiesbaden, monthly). Coal imports include coal for household consumption.

The French imports in current values, shown in Appendix Tables V–G and V–H were deflated by import-price indices, constructed from the import current value and volume indices found in INSEE, "Indices du commerce extérieur de la France," *Études statistiques*, 1:49–50, 52–55 (Paris, January–March 1958). The indices correspond exactly to most of the component series used in this chapter, since the INSEE index itself follows the Standard Industrial Trade Classification nomenclature (*ibid.*, p. 7, and Appendix Table V–G). In a few cases, the INSEE index is not sufficiently detailed, and exact correspondence between the coverage of the index and the figures to be deflated could not be ensured. This was serious only for the category "other semimanufactures." The figures in column 9 of Appendix Table V–H were deflated by a price index for all the specified semimanufactures.

TABLE 20. *British, West German, and French Exports of Raw Materials*
(in millions of dollars at 1950 prices)

Year	Country	(1) Oils & greases	(2) Rubber	(3) Wood & timber	(4) Pulp & paper	(5) Textile materials	(6) Ores & metals	(7) Crude petroleum	(8) Coal	(9) Skins & hides	(10) Other	(11) Total
1950	Germany	2.4	0.4	9.6	6.9	33.3	34.5	1.2	317.1	0.2	31.5	437.1
	Britain	14.6	3.4	0.6	0.6	188.6	4.0	0	169.4	2.7	27.6	411.5
	France	14.3	0.9	50.5	1.5	130.3	39.1	0.2	85.5	9.8	47.8	379.9
1951	Germany	3.5	0.3	6.3	7.3	32.3	29.5	0.1	305.8	0.1	35.3	420.5
	Britain	9.7	2.0	0.7	0.4	155.0	3.8	0	130.8	2.7	27.5	332.6
	France	13.7	0.9	46.3	0.9	101.0	38.2	1.2	81.7	6.3	46.1	336.3
1952	Germany	2.2	0.6	1.8	3.2	29.8	22.8	0.3	309.7	0.3	27.5	398.2
	Britain	5.8	2.2	2.6	0.5	185.0	4.6	0	196.1	3.7	24.0	424.5
	France	16.7	0.7	21.0	1.5	133.3	38.9	0.4	75.0	9.1	41.7	338.3
1953	Germany	6.1	1.2	4.7	3.8	39.1	20.3	0.1	308.2	0.5	31.2	415.2
	Britain	13.3	2.5	0.8	1.6	193.0	3.5	0	224.3	3.6	25.0	467.6
	France	21.3	1.2	25.2	2.0	129.2	53.4	0	95.1	8.9	37.8	374.1
1954	Germany	8.7	1.3	7.7	6.0	48.7	27.8	0.1	350.7	2.2	39.2	492.4
	Britain	21.4	3.3	0.8	1.9	211.0	2.9	0	222.1	4.0	28.2	495.6
	France	14.7	0.8	38.9	2.0	153.4	67.6	0	100.5	12.5	46.1	436.5
1955	Germany	6.8	1.3	12.6	6.0	72.3	26.6	0	329.1	5.3	38.7	498.7
	Britain	24.6	2.8	1.1	2.2	260.5	3.6	3.5	205.4	5.7	27.4	536.8
	France	13.0	1.5	50.9	0.7	159.5	68.0	0	166.3	18.1	41.4	519.4

Source: See sources for Appendix Table V-K. The data of Table V-K have been deflated by price indices derived from export current value and volume indices found in INSEE, "Indices du commerce extérieur de la France," pp. 49–50, 52–55.

ports of industrial materials for the three countries in 1950 prices. Appendix Table V-K gives the three countries' exports at current prices, and Table 20 gives them at 1950 prices. There is a possibility that the values of French and British raw-material imports, reported in Appendix Table V-G, are too high. Both countries possessed colonial empires which they accorded certain preferences. As a result, selected imports from these areas may have been overvalued. The prices of most raw-material imports into France and Great Britain must have been competitive, however. Colonial agriculture, but not colonial industry, received favorable treatment from the French metropole.[9] Agricultural commodities comprised most of the roughly 40 percent of total French imports that originated in the colonies between 1950 and 1955. Only some 11 percent of total raw materials used in French industry came from the colonies in 1950; thus only a considerable overvaluation of that portion could affect the results.[10]

RAW-MATERIAL INPUTS RELATED TO VALUE
ADDED BY INDUSTRY

The estimates of imports of industrial materials, exports, and domestic production of raw materials can be combined into an estimate of total availabilities of industrial materials in each of the three countries. The increases in stocks of raw materials in some years were certainly offset by decreases in others over the period 1950-1955. Therefore, the estimates of availabilities can

[9] Wine, sugar, peanut oil, bananas, vegetables, wheat, coffee, sardines, and tobacco are the main colonial products to which the French have granted preferential treatment.

[10] Moreover, among industrial materials, only colonial jute, manioc, peanut oil, nickel, cork, cotton, some types of wood, zinc, and sisal enjoyed supported prices in 1950, and the price supports were in fact very low. See Pierre Moussa, *Les Chances économiques de la Communauté Franco-Africaine* (Paris, 1957), pp. 77–79. Peanut oil received by far the greatest price benefit: about 20 to 30 percent. But this support represented only an additional $16 million for the category of "oils and greases." Among the other industrial materials, only nickel received an appreciable price support. This amounted to only about $2 million. A rough calculation from my own and Moussa's data indicates that the overestimation of French industrial-material availabilities because of colonial price supports could not have been more than 1 percent.

TABLE 21. *Industrial-Material Use* — *Imports of Raw Materials plus Imports of Semimanufactures plus Domestic Production of Raw Materials minus Exports of Raw Materials* — *in West Germany, Great Britain, and France*
(in millions of dollars at 1950 prices)

Year	(1) Oils & greases	(2) Rubber	(3) Wood & timber	(4) Pulp & paper	(5) Textile materials	(6) Ores & metals	(7) Crude petroleum	(8) Coal	(9) Skins & hides	(10) Chemicals	(11) Other	(12) Total
West Germany												
1950	220.5	56.4	270.6	113.2	494.7	215.4	64.5	829.1	113.7	46.2	148.4	2572.7
1951	212.6	57.9	296.9	139.4	351.0	278.8	98.0	922.7	104.9	53.6	110.8	2626.6
1952	160.3	63.0	324.8	119.5	403.4	395.1	113.5	986.4	111.8	60.7	162.0	2900.5
1953	222.8	79.0	301.7	132.2	498.5	440.7	154.0	988.4	119.1	70.5	193.4	3200.3
1954	258.9	96.4	342.1	176.6	540.8	588.0	184.6	993.5	118.8	102.8	228.4	3630.9
1955	280.5	112.3	424.3	192.5	593.3	816.0	218.9	1118.9	137.8	122.8	286.7	4304.0
	1355.6	465.0	1960.4	873.4	2881.7	2734.0	833.5	5889.0	706.1	456.6	1129.7	19,235.0
Great Britain												
1950	340.0	140.9	367.8	202.4	966.6	645.4	207.9	1284.4	180.4	141.9	304.0	4781.7
1951	346.8	202.5	511.5	269.5	921.5	687.2	368.3	1393.7	218.3	231.1	330.7	5481.1
1952	318.4	121.3	338.2	202.3	768.9	856.2	495.6	1362.0	186.6	146.2	237.0	5032.7
1953	299.1	147.3	406.6	221.8	949.5	743.5	530.5	1382.0	171.9	143.8	288.0	5284.0
1954	285.5	169.3	435.4	291.7	867.0	747.8	570.0	1393.1	177.8	186.0	309.1	5432.7
1955	274.7	205.8	494.9	347.9	799.5	968.5	591.9	1444.3	171.6	202.8	309.5	5811.4
	1864.5	987.1	2554.4	1535.6	5273.0	4648.6	2764.2	8259.5	1106.6	1051.8	1778.3	31,823.6
France												
1950	139.1	59.8	154.4	74.0	410.5	269.8	301.0	518.6	112.8	83.1	76.3	2199.4
1951	226.5	77.0	203.7	114.4	419.9	336.9	356.3	608.4	122.2	94.0	79.6	2638.9
1952	158.1	77.8	221.4	98.0	354.3	402.7	442.1	593.2	132.4	110.6	60.7	2651.3
1953	176.4	73.4	299.2	89.4	435.9	365.1	486.4	545.3	121.5	86.8	77.6	2757.0
1954	226.0	86.0	301.7	114.7	429.4	403.3	538.1	551.3	122.2	108.0	90.5	2971.2
1955	249.1	98.7	352.6	139.7	410.5	536.8	559.6	592.2	127.7	190.3	133.6	3390.8
	1175.2	472.7	1533.0	630.2	2460.5	2314.6	2683.5	3409.0	738.8	672.8	518.3	16,608.6

TABLE 22. *Availabilities of Industrial Materials in Relation to Industrial Value Added in West Germany, Great Britain, and France*

(in ratios and in millions of dollars at 1950 prices)

Year	(1) Domestic output of raw materials	(2) Index	(3) Imports of raw materials	(4) Index	(5) Exports of raw materials	(6) Index	(7) Availabilities of raw materials	(8) Index	(9) Value added by industry	(10) Index	(11) Col. 1 ÷ Col. 9	(12) Col. 3 ÷ Col. 9	(13) Col. 7 ÷ Col. 9
West Germany													
1950	1740.5	100.0	1466.8	100.0	437.1	100.0	2572.7	100.0	7200.0	100.0	.2417	.2037	.3573
1951	1891.0	108.6	1414.5	96.4	420.5	96.2	2626.6	102.1	8500.0	118.0	.2224	.1663	.3090
1952	1932.3	111.0	1632.9	111.3	398.2	91.1	2900.5	112.7	9000.0	125.0	.2147	.1814	.3223
1953	1939.1	111.4	1979.5	136.0	415.2	95.0	3200.3	124.4	10,000.0	139.0	.1939	.1980	.3200
1954	2011.6	115.6	2356.8	160.7	492.4	112.7	3630.9	141.1	11,100.0	154.0	.1812	.2123	.3271
1955	2106.0	121.0	2940.5	200.5	498.7	114.1	4304.0	167.3	12,900.0	179.0	.1633	.2279	.3336
	11,620.5		11,791.0		2,662.1		19,235.0		58,700.0		.1980	.2009	.3277
Great Britain													
1950	2203.8	100.0	3498.4	100.0	411.5	100.0	4781.7	100.0	13,400.0	100.0	.1644	.2611	.3568
1951	2286.6	102.8	4064.0	116.2	332.6	80.8	5481.1	114.6	13,900.0	104.0	.1630	.2924	.3943
1952	2296.7	104.2	3662.4	104.7	424.5	103.2	5032.7	105.6	13,400.0	100.0	.1713	.2733	.3756
1953	2276.2	103.3	3908.9	111.7	467.6	113.6	5284.0	110.5	14,300.0	107.0	.1591	.2733	.3695
1954	2279.3	103.4	4112.3	117.6	495.6	120.4	5432.7	113.6	15,500.0	116.0	.1470	.2653	.3505
1955	2268.8	102.9	4614.3	131.9	536.8	130.5	5811.4	121.5	16,400.0	122.0	.1383	.2814	.3544
	13,591.4		23,860.3		2,668.6		31,823.6		86,900.0		.1564	.2746	.3662
France													
1950	1035.0	100.0	1704.7	100.0	379.9	100.0	2199.4	100.0	6099.0	100.0	.1696	.2795	.3606
1951	1157.4	111.8	1983.5	116.4	336.3	88.5	2638.9	120.0	7001.0	114.8	.1653	.2833	.3770
1952	1200.8	116.0	2006.6	117.7	338.3	89.0	2651.3	120.5	7018.0	115.1	.1711	.2859	.3778
1953	1270.6	122.8	2024.7	118.8	374.1	98.5	2757.0	125.4	7085.0	116.2	.1793	.2858	.3891
1954	1327.5	128.3	2255.9	132.3	436.5	114.9	2971.2	135.1	7774.0	127.5	.1707	.2902	.3822
1955	1422.3	137.4	2602.3	152.7	519.4	136.7	3390.8	154.2	8464.0	138.8	.1686	.3075	.4006
	7,413.6		12,577.7		2,384.5		16,008.6		43,441.0		.1706	.2895	.3823

be taken as estimates of the actual inputs of raw materials for the period. Table 21 shows the detailed breakdown of raw-material availabilities for the three countries. Table 22 presents synoptically the information contained in the preceding tables of this chapter.

The ratio of total availabilities of industrial materials to industrial value added, given in column 13 of Table 22, supports the thesis which Figure V-1 illustrated. France, the most protectionist of the three countries, used more raw materials, per unit of capital and labor adding value, than did either Germany or Great Britain. Moreover, during a period in which French commercial policy grew more restrictive and the ratio of wages to raw-material prices rose, the ratio of raw materials to primary-factor inputs in French industry increased. The same ratio was stable in Germany and Great Britain. These tendencies show up clearly, despite the unfavorable weighting of questionable or doubtful estimates.

The French ratio of raw-material inputs to industrial value added is, relative to Germany and Great Britain, higher than the figures of Table 22 indicate, since the industrial materials used by France contained a relatively lower percentage of imported semimanufactures. It is possible to correct fairly successfully for this difference with the aid of the inverse of a working draft of the French 1956 input-output table.[11] Appendix Table V-L reports the raw-material content of French semimanufactures as calculated from the input-output table. The coefficients of Table V-L were weighted by the appropriate semimanufactured imports for the three countries to obtain estimates of their raw-material content. The corrected ratios are given in Table 23.

Table 23 indicates that between 1950 and 1955 French industry required about 25 percent more raw materials per dollar's worth of value added in industry than West Germany did, and about 16 percent more than Britain did. This discrepancy certainly supports the thesis that a high-tariff country uses more raw materials per unit of industrial value added, but it does not necessarily prove it. It is possible, for example, that France has

[11] I am indebted to the Ministère des Finances, and particularly to M. Nivollet, for making this table available to me.

TABLE 23. *Availabilities of Raw Materials in Relation to Industrial Value Added in West Germany, Great Britain, and France, 1950–1955*

Country	Ratio
West Germany	.2707
Great Britain	.2927
France	.3376

Source: The coefficients of Table V-L in Appendix V were weighted by the corresponding semimanufacture imports of the three countries.

a comparative advantage in activities that, even under free trade, are associated with high raw-material inputs per unit of labor and capital. Moreover, it is quite possible that, since French imports of semimanufactures were relatively less important than those of the other two countries, its domestic production of them was relatively higher and therefore its raw-material requirements were greater. It is necessary to check whether the former possibility is true; but no correction is indicated for the second. If the effect of a commercial policy is to make raw materials relatively cheap, it will at the same time increase the profitability of those industries whose final products contain a high proportion of raw materials. French commercial policy probably encouraged the semimanufacturing activities listed in Appendix Table V-L in roughly the order in which they are listed,[12] and this increased the total raw-material dependence of the economy.

It would probably be futile to attempt to separate, and to measure the influence of, those differences in industrial structure which do and do not depend upon differences in commercial policy. An examination of the differences in the structure of production between France and Germany will show the extent to which each separate industry in France is, or is not, lavish in its usage of raw materials compared to its German counterpart. A number of approaches to this task are possible; two are presented here.

One approach consists simply of examining the structure of

[12] That is, the encouragement is roughly correlated with the raw-material content of the activity's product.

industrial-material use in the three countries, which presumably bears some relationship to the structure of transforming industries. Table 24 presents the total consumption of each type of industrial material at 1950 prices, expressing these totals as percentages of value added by industry, for the years 1950–1955. A marked similarity appears in the patterns of consumption in the three countries. The important differences concern only coal, petroleum, and chemicals. The last of these arises only for imports of chemical semimanufactures, and Germany's low imports were clearly related to its important chemical industry. The differences in coal and crude-petroleum consumption separately were much greater than that in the consumption of the two fuels taken together. France, evidently because it lacks coal, has substituted petroleum to a large extent. In addition, French throughput capacity is high, partly because, as early as 1929, the government obliged companies selling in France to refine their petroleum there.

A second method consists of comparing raw-material use in France and Germany on the assumption that, if the industrial structures of both countries were identical, the ratio of raw-material use to industrial value added would also be identical. The sixty-five sectors of the French input-output table were classified into industrial and raw-material-producing sectors according to the same principle of classification used earlier in this chapter. The ratio of the input of raw materials to value added for each French industrial sector was then computed. The resulting coefficients were used, along with estimates of value added in Germany by corresponding industries, to estimate what Germany's consumption of raw materials would have been had each of its industries used raw materials in the same proportion to value added as did the corresponding French industry. Section 2 in Appendix V describes in detail the methods used to establish correspondence between French and German industrial sectors. This was a difficult task, and the reader must judge for himself what degree of confidence to place in the results. They indicate, at least, that the higher rate of raw-material utilization in France was not associated with its industrial structure. According to the computation in Appendix V, the ratio of raw-material consump-

TABLE 24. *Availabilities of Industrial Materials as Percentages of Industrial Value Added in West Germany, Great Britain, and France*

Year	(1) Oils & greases	(2) Rubber	(3) Wood & timber	(4) Pulp & paper	(5) Textile materials	(6) Ores & metals	(7) Crude petroleum	(8) Coal	(9) Skins & hides	(10) Chemicals	(11) Other	(12) Total
West Germany												
1950	3.06	0.78	3.76	1.57	6.87	2.99	0.91	11.52	1.59	0.64	2.06	35.73
1951	2.50	0.68	3.49	1.64	4.14	3.28	1.15	10.86	1.19	0.63	1.30	30.90
1952	1.78	0.70	3.61	1.33	4.48	4.39	1.26	10.96	1.24	0.67	1.80	32.23
1953	2.23	0.79	3.02	1.32	4.99	4.41	1.54	9.88	1.19	0.71	1.93	32.00
1954	2.33	0.87	3.08	1.59	4.87	5.30	1.66	8.95	1.07	0.93	2.06	32.71
1955	2.17	0.87	3.29	1.49	4.60	6.33	1.70	8.67	1.07	0.95	2.99	33.36
1950-55	2.31	0.79	3.33	1.49	4.91	4.66	1.42	9.95	1.20	0.78	1.93	32.77
Great Britain												
1950	2.54	1.05	2.74	1.51	7.21	4.82	1.55	9.59	1.35	1.06	2.27	35.68
1951	2.49	1.46	3.68	1.94	6.63	4.94	2.65	10.02	1.57	1.66	2.38	39.43
1952	2.38	0.91	2.52	1.51	5.74	6.39	3.70	10.16	1.39	1.09	1.77	37.56
1953	2.09	1.03	2.84	1.55	6.64	5.20	3.71	9.66	1.20	1.01	2.01	36.95
1954	1.84	1.09	2.81	1.88	5.59	4.82	3.68	8.99	1.15	1.20	1.99	35.05
1955	1.68	1.25	3.02	2.12	4.88	5.91	3.61	8.81	1.05	1.24	1.89	35.44
1950-55	2.15	1.14	2.94	1.77	6.07	5.35	3.18	9.51	1.27	1.21	2.05	36.62
France												
1950	2.28	0.98	2.53	1.21	6.73	4.42	4.94	8.50	1.85	1.36	1.25	36.06
1951	3.24	1.10	2.91	1.63	6.00	4.81	5.09	8.69	1.75	1.34	1.14	37.69
1952	2.25	1.11	3.15	1.40	5.05	5.74	6.30	8.45	1.89	1.58	0.86	37.78
1953	2.49	1.04	4.22	1.26	6.15	5.15	6.87	7.70	1.71	1.23	1.10	38.91
1954	2.91	0.99	3.88	1.48	5.55	5.19	6.95	7.12	1.57	1.40	1.16	38.22
1955	2.95	1.06	4.17	1.65	4.85	6.34	6.61	7.00	1.51	2.25	1.58	40.06
1950-55	2.71	1.09	3.53	1.45	5.66	5.33	6.18	7.85	1.70	1.55	1.19	38.23

tion to value added by industry is 0.2180 under the French and would be 0.2234 under the German structure of industrial value added. The difference between these figures is probably not significant.

Notice, however, that the value of raw-material inputs in France is a lesser proportion of industrial value added according to the input-output calculation in Appendix Table V-N than it is according to Table 23. The difference between the two coefficients, 0.2180 and 0.3376, reflects the greater increase of labor and capital prices than of raw-material prices between 1950 and 1956. Table 23 is based on 1950 prices, corrected for the overvaluation of the franc at that time, whereas the input-output table underlying Appendix Table V-N is based on 1956 prices. According to Table 16, wages rose 68 percent with respect to raw-material prices between 1950 and 1956, and this amount is consistent with the difference between the two estimates. Those estimates thus confirm the argument that French commercial policy has lowered the prices of raw materials in relation to the prices of the primary factors working in industry.

PROTECTION AND THE SPREAD
OF ECONOMIC DEVELOPMENT

ONLY a small fraction of the world is wealthy. The United States alone earns about 40 percent of world income, and Europe, excluding the Soviet Union, earns another 27 percent. The other wealthy areas are recently discovered territories, almost entirely inhabited by Europeans. Economic development must therefore be regarded as the experience of a small segment of mankind, and even today it shows few signs of spontaneously spreading elsewhere. Japan is the single non-European country which is growing fast enough to close the gap between its per capita income and that of the wealthiest countries. The rest of the world seems unable to make significant economic progress.

Yet, according to the factor-price equalization theorem, high incomes in one area should spread through trade to others. The rise in per capita incomes as factor prices tend to be equalized should eventually permit poor areas to accumulate capital. In addition, if the wealthy countries invest directly abroad, the spread of high incomes should be even more rapid. The Heckscher–Ohlin theory thus indicates that under free trade economic development should spread evenly over the entire inhabited globe.

A PHYSIOCRATIC VIEW OF TRADE AND ECONOMIC GROWTH

There is, I believe, a simple explanation for the restriction of economic development. The most favorable agricultural land lies between the thirtieth and fiftieth parallels. There are relatively narrow bands of favorable farmland in higher latitudes along western coasts, particularly in Western Europe. Elsewhere, the short growing season and the permanently frozen subsoil render vast areas of more northerly land valueless for anything but shallow root crops. The tropics are equally unsuited for general agriculture because of insects, crop and livestock diseases, violent alternations of wet and dry seasons, and thin topsoil. Good agricultural land is virtually a North American and Western European monopoly.

The ease with which people can procure food, the primary necessity, determines the amount of labor and other resources that they can devote to industry and culture. A population that must devote 95 percent of its resources to feeding itself will have fewer allocable resources for other pursuits than will one of equal size that must devote only 90 percent to procuring necessities. The latter society can grow twice as fast at the outset, and the resulting capital accumulation will constantly raise the proportion of resources which it can use for further development. After a time, therefore, the two populations will occupy entirely different economic and cultural levels. When one considers that many societies today spend practically their total resources in securing the barest necessities of life, while others spend less than 10 percent for needs of the same urgency, observed differences in the levels of development of the two groups are not surprising (unless the two areas trade freely with one another).

The physiocrats, in thinking that agriculture was the only truly productive occupation, seemed to be making the same point. They observed that manufacturing added only enough value to the materials which the agriculturists advanced to repay the necessary living expenses of the artificers, and so seemed unable to enrich anyone. What they observed among classes they applied to nations. Some, like Holland, had to manufacture to eat while others, like France, could profitably leave the burdensome tasks of manufacturing to mercantile, or menial, nations:

It can never be to the interest of those landed nations, if I may call them so, to discourage or distress the industry of such mercantile states, by imposing high duties upon their trade, or upon the commodities which they furnish. Such duties, by rendering those commodities dearer, could serve only to sink the real value of the surplus produce of their own land, with which, or, what comes to the same thing, with the price of which, those commodities are purchased. Such duties could serve only to discourage the increase of that surplus produce, and consequently the improvement and cultivation of their own land. The most effectual expedient, on the contrary, for raising the value of that surplus produce, for encouraging its increase, and consequently the improvement and cultivation of their own land, would be to allow the most perfect freedom to the trade of all such mercantile nations.[1]

It is not hard to determine whether a country is, in Smith's phrase, a landed nation or what might today more appropriately be called a proletarian nation. Japan, for instance, obviously has little arable land, compared to the United States, but it is a very good workshop. India and Pakistan, as well as many Latin American countries — notably Mexico, Puerto Rico, and Cuba — would seem to have more promise as proletarian nations. Parts of Africa and South America have some promise as landed nations, particularly if new techniques for tropical agriculture are developed. In most cases, however, the high proportion of raw materials in the exports of underdeveloped countries gives a false impression that they are landed nations.

This high proportion stems instead from the unwillingness of the landed nations to accept products that compete with their protected manufacturing industries. The countries studied in the preceding chapters have nearly identical industrial structures, despite the large differences in their endowments of capital per worker. They trade primarily to match dissimilar natural-resource endowments to their similar patterns of raw-material consumption. Even the United States fails to exchange capital services for those of labor. The commercial policies of the industrial countries were originally erected as barriers against each other's commerce. Now they prevent competition from countries which, because of poor land resources, can grow only through industrialization. They particularly discourage the establishment of the highly labor-intensive commodities in which the proletarian nations possess a comparative advantage.[2] If manufactur-

---

[1] Adam Smith, *Wealth of Nations*, pp. 634–635.

[2] By allowing only raw materials to enter their markets freely, the industrial countries' commercial policies give the false impression that many underdeveloped countries have a comparative advantage in raw-material production. One cannot infer comparative advantage from trade flows under protection, as the discussion of the Leontief paradox in Chapters Three and Four shows. Not only trade policies, but also the investment policies of firms in the developed countries, which are anxious to assure their sources of raw materials and to capture the external economies of their demand for them, help to account for the relative overdevelopment of raw-material extraction in underdeveloped countries. In addition, one must not forget the conscious policies of the colonial powers to develop primary industry

ing industries were established there, the proletarian nations would be important net importers of both agricultural products and industrial materials, including capital-intensive processed raw materials and semimanufactures to be worked into elaborate final products.

There are two tragic ironies in this physiocratic account of trade and growth. One is that productive agriculture, as it happens, requires not only land, but also much capital and technical skill, while it can make but little use of large amounts of labor. But the restrictive commercial policies of the landed nations oblige the proletarian nations to employ nearly their entire labor force in an attempt to secure food. This is why agriculture appears labor-intensive in those countries. Such subsistence farming, however, has less to do with modern, highly capitalized and rationalized agriculture, like that of the United States, than the latter has to do with industry. The advanced sector of American agriculture, in fact, uses more scientific knowledge, technique, and capital per dollar's worth of output than do most manufacturing industries. It is obvious, therefore, that agriculturalization is more difficult for a developing country than industrialization.

The second irony is that the proletarian countries themselves, by protecting industry, prevent their own industrialization. Their import restrictions keep out the capital-intensive heavy manufactures that are necessary to build, and provide materials for, labor-intensive industries. Domestic production of capital-intensive manufactures raises the economy's capital requirements and thus raises the amount of domestic saving required to achieve a given growth rate. But the reduction in national income accompanying protection makes savings scarcer. Only landed countries can industrialize through protection because only they can afford it.

---

in the colonies and to discourage competing manufactures. See Richard Pares, "Economic Factors in the History of the Empire," in E. M. Carus-Wilson, ed., *Essays in Economic History* (London, 1954), pp. 416–438.

THE FUTURE OF TRADE AND PROTECTION

The uneven distribution of factors among countries would cause world trade to increase greatly if all countries, or even only the very rich and the very poor, abolished protection. The resulting increased volume, and improved patterns, of world trade would give the poor countries an opportunity to develop by reducing the effort they devote to the pursuit of necessities. The quickest and best way to reduce differences in per capita incomes, however, would be to reshuffle the movable supplies of labor and capital among countries. Factor movements are better than commodity trade because they greatly reduce transport requirements. In addition, the ability of trade to equalize factor returns and thus to allocate world production optimally is limited, even if transport costs are zero. National prejudices, of course, preclude the rational redistribution of the world's labor force among countries. The redistribution of capital stocks through foreign investment, however, would be almost as good a measure.

A nearly optimal plan for world economic development would involve the investment of the total savings, and as much as possible of the depreciation allowances, of all countries with more capital per worker than the world average in those countries with less. The investment would be made in such a way as to give each part of the world a similar production structure in order to minimize transport requirements. But in allocating capital to a country, and in determining its exact production structure, allowance would have to be made for its peculiar endowment of natural resources. Ironically, each country would tend to realize the protectionist goal of operating every possible industry domestically.

Although it is possible to imagine how the world would appear if it became a completely integrated economy, it is difficult to tell whether the world is tending toward or away from global economic integration. The formation of regionally integrated trading blocs appears to many to be a beneficial and necessary preliminary stage in this process. Unfortunately, the regional blocs tend to group countries similar in relative factor endowments and in other important characteristics. This promises little increase in economic efficiency, a consideration which empirical studies seem to corroborate.[3] Economic efficiency and the spread of economic development require that trading blocs, if they must be formed, embrace countries possessing markedly dissimilar factor endowments. If countries with extreme factor endowments, like the United States and India, say, were joined in a customs union, the effect on their structures of production and factor prices would be nearly equivalent to that of universal free trade. The actual development of regional blocs seems likely, on the contrary, to consolidate the protectionism of rich and poor countries against each other, to arouse and reinforce political and commercial suspicions, and thus to make the task of world economic integration all the more difficult.

The General Agreement on Tariffs and Trade, which negotiates tariff reductions and assures their general adoption by all member countries, represents a far more promising development. Its attempt to move away from product-by-product tariff negotiation is particularly encouraging because that approach was unnecessarily costly and disruptive to existing national production structures and was therefore detrimental to the swift reduction of trade restrictions. The indeterminacy of domestic production structures implies that most industries are extremely sensitive to their equilibrium degrees of protection. Negotiating the percentage by which countries would lower all tariffs tends to eliminate at each stage only those industries most lacking in comparative advantage in each country. It thus ensures that all resulting adjustments in a country's structure of production are necessary and final. This in turn assures the greatest real benefits from trade liberalization with a minimum disruption of the country's economy.[4]

Because freer trade is the only hope of so many countries, it is remotely possible that one day a landless proletarian country may decide to develop according to its comparative advantage. To this end, it would be obliged to dismantle its own tariffs

[3] Tibor Scitovsky, *Economic Theory and Western European Integration* (London, 1958), p. 67.

[4] The use of this type of tariff reduction, as well as the similarity of relative factor endowments, accounts for the ease with which the European Economic Community has been able to reduce its internal tariffs on industrial products.

without awaiting tariff concessions from the other countries. This policy, while desirable in itself, would work only if the others did not raise their duties. Retaliation on the part of its wealthy trading partners would be likely, however, if a large poor country like India began to trade freely and to specialize in labor-intensive manufactures for export. It would very palpably displace those industries in America and Europe unless higher tariffs were imposed there. In the end, India would be prevented from specializing in the desirable way, since foreign restrictions would substitute entirely for its previous protection. The essential task of international economic cooperation will be, therefore, to make sure that countries which want free trade can have some opportunity to practice it.

APPENDICES

INDEX

APPENDIX I

DICTIONARY OF SYMBOLS

ENGLISH SYMBOLS

A As a superscript, denotes country A in all two-country examples. Superscripts are omitted when a variable forcibly has the same value in all countries. Also the matrix of coefficients a_{ij}, when all imports are competitive.

a As a superscript, denotes country a in all m-country examples $(a = 1, \ldots, m)$.

$a_{ij}{}^a$ Equal to $p_i{}^a x_{ij}{}^a / c_j{}^a x_j{}^a$ if country a produces x_i and to $p_{n_i}{}^a x_{ij}{}^a / c_j{}^a x_j{}^a$ if country a produces no x_i.

$A_d{}^a$ Equal to diag $p^a A_d{}'^a$ diag $c^{a^{-1}}$.

$A_n{}^a$ Equal to diag $p_n{}^a A_n{}'^a$ diag $c^{a^{-1}}$.

A' Matrix of coefficients $a_{ij}{}'$ when all imports are competitive.

$A_d{}'^a$ Country a's matrix of intermediate-commodity input coefficients when it specializes but produces domestically the commodity i to which the typical input coefficient, $a_{ij}{}'^a$, in $A_d{}'^a$ corresponds.

$A_n{}'^a$ Country a's matrix of intermediate-commodity input coefficients when it specializes but does not produce domestically the commodity i to which the typical input coefficient, $a_{ij}{}'^a$, in $A_n{}'^a$ corresponds.

$a_{ij}{}'$ Equal to x_{ij}/x_j.

B Superscript denoting country B in all two-country examples.

b Superscript denoting country b in all m-country examples $(b = 1, \ldots, m)$.

$C_i{}^{ab}$ The functional relation of protection coefficients that holds between $c_i{}^a$ and $c_i{}^b$ when country a and country b produce and trade commodity i.

$C_{ok}{}^{ab}$ The functional relation of protection coefficients that holds between $c_{ok}{}^a$ and $c_{ok}{}^b$ when country a and country b trade directly the services of factor k.

c	Column vector of production costs, c_j.
c_j	The cost of producing one unit of x_j.
c_{ok}	The price which the owners of factor k receive net of factor taxes and subsidies for the services of each unit of that factor.
D^{ab}	The degree of indeterminacy in the localization of production in country a and country b.
D_i	The final demand function for commodity i, or r_i.
diag	Indicates a diagonal matrix, that is, one whose off-diagonal elements are all zero.
F	Column vector of primary factor supplies, F_k.
F_k	The supply of factor k.
F_{kj}	The amount of factor k which industry j employs.
F_1	Column vector of elements F_{1j}, the amount of labor, factor 1, which industry j employs. Also, as a scalar, the supply of labor.
F'	Matrix of coefficients F_{kj}'.
F_{kj}'	Equal to F_{kj}/x_j.
F''	Matrix of coefficients F_{kj}'' and equal to $F'(I - A')^{-1}$ if there are no production excise taxes or subsidies so that all $h_i^{aa} = 1$.
F_{kj}''	The amount of factor k which industry j uses directly and indirectly to produce one unit of x_j.
F_r^A	Equivalent to F_r^* under free trade.
F_r^a	Equal to $F'^a(I - A'^a)^{-1}r^a$, to $F''^a r^a$, to $f'^a(I - A^a)^{-1}$ diag $p^a r^a$, etc. It is the column vector of coefficients $F_{r_k}^a$.
$F_{r_k}^a$	The Leontief test estimate of the amount of factor k whose services country a's final demand contains directly and indirectly.
F_r^*	Column vector of coefficients $F_{r_k}^*$.
$F_{r_k}^*$	The amount of factor k the services of which country a's final demand would contain directly and indirectly under factor-price equalization.
F_t^A	Equivalent to F_t^* under factor-price equalization.
F_t^a	Equal to $F''^a t^a$, to $F'^a(I - A'^a)^{-1}t^a$, to $f'^a(I - A^a)^{-1}$ diag $p^a t^a$, etc. It is the column vector of coefficients $F_{t_h}^a$.

$F_{t_k}{}^a$ — The Leontief test estimate of the amount of factor k whose services country a's foreign trade brings in directly and indirectly.

$F_t{}^*$ — Equal to $F_r{}^* - F^a$. It is the column vector of coefficients $F_{t_k}{}^*$.

$F_{t_k}{}^*$ — The amount of factor k the services of which country a's foreign trade would bring in directly and indirectly under factor price equalization.

f — Equal to diag $p_o F'$ diag c^{-1}; the matrix of coefficients f_{kj}.

f_{kj} — Equal to $F_{kj} p_{ok}/x_j c_j$.

f' — Equal to F' diag c^{-1}, to diag $p_o{}^{-1} f$, etc.; the matrix of coefficients f_{kj}'.

f_{kj}' — Equal to $F_{kj}/x_j c_j$.

f'^* — The matrix of coefficients $f_{kj}'^*$.

$f_{kj}'^*$ — The amount of factor k which industry j would use to produce one dollar's worth of x_j under factor price equalization.

f'' — The matrix of coefficients f_{kj}'' and equal to $f(I - A)^{-1}$ if all $h_i{}^{aa} = 1$.

f_{kj}'' — The direct and indirect contribution of factor k to the cost of commodity j.

$g(p_o)$ — The general mapping of factor prices into commodity prices: $p = g(p_o)$.

$g'(p_o)$ — The Jacobian matrix, $\partial g/\partial p_o = (\partial g_j/\partial p_{ok})$, of $p = g(p_o)$. When all production functions are homogeneous of degree one and have continuous first derivatives, $g'(p_o) = F''^T$.

g^a — Equal to diag $p_o{}^a$ diag $p_o{}^*$; the column vector of coefficients $g_k{}^a$.

$g_k{}^a$ — Equal to $p_{ok}{}^a/p_{ok}{}^*$.

h^{AB} — Column vector of coefficients $h_j{}^{AB}$.

$h_j{}^{AB}$ — Equal to one plus the *ad valorem* tax, which may be negative, that country A levies on imports from or exports to country B of commodity j.

$h_i{}^{aa}$ — Equal to one plus the *ad valorem* excise tax rate, which may be negative, on the production cost, $c_i{}^a$, of commodity i in country a.

$h_j{}^{ab}$ Equal to one plus the *ad valorem* tax which country a levies on imports from or exports to country b $(b = 1, \ldots, m)$ of commodity j.

$h_{ok}{}^{aa}$ Equal to one plus the *ad valorem* rate of whatever tax country a applies to its factors working in country a.

$h_{ok}{}^{ab}$ Equal to one plus the *ad valorem* tax rate which country a levies on the services of factor k which country a and country b trade directly.

i Commodity subscript $(i = 1, \ldots, n)$.

j Commodity subscript $(j = 1, \ldots, n)$.

k Factor subscript $(k = 1, \ldots, r)$.

$MPPF_{kj}$ The marginal physical productivity of factor k in industry j.

m The number of countries.

m_j The price of commodity j which its final consumers face; $m_j{}^a = s_j{}^a c_j{}^a$.

n The number of commodities the world produces.

n^a The number of commodities country a produces. Also the column vector of country a's noncompetitive imports, $n_i{}^a$.

n^{ab} The number of commodities which country a and country b produce in common.

o A supplementary subscript denoting openness.

p The column vector of prices, p_j.

p_i, p_j The price of the ith or jth commodity; $p_i{}^a = h_i{}^{aa} c_i{}^a$.

$p_n{}^a$ The vector of the prices, $p_{n_i}{}^a$, of country a's noncompetitive imports.

$p_{n_i}{}^a$ The price to country a's consumers of commodity i when country a does not produce commodity i;
$$p_{n_i}{}^a = \frac{h_i{}^{ab} c_i{}^b}{h_i{}^{ba}} + u_i{}^{ba}.$$

p_o Column vector of primary-factor prices, p_{ok}.

p_{ok} The price of the services of factor k; $p_{ok}{}^a = h_{ok}{}^{aa} c_{ok}{}^a$.

q Equal to $(I - A')x$; the column vector of amounts q_i.

q_i Equal to $x_i - \sum_{j=1}^{n} x_{ij}$, the net output of commodity i.

R^a The column vector of consumption coefficients $R_i{}^a$.

$R_i{}^a$ Equal to $r_i{}^a p_i{}^a / Y^a$, the proportion of their income which final consumers in country a spend to purchase commodity i.

r The number of primary factors. Also the column vector of final domestic consumption amounts, r_i.

r_i The amount of commodity i going to final domestic consumers.

s_j Equal to one plus the *ad valorem* rate of the domestic retail tax or subsidy on commodity j.

$S_k{}^a$ The supply function of primary-factor services; the total amount of factor k which country a supplies.

T Superscript indicating the transpose of the matrix to which it is attached; the transformation function.

t^a Column vector of the amounts, t^a, of commodities which country a imports or exports competitively.

$u_j{}^{ba}$ Transport costs per unit of shipping commodity j from country b to country a.

$u_{ok}{}^{ba}$ The cost of transporting directly the services of one unit of factor k from country b to country a.

v_j Equal to one plus the *ad valorem* tax rate on the value added of industry j.

diag v Scalar matrix, equal to diag w diag y^{-1}.

W Superscript refering to the world as a whole. Thus $F_k{}^W$ is the world supply of factor k. When the world is considered as an integrated economy, Y^W is world income, $p_j{}^W$ the world-wide price of commodity j, $p_{ok}{}^W$ that of factor k, etc.

w A scalar, equal to the ratio between country a's income and the income of the whole world under factor-price equalization.

diag w A scalar matrix of w.

x The column vector of gross domestic outputs, x_i or x_j.

x_i The gross domestic output of the ith industry.

x_j The gross domestic output of the jth industry.

x_{ij} The amount of x_i which the jth industry uses up in producing x_j.

Y^a Country a's national income at its own market prices. Equal to $\sum\limits_{i=1}^{r} r_i{}^a p_i{}^a$.

Y^*	Country a's national income, under factor-price equalization.
y	A scalar, equal to Y^*/Y^a.
diag y	A scalar matrix of y.
z	A scalar, equal to w/y.
diag z	Scalar matrix, equal to diag w diag y^{-1}.

GREEK SYMBOLS

$\theta(\pi_o)$	The general mapping of the logarithms of factor prices into the logarithms of commodity prices: $\pi = \theta(\pi_o)$.
$\theta'(\pi_o)$	The Jacobian matrix of the equation system $\pi = \theta(\pi_o)$.
λ	The vector of Lagrangian undetermined multipliers, λ_j, corresponding to commodity prices.
λ_i, λ_j	The Lagrangian undetermined multiplier corresponding to commodity prices.
ρ	The matrix of the coefficients ρ_{kj}.
ρ_{kj}	Equal to F_{kj}/F_{1j}, the ratio of the amount of factor k which industry j employs to the amount of factor 1 (labor) which it employs.
π	The vector of the logarithms of commodity prices, π_j.
π_j	Equal to log p_j.
π_o	The vector of the logarithms of factor prices, π_{ok}.
π_{ok}	Equal to log p_{ok}.
ϕ	The vector of Lagrangian undetermined multipliers, ϕ_k, corresponding to factor prices.
ϕ_k	The Lagrangian undetermined multipliers corresponding to factor prices.
ψ_j	The general form of the gross output function of commodity j; $x_j = \psi_j(F_{1j}, \ldots, F_{rj}; x_{1j}, \ldots, x_{nj})$.

CONSTRUCTING THE EMPIRICAL
EQUALIZATION REGION

TABLE II-A here provides the data from which Figure II-10 has been drawn, using the industry classification described on page 64 above. The capital and labor coefficients in Table II-A are taken from Leontief's study of factor proportions and the structure of American foreign trade.[1] Leontief attempted to establish incremental, as opposed to average, ratios of capital and labor to output. These represent the amounts of additional capital and labor which an industry would have employed in 1947 had it produced an extra million dollars' worth of its output. In general, these coefficients will differ from those representing the ratio between the capital and labor which industries actually employed in 1947 and their total gross domestic outputs.[2]

It is appropriate to use the incremental coefficients in constructing an empirical equalization region, since average coefficients reflect factor proportions deriving partly from historical technologies and relative factor prices. Table II-A does not, therefore, estimate the actual division of capital and labor between different sectors in 1947, but rather the most desirable, or efficient, division given the available techniques and relative factor prices of that year.

In fact, where incremental coefficients could be calculated separately, these were nearly the same as the average coefficients in most sectors, and the estimates of the total capital stock and man-year employment in 1947 which Table II-A reports are similar to other estimates of these quantities. The agricultural labor coefficient which Leontief obtained is, however, an exception. It was established on the assumption that the number of

[1] Wassily Leontief, "Factor Proportions and the Structure of American Trade," *Review of Economics and Statistics*, 38.4:403–407 (November 1956).

[2] For descriptions of the concepts of incremental and average coefficients used in Leontief's study, and of the methods used to obtain the capital coefficients, see "Estimates of the Capital Structure of American Industries, 1947," prepared by James M. Henderson and others, Harvard Economics Research Project (Cambridge, Mass., June 1953), p. 5 and *passim*.

self-employed workers in agriculture (50 percent of the agricultural labor force in 1947) could not increase in proportion to increases in output, but that only hired hands and unpaid family workers could so increase.[3] The labor coefficient derived under this assumption risks being too small, because if agricultural output should increase without a simultaneous change in technique, either the number of self-employed would have to increase or the number of hired laborers and unpaid family help would have to increase more than in proportion to the increase in output. I have accordingly taken the larger Department of Commerce figure of 6,785,000 persons engaged in agriculture in 1947, although this estimate undoubtedly exaggerates the equilibrium incremental labor coefficient — the number of persons engaged in agriculture has subsequently fallen to less than 4,000,000 despite great increases in agricultural production and an increase in the national labor force. This indicates that many of the persons engaged in agriculture in 1947 were badly underemployed, given the opportunities for employment in other sectors and the possibilities for widespread economic substitution of capital for labor in agriculture at that time.

The first step in constructing the empirical equalization boundaries for country A in Figure II-10 is to add cumulatively, for Group II only, the total world amounts of labor and capital used by each sector, ranked in descending order of capital-labor ratios. Two new columns are thus obtained, showing for each sector the amount of labor and capital used by that sector and all sectors more capital-intensive than it. Further, for each entry in the cumulative labor column, the corresponding entry in the cumulative capital column shows the maximum amount of capital which can be employed without disturbing world factor prices, given the existing technology and assuming that only Group II goods are produced. In the same way, for each entry in the cumulative capital column, the corresponding entry in the cumulative labor column gives the minimum amount of labor which can be employed under the same assumptions.

If country A produced only Group II goods, the above information would be sufficient to plot its upper specialization boundary. In addition, by reversing the order of the sectors so that they are ranked in ascending order of capital-labor ratios, the same process would secure country A's lower specialization boundary as well. Any amount of Group II activity in country A, however, will also foster some Group III activity. Figure II-10 is constructed under the special but reasonable assumption that each Group III sector is found in country A, and further that the amount of each Group III sector's activity in A bears the same proportion to its total activity in the world that the number of workers producing tradables in A bears to the number of workers producing tradables in the world. One consequence of this assumption is that the aggregate Group III capital-labor ratio in country A is the same as the world Group III capital-labor ratio. Accordingly, if country A uses one half (or x percent) of the world supply of labor producing tradables, it will also use one half (or x percent) of the world's supply of Group III labor and, since the Group III capital-labor ratio in country A is the same as that for the entire world, it will also use one half (or x percent) of the world's supply of capital that Group III employs.

Now it is possible to draw the upper and lower specialization boundaries for the case in which country A owns none of the world's specific resources. To each entry in the cumulative labor and capital columns for Group II must be added some Group III labor and capital, and in each case the amount to be added will bear the same proportion to the total Group III labor or capital as the amount of Group II labor in country A bears to the total amount of labor producing tradables (Group I plus Group II) in the world. In Figure II-10, RZ is the upper specialization boundary obtained in this fashion, while UZ is the lower specialization boundary.

Curves $VWQS$ and $VWPS$ are country A's specialization boundaries when it owns the entire world supply of factors specific to Group I goods. Factor prices cannot be equalized between country A and the rest of the world unless A also possesses enough capital and labor to produce the world output of these Group I goods. In addition, it must devote capital and labor to Group III services, and this capital and labor must bear

260 APPENDIX II

TABLE II-A. *Estimated Capital Stocks and Employment in the United States
by Groups of Productive Activities Ranked According to Their
Capital-Labor Intensities, 1947*

Input-output number	Sector	Amount of capital employed (in units of $1,000 at 1947 prices)	Man-years employed	Capital-labor intensity
Group I. Activities requiring specific resources and producing tradable commodities				
17	Crude petroleum, natural gas	6,653,919	164,009	40.57
20	Other nonmetallic minerals	254,558	13,300	19.14
19	Sulphur	94,240	5,500	17.14
12	Copper mining	453,231	27,499	16.48
15	Other nonferrous mining	261,237	17,300	15.10
11	Iron ore mining	480,635	34,301	14.01
18	Stone, sand, clay, abrasives	965,796	96,098	10.05
1–9	Agriculture	64,240,556	6,785,000	9.47
14	Bauxite mining	8,652	1,000	8.65
13	Lead & zinc mining	170,410	22,900	7.44
36	Logging	453,965	81,104	5.60
16	Coal mining	2,456,751	505,014	4.86
10	Fisheries, hunting, trapping	456,259	141,002	3.24
	Group I totals	76,950,209	7,894,027	9.74
Group II. Activities requiring no specific resources and producing tradable goods and services				
63	Coke & products	2,645,423	43,097	61.38
44	Pulp mills	2,470,797	48,403	51.05
173	Other water transportation	3,704,704	74,696	49.60
167	Electric light & power	14,631,133	317,210	46.12
84	Primary lead	270,739	6,101	44.38
82	Primary copper	811,346	18,704	43.38
88	Primary aluminum	457,637	11,501	39.79
62	Petroleum products	7,119,095	186,440	38.18
78	Blast furnaces	1,796,546	48,196	37.28
90	Secondary nonferrous metals	644,734	18,400	35.04
86	Primary metals, n.e.c.	76,321	2,800	27.26
51	Synthetic rubber	165,061	7,801	21.16
27	Sugar	715,677	38,398	18.64
49	Industrial organic chemicals	1,566,276	84,702	18.49
172	Overseas transportation	3,910,810	220,894	17.70
87	Nonferrous metal rolling, n.e.c.	152,510	9,100	16.76
71	Cement	589,868	38,100	15.48
79	Steel works, rolling mills	8,281,673	568,975	14.56
83	Copper rolling & drawing	1,011,342	69,496	14.55
50	Plastic materials	410,099	29,201	14.04
85	Primary zinc	194,149	16,001	12.13

TABLE II-A (*continued*)

Input-output number	Sector	Amount of capital employed (in units of $1,000 at 1947 prices)	Man-years employed	Capital-labor intensity
64	Paving & roofing materials	288,807	25,200	11.46
45	Paper & board mills	1,985,062	185,604	10.70
52	Synthetic fiber	763,624	74,401	10.26
93	Tin cans, other tin ware	444,389	47,698	9.32
105	Metal barrels, drums, etc.	108,387	11,899	9.11
104	Fabricated wire products	470,812	55,398	8.50
28	Alcoholic beverages	1,013,588	123,211	8.23
108	Steel springs	68,275	8,500	8.03
126	Valves, fittings	629,988	81,301	7.75
128	Machine shops	404,908	53,300	7.60
55	Soap & related products	418,312	55,095	7.59
57	Gum & wood chemicals	87,631	11,701	7.489
59	Vegetable oils	264,321	35,307	7.486
118	Special industrial machinery	1,576,503	214,102	7.363
142	Storage batteries	108,162	14,701	7.357
123	Industrial machinery, n.e.c.	298,000	40,699	7.32
58	Fertilizers	261,975	36,701	7.14
48	Industrial inorganic chemicals	468,251	66,599	7.03
70	Glass	1,004,317	143,796	6.98
89	Aluminum rolling & drawing	222,018	32,500	6.83
26	Misc. food products	2,259,931	336,834	6.71
119	Pumps, compressors	360,704	54,698	6.594
112	Farm & industrial tractors	592,988	90,000	6.589
145	Motor vehicles	4,853,888	754,312	6.43
120	Elevators, conveyors	223,133	34,799	6.412
161	Plastic products	303,732	47,403	6.407
107	Misc. fabricated steel products	78,863	12,400	6.36
121	Blowers, fans	92,733	14,800	6.27
61	Misc. chemical industries	608,075	98,509	6.17
155	Medical & dental instruments & supplies	227,760	37,501	6.07
103	Lighting fixtures	281,993	46,801	60.3
136	Insulated wire & cable	359,602	61,450	5.85
98	Heating equipment	774,174	134,895	5.74
42	Metal furniture	470,118	82,004	5.73
114	Construction & mining machinery	509,688	89,402	5.70
147	Automobile trailers	53,619	9,599	5.59
156	Watches, clocks	229,151	41,302	5.55
24	Grain-mill products	626,329	116,929	5.36
106	Tubes, foils	47,384	8,900	5.32
22	Processed dairy products	777,112	148,020	5.25

APPENDIX II

TABLE II-A (*continued*)

Input-output number	Sector	Amount of capital employed (in units of $1,000 at 1947 prices)	Man-years employed	Capital-labor intensity
60	Animal oils	06 ,476	20,403	5.22
113	Farm equipment	511,797	98,205	5.21
151	Railroad equipment	269,597	51,999	5.18
146	Truck trailers	63,583	12,300	5.17
75	Abrasive products	112,974	22,225	5.08
122	Power-transmission equipment	271,617	54,298	5.00
174	Air transportation	457,896	91,901	4.98
97	Metal plumbing, vitreous fixtures	226,518	47,100	4.81
149	Ships, boats	758,555	159,400	4.759
115	Oilfield machinery & tools	146,479	30,801	4.756
92	Iron & steel forgings	164,024	34,603	4.74
74	Concrete & plaster products	384,558	81,502	4.72
53	Explosives, fireworks	65,505	13,900	4.71
134	Electrical welding apparatus	89,027	19,301	4.61
96	Hardware, n.e.c.	343,078	77,599	4.42
153	Instruments, etc.	334,069	75,798	4.4074
95	Tools, general hardware	257,345	58,400	4.4066
65	Tires, inner tubes	580,446	132,402	4.384
150	Locomotives	143,735	32,799	4.382
76	Asbestos products	156,655	36,701	4.268
100	Boiler-shop products & pipe bending	328,083	76,897	4.267
46	Converted paper products	977,288	230,791	4.23
77	Other misc. nonmetallic mineral products	112,003	26,701	4.19
135	Electrical appliances	470,281	113,002	4.16
56	Paints & allied products	283,261	68,301	4.15
54	Drugs, medicines	377,990	93,602	4.04
94	Cutlery	81,121	20,499	3.96
21	Meat packing, poultry	1,060,633	272,544	3.89
29	Tobacco manufactures	403,794	104,001	3.88
129	Wiring devices, graphite products	184,868	48,701	3.80
124	Commercial machines & equip., n.e.c.	505,321	133,301	3.79
144	X-ray apparatus	23,431	6,200	3.779
125	Refrigeration equipment	409,949	108,496	3.778
23	Canning, preserving, freezing	840,483	223,502	3.76
162	Cork products	10,451	2,800	3.73
132	Transformers	141,455	38,801	3.65
72	Structural clay products	276,961	76,102	3.64
101	Metal stampings	483,542	133,501	3.62
91	Nonferrous foundries	308,526	85,901	3.59
143	Primary batteries	31,239	9,000	3.47

TABLE II-A (*continued*)

Input-output number	Sector	Amount of capital employed (in units of $1,000 at 1947 prices)	Man-years employed	Capital-labor intensity
47	Printing, publishing	2,581,567	747,213	3.45
111	Internal combustion engines	245,740	71,398	3.44
102	Metal coating & engraving	133,987	39,220	3.42
32	Jute, linen, cordage, twine	869,417	25,600	3.40
31	Special textile products	281,008	83,300	3.37
37	Sawmills, planing, veneer mills	1,695,362	505,217	3.36
25	Bakery products	1,087,421	324,617	3.35
154	Optical, ophthalmic & photo equipment	363,397	110,299	3.29
133	Electrical control apparatus	254,673	78,400	3.25
109	Nuts, bolts, & screw machine products	270,138	85,202	3.17
130	Electrical measuring instruments	49,202	16,029	3.07
66	Misc. rubber products	421,175	137,999	3.05
164	Misc. manufactured products	550,129	182,001	3.023
67	Leather tanning & finishing	168,269	55,695	3.021
138	Electric lamps	110,013	37,300	2.95
35	House furnishings & other nonapparel	287,090	97,502	2.94
141	Communication equipment	283,732	98,201	2.89
148	Aircraft & parts	652,071	228,602	2.85
80	Iron foundries	536,375	193,095	2.78
30	Spinning, weaving, dyeing	2,520,316	931,375	2.71
81	Steel foundries	171,710	63,702	2.70
127	Ball & roller bearings	139,088	53,000	2.6243
43	Partitions, screens, shades, etc.	159,150	61,402	2.59
152	Motorcycles, bicycles	43,447	17,000	2.56
99	Structural metal products	331,324	139,506	2.37
160	Office supplies	79,927	33,799	2.36
110	Steam engines, turbines	47,455	21,700	2.19
139	Radio & related products	413,671	201,005	2.06
158	Musical instruments & parts	33,965	16,700	2.03
159	Toys, sporting goods	159,880	80,000	2.00
38	Plywood	628,699	31,801	1.98
116	Machine tools & metalworking machinery	285,806	145,501	1.96
137	Engine electrical equipment	139,040	74,300	1.87
163	Motion-picture production	68,747	37,702	1.82
39	Fabricated wood products, excl. furniture	238,838	132,901	1.80
157	Jewelry, silverware	142,720	81,688	1.75
117	Cutting tools, jigs, fixtures	178,498	102,799	1.74
131	Motors, generators	219,776	128,899	1.71

TABLE II-A (*continued*)

Input-output number	Sector	Amount of capital employed (in units of $1,000 at 1947 prices)	Man-years employed	Capital-labor intensity
	Sectors ranked in descending order of capital-labor intensity, by groups			
73	Pottery & related products	97,714	58,801	1.66
40	Wood containers, cooperage	141,532	87,300	1.62
140	Tubes	49,404	30,701	1.6092
41	Wood furniture	316,289	196,597	1.6088
33	Canvas products	15,652	10,100	1.55
34	Apparel	1,825,988	1,315,029	1.39
69	Footwear (excl. rubber)	292,775	277,597	1.05
68	Other leather products	76,483	75,199	1.02
181	Banking, finance, insurance	362,359	1,189,070	0.30
	Group II totals	109,808,559	17,132,831	6.409
	Group III. Activities producing nontradable goods and services			
168	Natural, manufactured, mixed gas	2,266,895	93,908	24.14
169	Railroads	33,253,970	1,530,095	21.73
179	Telephone and telegraph	11,941,863	608,003	19.64
175	Pipeline transportation	418,397	29,002	14.43
192	Nonprofit institutions	28,011,099	2,433,008	11.51
171	Warehousing & storage	1,750,487	178,388	9.81
191	Medical, dental & other prof. services	9,777,002	1,391,577	7.03
182	Hotels	2,143,890	359,296	5.97
190	Motion picture & other amusements	2,468,246	491,412	5.02
177	Retail trade	21,139,846	4,685,200	4.51
180	Eating & drinking places	7,348,094	1,663,471	4.42
170	Trucking	1,708,095	418,019	4.09
184	Laundries, dry cleaning	1,975,402	518,495	3.81
176	Wholesale trade	8,327,850	2,241,692	3.71
185	Other personal services	1,446,631	402,901	3.59
178	Local & highway transportation	1,175,682	409,901	2.87
186	Advertising, incl. radio, television	237,775	120,107	1.98
188	Automobile repair services, garages	1,287,630	684,009	1.88
211–12	Construction	4,512,274	3,007,000	1.50
189	Other repair services	247,688	206,303	1.20
187	Business services	139,332	302,704	0.46
183	Real estate, rentals	182,274	472,177	0.39
	Group III totals	141,760,422	22,246,668	6.372

Source: The entries in column 2 are the products of the coefficients of direct capital requirements (per million dollars' of gross output) and the gross domestic outputs of the respective sectors. The entries in column 3 are, with a few exceptions, the products of the labor coefficients and the gross domestic outputs. The capital and labor coefficients are from Leontief, "Factor Proportions," appendix 3 (pp. 403–407), columns 1 and 2. The exceptions are as follows: the entry for column 3, sectors 1–9, is from U.S. Department of Commerce, *National Income* (supplement to *Survey of Current Business*), 1954, pp. 202–203.

the same proportion to the world Group III capital and labor that the number of workers necessary to produce Group I goods bears to the total number of workers producing tradables. As a result, the upper and lower specialization boundaries will at first coincide along the straight horizontal line, VW. Its length, equal to HN on the horizontal axis, sums the number of workers necessary to produce the world supply of Group I goods plus the number of Group III workers necessary to service the Group I workers, both as percentages of the total world labor supply. Its height, OV, represents the ratio of capital to labor devoted both to the Group I goods and the accompanying Group III services.

Beyond WH', country A produces Group II goods in addition to the world output of Group I goods and accompanying Group III services. The upper and lower specialization boundaries, WQS and WPS, are analogous to the boundaries RZ and UZ in the case where country A produced no Group I goods. The coordinates for WQS are obtained by taking the coordinates for RZ and adding, for the ordinate, the amount of capital and labor employed at point W, and for the abscissa, the percentage of labor employed at H'. The curve WPS is obtained by adding the same amounts to the coordinates of UZ.

THE CAPITAL-LABOR INTENSITY OF THE UNITED STATES ECONOMY AND THE IMPLIED CAPITAL-LABOR INTENSITY OF THE FRENCH ECONOMY

Sector	(1) Percent of U.S. man-hours	(2) Percent of French workers engaged	(3) U.S. labor (in man-years)	(4) U.S. capital (in $10,000)	(5) Capital-labor ratio in U.S.	(6) Number of French workers engaged	(7) = (5) × (6) Computed capital for France
			Group I				
Agriculture, hunting, fishing, forestry							
Total	100.000	100.000	6,926,002	6,469,682	0.934	4,684,500	4,375,861
Mining							
Coal	56.940	73.377	505,014	245,675	0.486	247,500	120,384
Lead, zinc	2.582	1.023	22,900	17,041	0.744	3,450	2,567
Bauxite	0.113	0.205	1,000	865	0.865	690	597
Stone, clay, sand, adhesives	10.835	12.719	96,098	96,580	1.005	42,900	43,115
Iron ore	3.867	4.915	34,301	48,064	1.401	16,700	23,400
Other nonferrous	1.951	0.878	17,300	26,124	1.510	2,960	4,470
Copper	3.101	0.0	27,499	45,323	1.648	—	—
Sulphur	0.620	0.0	5,500	9,424	1.714	—	—
Other nonmetallic	1.500	5.366	13,300	25,456	1.914	18,100	34,642
Crude petroleum, natural gas	18.492	1.482	164,009	665,400	4.057	5,000	20,285
Total	100.000	100.000	886,921	1,179,952	1.330	337,300	249,460

Group II
Tradables not dependent on specific resources

Coke	0.252	0.024	43,097	264,542	6.138	1,200	7,403
Electric power, light	1.851	2.064	317,210	1,463,113	4.612	102,500	472,730
Aluminum	0.067	0.181	11,501	45,764	3.979	8,980	35,731
Petroleum refining & products	1.088	0.634	186,440	711,910	3.818	31,510	120,305
Copper, lead, zinc	0.238	0.050	40,806	127,624	3.128	2,480	7,757
Primary metals, n.e.c.	0.016	0.076	2,800	7,632	2.726	3,770	10,277
Water transportation	1.725	1.176	295,590	761,551	2.576	58,400	150,438
Sugar refining	0.224	0.699	38,398	71,568	1.864	34,710	64,699
Iron & steel	3.602	2.507	617,171	1,007,822	1.633	124,500	203,309
Organic chemicals, rubber, plastics	1.145	0.324	196,105	290,506	1.481	16,090	23,829
Pulp, paper & paper products	2.713	2.306	464,798	543,315	1.169	114,500	133,851
Nonferrous transformation	1.257	0.684	215,397	233,913	1.086	33,950	36,870
Tin cans & wares	0.278	0.608	47,698	44,439	0.932	30,200	28,146
Construction materials	0.845	1.182	144,802	126,324	0.872	58,700	51,186
Alcoholic beverages	0.719	1.039	123,211	101,359	0.823	51,600	42,467
Springs	0.050	0.104	8,500	6,828	0.803	5,160	4,143
Machine shops	0.311	1.920	53,300	40,491	0.760	95,340	72,458
Soap & cleaning agents	0.322	0.562	55,095	41,831	0.759	27,900	21,176
Vegetable oils & fats	0.206	0.203	35,307	26,432	0.749	10,100	7,565
Gum, wood & natural extract chemicals	0.068	0.193	11,701	87,631	0.749	9,590	7,183
Glass	0.839	0.969	143,796	100,432	0.698	48,100	33,574
Misc. food processing	1.966	0.932	336,834	225,993	0.671	46,300	31,067
Plumbing, valves & fixtures	0.749	0.217	128,401	85,651	0.667	10,800	7,204
Pumps, compressors, fans	0.406	0.422	69,498	45,343	0.652	20,980	13,679
Misc. chemicals & chemical products	0.759	1.752	130,001	84,223	0.648	86,990	56,370
Motor vehicles & parts	4.403	4.832	754,312	485,389	0.643	239,990	154,314
Elevators, conveyors	0.203	0.734	34,799	22,313	0.641	36,430	23,352

Group II (continued)

Sector	(1) Percent of U.S. man-hours	(2) Percent of French workers engaged	(3) U.S. labor (in man-years)	(4) U.S. capital (in $10,000)	(5) Capital-labor ratio in U.S.	(6) Number of French workers engaged	(7) = (5) × (6) Computed capital for France
Plastic products	0.277	0.306	47,403	30,373	0.641	15,210	9,750
Misc. machinery	2.606	0.833	446,402	277,641	0.622	41,370	25,732
Misc. chemicals, specialties	0.575	0.607	98,509	60,808	0.617	30,150	18,603
Medical equipment	0.219	0.184	37,501	22,776	0.607	9,150	5,554
Batteries	0.138	0.148	23,701	13,940	0.588	7,370	4,334
Farm tractors & machinery	1.099	0.836	188,205	110,479	0.587	41,520	24,372
Insulated wire & cable	0.359	1.167	61,450	35,960	0.585	57,970	33,912
Heating equipment	0.787	0.384	134,895	77,417	0.574	19,050	10,935
Metal furniture	0.479	0.265	82,004	47,012	0.573	13,180	7,552
Clocks, watches	0.241	0.455	41,302	22,915	0.555	22,590	12,537
Grain-mill products	0.682	0.745	116,929	62,633	0.536	37,000	19,832
Trailers	0.128	0.466	21,899	11,720	0.535	23,160	12,391
Dairy products	0.864	0.971	148,019	77,711	0.525	48,200	25,305
Animal oils & fats	0.119	0.095	20,403	10,648	0.522	4,620	2,464
Abrasive products	0.130	0.085	22,225	11,297	0.508	4,220	2,144
Air transport	0.536	0.246	91,901	45,790	0.498	12,200	6,076
Railroad equipment	0.495	1.248	84,798	41,333	0.487	61,960	30,175
Misc. metal construction	1.605	0.760	274,904	131,876	0.480	37,720	18,106
Ships, boats	0.930	1.357	159,400	75,856	0.476	67,400	32,082
Explosives	0.081	0.271	13,900	6,551	0.471	13,480	6,349
Hardware	0.794	0.813	135,999	60,042	0.441	40,380	17,808
Instruments, precision equipment	0.442	0.459	75,798	33,407	0.441	22,810	10,059
Tires, tubes	0.773	0.657	132,402	58,045	0.438	32,640	14,296

Boiler-shop products	0.449	1.063	76,897	32,808	0.427	52,840	22,563
Asbestos products	0.214	0.063	36,701	15,666	0.427	3,090	1,319
Appliances	0.660	0.597	113,002	47,028	0.416	29,650	12,334
Paints, pigments, inks	0.399	0.390	68,301	28,326	0.415	19,370	8,039
Drugs, medicines	0.546	0.981	93,602	37,799	0.404	48,720	19,683
Wood products, excl. furniture	1.471	1.175	252,002	100,907	0.400	58,360	23,344
Cutlery	0.120	0.177	20,499	8,112	0.396	8,780	3,477
Meat packing & poultry	1.591	0.443	272,544	106,063	0.389	21,990	8,554
Tobacco products	0.607	0.006	104,001	40,379	0.388	300	116
Refrigeration equipment	0.633	0.207	108,496	40,995	0.378	10,280	3,886
Canning, preserving	1.305	1.081	223,502	84,048	0.376	53,700	20,191
Cork products	0.016	0.098	2,800	1,045	0.373	4,890	1,824
Metal stampings	0.779	0.781	133,501	48,354	0.362	38,800	14,046
Office equipment	0.975	0.342	167,100	58,525	0.350	16,990	5,946
Printing, publishing	4.361	3.262	747,213	258,157	0.345	162,000	55,890
Metal coating & treating	0.229	0.252	39,220	13,399	0.342	12,430	4,251
Jute, cordage, etc.	0.149	0.526	25,600	86,942	0.340	26,000	8,840
Special textile products	0.486	3.850	83,300	28,101	0.337	190,300	64,131
Saw mills	2.949	0.565	505,217	169,536	0.336	28,080	9,435
Bakery products	1.895	2.310	324,617	108,742	0.335	114,700	38,425
Optical & photo	0.644	0.408	110,299	36,340	0.329	20,240	6,659
Electrical measuring, control equipment	0.551	0.113	94,429	30,388	0.322	5,600	1,803
Nuts, bolts, screws	0.497	0.517	85,202	27,014	0.317	25,690	8,144
Misc. rubber products	0.805	0.684	137,999	42,118	0.305	33,950	10,355
Misc. manufactured products	1.062	1.198	182,001	55,013	0.302	59,500	17,969
Leather tanning and finishing	0.325	0.459	55,695	16,827	0.302	22,800	6,886
Iron & steel products	1.701	4.719	291,400	87,211	0.299	234,360	70,073
Electrical machinery	1.408	2.022	241,299	72,188	0.299	100,430	30,029
Electrical bulbs & lamps	0.218	0.208	37,300	11,001	0.295	10,320	3,044

Group II (continued)

Sector	(1) Percent of U.S. man-hours	(2) Percent of French workers engaged	(3) U.S. labor (in man-years)	(4) U.S. capital (in $10,000)	(5) Capital-labor ratio in U.S.	(6) Number of French workers engaged	(7) = (5) × (6) Computed capital for France
Aircraft & parts	1.334	1.617	228,602	65,207	0.285	80,300	22,886
Nonapparel textiles	0.628	0.132	107,602	30,274	0.288	6,580	1,895
Ceramics, pottery & clay	0.787	1.341	134,903	37,468	0.278	66,600	18,515
Spinning, weaving, dyeing	5.436	7.951	931,375	252,032	0.271	394,900	107,018
Graphite, insulators, wiring devices, etc.	0.718	0.883	123,001	32,391	0.263	43,850	11,533
Ball & roller bearings, measuring equipment	0.309	0.228	53,000	13,909	0.262	11,320	2,966
Motorcycles, bicycles	0.099	0.602	17,000	4,345	0.256	26,910	7,657
Radio tubes & equipment	1.962	1.013	336,107	77,024	0.229	50,330	11,526
Steam engines, turbines	0.127	0.001	21,700	4,746	0.219	50	11
Musical instruments	0.097	0.181	16,700	3,397	0.203	9,000	1,827
Toys, sporting goods, firearms	0.467	0.554	80,000	15,988	0.200	27,530	5,506
Machine tools, metalworking machinery	1.449	1.049	248,300	46,430	0.187	52,090	9,741
Furniture	1.506	1.689	257,999	47,544	0.184	83,900	15,438
Motion-picture production	0.220	0.370	37,702	6,875	0.182	18,400	3,349
Jewelry, silverware	1.477	0.443	81,688	14,272	0.175	22,000	3,850
Apparel, furs	7.675	6.204	1,315,029	182,599	0.139	308,120	42,829
Leather footwear	1.620	2.020	277,597	29,278	0.105	100,300	10,532
Misc. leather products	0.439	0.759	75,199	7,648	0.102	37,700	3,845
Banking, finance, insurance	6.940	4.734	1,189,070	36,236	0.030	235,100	7,053
Total	100.000	100.000	17,132,831	10,980,856	0.641	4,966,360	2,940,684

Source: Appendix II and Ministère des Finances, "Les Salaires déclarés en 1957," *Statistiques et études financières*, 122:160–185 (February 1959).

EVOLUTION OF THE SPECIAL TEMPORARY IMPORT TAX

The following tables show value in millions of 1948 francs and the percentage of liberated trade in France affected by the tax rates as of the different periods specified.

TABLE IV-A. *Taxes on Products Liberated by April 1954*

Tax rate	End of April 1954		End of Nov. 1954		End of Aug. 1954		End of Oct. 1954	
	Value	Percent	Value	Percent	Value	Percent	Value	Percent
Category I. Agricultural products								
15%	760.6	7.1	0	0	0	0	0	0
11%	0	0	760.6	7.1	760.6	7.1	301.5	2.8
10%	7,284.0	67.7	0	0	0	0	0	0
7%	0	0	6,027.1	56.0	6,027.1	56.0	6,302.9	58.6
0%	2,714.2	25.2	3,971.2	36.9	3,971.2	36.9	4,154.5	38.6
Total	10,758.9	100.0	—	—	—	—	—	—
Category II. Raw materials								
15%	1,329.4	3.8	0	0	0	0	0	0
11%	0	0	1,329.4	3.8	1,180.4	3.4	1,180.4	3.4
10%	220.7	0.6	0	0	0	0	0	0
7%	0	0	220.7	0.6	220.7	0.6	220.7	0.6
0%	33,260.3	95.5	33,260.3	95.5	33,409.3	96.0	33,409.3	96.0
Total	34,810.4	—	—	—	—	—	—	—
Category III. Manufactures and semimanufactures								
15%	6,036.8	30.8	0	0	18.3	0.1	18.3	0.1
11%	0	0	5,525.1	28.2	5,414.8	27.6	4,544.9	23.2
10%	4,555.4	23.3	0	0	0	0	0	0
7%	0	0	4,461.9	22.8	4,543.2	23.2	5,219.7	26.6
0%	9,000.6	45.9	9,605.8	45.9	9,616.4	49.1	9,809.8	50.1
Total	19,592.8	—	—	—	—	—	—	—

TABLE IV-B. *Taxes on Products Liberated in September-October 1954*

Tax rate	Sept.–Oct. 1954		End of Nov. 1954		End of Aug. 1954		End of Nov. 1955	
	Value	Percent	Value	Percent	Value	Percent	Value	Percent
Category I. Agricultural products								
15%	2,133.0	99.1	0	0	0	0	0	0
11%	0	0	2,133.0	99.1	2,133.0	99.1	0	0
7%	0	0	0	0	0	0	2,133.0	99.1
0%	19.9	0.9	19.9	0.9	19.9	0.9	19.9	0.9
Total	2,152.0	100.0	—	—	—	—	—	—

Tax rate	Sept.–Oct. 1954		Nov. 1954		Dec. 1954		Oct.–Nov. 1955	
	Value	Percent	Value	Percent	Value	Percent	Value	Percent
Category II. Raw materials								
10%	60.1	0.6	0	0	2,436.1[a]	23.6	0	0
7%	0	0	60.1	0.6	60.1	0.6	17.8	0.2
0%	10,276.3	99.4	10,276.3	99.4	7,839.7	75.8	10,318.6	99.8
Total	10,336.4	100.0	—	—	—	—	—	—

Tax rate	Sept.–Oct. 1954		Nov. 1954		Jan.–Aug. 1955		Oct.–Nov. 1955	
	Value	Percent	Value	Percent	Value	Percent	Value	Percent
Category III. Manufactures and semimanufactures								
15%	3,185.3	71.5	0	0	25.4	0.6	25.4	0.6
11%	0	0	3,185.3	71.5	3,048.8	68.5	2,831.5	63.6
10%	1,027.8	23.1	0	0	0	0	0	0
7%	0	0	1,027.8	23.1	1,110.3	24.9	1,034.6	23.2
0%	239.9	5.4	239.9	5.4	268.5	6.0	561.5	12.6
Total	4,453.0[b]	100.0	—	—	—	—	—	—

[a] 1948 value of the French tariff post, ex 767 A, "sawed pine logs."
[b] Excluding those steel products comprised under Chapter 73 of the French tariff list.

TABLE IV-C. *Taxes on Products Liberated in January-March 1955*

Tax rate	Jan.–March 1955		June 1955		Oct.–Nov. 1955	
	Value	Percent	Value	Percent	Value	Percent
	Category I. Agricultural products					
15%	25.3	2.1	25.3	2.1	25.3	2.1
0%	1,176.9	97.9	1,176.9	97.9	1,176.9	97.9
Total	1,202.2	100.0	—	—	—	—
	Category II. Raw materials					
15%	1,536.3	30.2	36.1	7.1	105.3	2.1
11%	0	0	0	0	235.8	4.6
10%	905.3	17.8	2,051.6	40.3	1,968.6	38.6
7%	0	0	0	0	83.0	1.6
0%	2,651.9	52.1	2,680.8	52.6	2,700.8	53.0
Total	5,093.5	100.0	—	—	—	—
	Category III. Manufactures and semimanufactures					
15%	7,166.5	93.8	6,085.2	79.6	4,451.8	58.2
11%	0	0	0	0	1,631.0	21.3
10%	302.3	4.0	308.8	4.0	11.5	0.2
7%	0	0	1,033.5	13.5	1,317.7	17.2
0%	174.9	2.3	216.2	2.8	231.7	3.2
Total	7,643.7	100.0	—	—	—	—

Source: For all three tables, OEEC, mimeographed document, SBC (55) 92 (1955).

CALCULATING RAW-MATERIAL USAGE

Table V-A shows the French domestic production of raw materials, for the period under consideration (1950–1955).

1. ESTIMATING THE VALUE OF COAL CONSUMPTION IN GERMANY, GREAT BRITAIN, AND FRANCE

Table V-B gives the total consumption of coal, by volume, for the three countries. The numbers in that table indicate the amount of hard and soft coal which industry consumed in each country. Coal mine and household consumption are omitted.

It is necessary to supplement the figures in Table V-B with figures for imports of transformed coal. Of these, imports of patent fuel were negligible in each country, so Table V-C presents figures only for "coke-oven coal" "brown-coal briquettes."

The main problem is to find a set of coal prices common to all three countries which nonetheless reflects the differences in the quality of coals consumed. It is generally thought, for example, that the quality of German and British exceeds that of French coal. Therefore, neither the simple internal price of any one nor the average price of all countries would be entirely appropriate. The imperfections of the international coal market during the period, as well as the impossibility of knowing what grades of coal moved in trade, prevent the use of average import values. The only recourse is to disaggregate national coal production, to apply a common but reasonable set of prices to each category, and to assume that production and consumption weights were roughly the same. The data do not permit a comparison of French and British coal production by homogeneous quality categories, but they do permit, thanks to the publications of the European Coal and Steel Community, such a comparison of French and German production.

The available data unfortunately give production figures for seven, but prices for only six, categories of hard coal. It is possible, though, to regroup the production figures, by means of data broken down by type of coal and coal field, into five categories that correspond exactly to the price data. The production

TABLE V-A. *French Domestic Production of Raw Materials, 1950-1955*

Year	Metal ores (metal content)				Wood and timber (millions of cubic meters)			Hides and skins (thousands of metric tons)			Mineral fuels (millions of metric tons)		Wool (thousands of metric tons)
	Iron (millions of metric tons) (1)	Bauxite (millions of metric tons) (2)	Lead (hundreds of metric tons) (3)	Zinc (4)	Soft wood (5)	Hard wood (6)	Pulp wood (7)	Cattle hides (8)	Calf skins (9)	Goat skins (10)	Coal (11)	Petro-leum (12)	(13)
1950	8.75	0.81	11.5	10.1	4.58	2.89	0.72	76.4	31.2	7.70	50.8	0.1	16
1951	10.27	1.12	10.5	10.4	5.57	3.51	1.63	77.1	27.4	7.70	53.0	0.3	19
1952	11.87	1.12	12.1	12.0	4.51	3.58	1.60	80.1	29.9	7.80	55.4	0.4	19
1953	12.36	1.17	11.5	9.2	6.14	5.23	1.33	79.6	31.3	7.16	52.6	0.4	21
1954	12.78	1.28	10.5	8.4	7.13	5.38	1.67	85.5	33.7	7.16	54.4	0.5	21
1955	14.68	1.50	8.6	8.9	8.08	6.04	1.82	87.4	34.9	7.29	55.3	0.7	22

Source: Metal ores—Iron: OEEC, Statistical Bulletins, *General Statistics* (Paris, May 1959), p. 26. Bauxite: OEEC, *Industrial Statistics, 1900–1957* (Paris, 1958), p. 110. The figures are for total production of crude ore. Lead: *Industrial Statistics*, p. 95. Zinc: *Industrial Statistics*, p. 100.
Wood and timber—Soft wood (sapins, épicés, pins et autres résineux): INSEE, *Annuaire statistique, 1958* (Paris, 1958), p. 39. Hard wood (chêne, hêtre, peuplier, et feuillus divers): *Annuaire statistique, 1958*, p. 39. Pulp wood: *Annuaire statistique, 1958*, p. 39.
Hides and skins—OEEC, *L'Industrie des cuires et peaux en Europe, Statistiques, 1957* (Paris, 1958), annex I.
Mineral fuels—Coal: *Industrial Statistics*, pp. 26, 51. Petroleum: *Industrial Statistics*, p. 24.
Wool—OEEC, *Agricultural and Food Statistics* (Paris, 1959), p. 37, table 22.

figures extend back only to 1953, the price data to 1952, so that it was necessary to take the proportion of total production that each of the five production categories represented between 1953 and 1957 as weights for the prices in 1952. Table V-D gives the production data by the seven categories. Table V-E shows the reduction of these seven categories to five categories sharing a common price. German prices were used exclusively because an inspection of the data showed them to be more representative of European coal prices in 1952 than the French prices were.

TABLE V-B. *Industrial Consumption*[a] *of Coal in West Germany, Great Britain, and France, 1950–1955*

(in millions of metric tons)

Year	Germany		Great Britain	France[b]	
	Hard coal	Soft coal	Hard coal	Hard coal	Soft coal
1950	83.91	64.93	144.84	53.60	1.47
1951	96.77	65.99	156.28	61.97	1.69
1952	102.98	70.33	153.03	59.46	1.66
1953	101.22	72.13	155.20	55.17	1.63
1954	100.59	75.34	156.74	56.26	1.69
1955	114.49	79.65	162.47	58.78	1.70

[a] Equals total consumption minus the consumption of mines, miners, and households.
[b] Includes the Saar, then part of the French customs territory.
Source: OEEC, *Industrial Statistics, 1900–1957* (Paris, 1958), tables 20, 22, 32, 34.

Weighting the prices of Table V-E by the tonnages of Table V-D yields an average price for German hard coal of $11.61 per metric ton, and for French of $11.92, in 1952. The 1950 prices were calculated by taking the German prices for *Fettkohlen, Gasflammkohlen, Esskohlen,* and *Anthrazitkohlen* for the years 1950–1952, weighting them appropriately by each country's output, and thus deriving a price index.[1] The 1950 prices were $9.33 and $9.58 for Germany and France, respectively.

It is impossible to compute the British price of hard coal from published data in the same manner as the German and French.

[1] The prices are from Statistische Bundesamt, *Statistisches Jahrbuch für die Bundesrepublik Deutschland* (Wiesbaden, 1956), p. 458.

TABLE V-C. *German, British, and French Net Imports of
Transformed Coal, 1950–1955*
(in millions of metric tons)

Year	Germany Coke	Germany Briquettes	Great Britain Coke	France[a] Coke	France[a] Briquettes
1950	8.12	−1.06	−0.88	2.16	0.38
1951	−10.21	−1.68	−0.18	3.36	0.45
1952	−10.67	−1.24	−0.44	4.14	0.42
1953	−9.34	−1.44	−0.38	3.27	0.51
1954	−9.94	0.77	−0.54	2.92	0.48
1955	−11.19	1.52	−0.64	4.58	0.57

[a] Includes the Saar.
Source: OEEC, *Industrial Statistics, 1900–1957*, Tables 26, 31.

TABLE V-D. *Hard-Coal Production by Quality Categories in
France and West Germany, 1954–1957*
(in thousands of metric tons)

Category[a]	France and the Saar 1954	1955	1956	1957	West Germany 1954	1955	1956	1957
I	1,849	1,969	2,314	2,641	5,875	5,967	6,720	6,729
II	8,972	8,987	9,002	9,593	4,572	5,264	5,488	5,747
III	5,879	5,880	5,537	4,596	9,726	9,693	9,332	10,634
IV	1,027	1,086	1,122	1,372	1,516	1,505	1,589	1,295
V	15,742	16,014	15,571	15,571	83,478	85,389	87,130	84,414
VIa	4,467	4,519	4,562	4,590	–	–	–	–
VIb	26,797	27,516	27,339	27,296	22,869	22,911	24,148	24,336
VII	6,359	6,571	6,639	7,156	–	–	–	–

[a] For the specifications of the categories to which the Roman numerals correspond, consult the source. For approximate names, see Table V-E.
Source: Communauté Européene du Charbon et de l'Acier, Haute Autorité, *Bulletin statistique, charbon et acier* (Luxembourg, September 1959), pp. 11–17. For the specifications of the categories, see *ibid.*, p. xxiv; and below, Table V-E.

British coal is undoubtedly of a quality comparable to that of the French, but its price in 1950 was only $8.67 per metric ton.[2] The values added in industry in each of the three countries were

[2] National Coal Board, *Quarterly and Annual Statement* (London, 1951). Price here equals "proceeds per ton."

expressed in British factor prices; for consistency the same should have been done for coal. It seemed more advisable, however, to average British and German prices for coal, and thereby to obtain a more reliable price than that for either country alone. The higher price, if inaccurate, will tend to bias the results against the argument that France used more raw materials in conjunction with the other factors than did Britain and Germany. This is

TABLE V-E. *German Coal Prices by Categories, May 1952*
(in U.S. dollars)

Category	Type	Size or grade	Coal field	1952 price
I	Anthracite	French nuts		$19.20
II	Low volatile	Small nuts		16.23
III	Semibituminous	Singles, $\frac{3}{4}$ Fettkohlen	Aachen	11.65
IV	Semibituminous	Singles, demi-gras	Nord/Pas de Calais	11.65
V	Bituminous	Washed duffs or coking fines		10.85
VIa	Bituminous	Washed duffs or coking fines	Saar, Lorraine & Centre Midi types	10.86
VIb	High volatile bituminous	Doubles	Nord/Pas de Calais	11.31
VII	High volatile bituminous	Doubles	Lorraine and Saar	11.31

Source: *Bulletin statistique, charbon et acier*, p. xxiv; and European Coal and Steel Community, High Authority, *Seventh General Report on the Activities of the Community* (Luxembourg, February 1, 1959), pp. 332–334.

because French coal consumption is markedly less than that of the other countries where coal prices will consequently have greater weights. Accordingly, average British and German prices of hard coal were taken as the price for both Germany and Britain, and French coal was valued at a price exceeding the German-British price by the same factor as the originally computed French price exceeded the German price. The British-German price, computed in this way, is $8.93 and the French $9.16.

The price of lignite, which is important in German coal

consumption, was computed from its hard-coal equivalent.[3] The net imports of coke into the three countries were weighted by the 1950 German price for *Hochofen* coke, and imports of brown-coal (or lignite) briquettes by the 1950 German price for

TABLE V-F. *Industrial Consumption of Coal in West Germany, Great Britain, and France, 1950–1955*
(in millions of dollars at 1950 prices)

Year	West Germany		Great Britain	France, incl. Saar	
	Industrial coal consumption				
	Hard coal	*Lignite*	*Hard coal*	*Hard coal*	*Lignite*
1950	749.30	167.12	1293.39	491.14	3.78
1951	864.13	169.85	1395.55	567.84	4.35
1952	919.59	181.02	1366.52	544.84	4.27
1953	903.87	185.91	1385.90	505.53	4.20
1954	898.25	193.92	1399.65	515.14	4.35
1955	1022.37	205.01	1450.82	538.60	4.38
	Net imports of transformed coal				
		Lignite			*Lignite*
	Coke	*briquettes*	*Coke*	*Coke*	*briquettes*
1950	− 83.13	−4.24	−9.01	22.11	1.52
1951	−104.53	−6.73	−1.84	34.40	1.80
1952	−109.24	−4.96	−4.50	42.39	1.68
1953	− 95.62	−5.77	−3.89	33.48	2.04
1954	−101.77	3.08	−5.53	29.90	1.92
1955	−114.56	6.09	6.55	46.89	2.28
	Total consumption				
1950	829.05		1284.38	518.55	
1951	922.72		1393.71	608.39	
1952	986.41		1362.02	593.18	
1953	988.39		1382.01	545.25	
1954	993.48		1393.10	551.31	
1955	1118.91		1444.27	592.15	

Braunkohlenbriketts.[4] Table V-F reports the value of coal consumption at 1950 prices, defined as above.

[3] The coefficient used to relate the two values was 0.28. See OEEC, *Industrial Statistics, 1900–1957* (Paris, 1958), p. 22, table 13, note.
[4] *Statistisches Jahrbuch, 1956*, p. 458.

TABLE V-G. *West German, British, and French Imports of Raw Materials, 1950–1955*
(in millions of current dollars)

Year	Country	(1) Oils & greases	(2) Rubber	(3) Wood & timber	(4) Paper pulp	(5) Textile materials	(6) Ores & metals	(7) Crude petroleum	(8) Coal	(9) Skins & hides	(10) Chemicals	(11) Other	(12) Total
1950	Germany	210.5	56.7	43.5	31.9	423.5	93.7	40.8	41.6	56.0	—	74.9	1073.1
	Britain	348.2	144.3	212.8	131.8	1021.3	241.2	207.9	0.1	97.9	—	155.3	2560.8
	France	147.2	59.9	23.4	49.4	486.6	52.9	299.0	153.9	49.1	—	84.4	1405.8
1951	Germany	288.8	104.7	77.3	94.5	522.5	180.9	84.2	173.5	56.7	—	94.8	1677.9
	Britain	483.0	369.7	525.8	392.6	1492.8	335.3	445.7	24.8	124.6	—	248.2	4442.5
	France	296.4	161.0	50.8	151.7	775.0	87.1	457.0	280.3	70.2	—	118.0	2447.5
1952	Germany	226.5	79.7	130.2	64.2	425.5	276.9	98.1	207.6	58.4	—	121.0	1688.0
	Britain	451.4	154.7	343.1	278.2	890.8	411.1	664.1	86.3	57.7	—	208.2	3545.6
	France	189.5	110.1	64.9	105.7	553.1	118.2	557.3	323.9	47.0	—	104.6	2174.3
1953	Germany	246.4	69.9	114.0	46.8	443.1	275.1	107.0	207.6	58.4	—	121.2	1689.5
	Britain	344.5	130.6	400.0	189.7	1030.0	395.6	610.1	98.8	83.9	—	171.8	3455.0
	France	205.5	76.1	34.1	65.4	573.1	92.7	482.0	229.9	63.9	—	94.9	1917.6
1954	Germany	271.0	75.6	161.5	65.9	482.0	301.5	130.1	119.7	55.4	—	153.1	1815.8
	Britain	320.1	133.3	400.7	242.5	1007.2	383.9	617.3	47.5	74.6	—	198.4	3425.5
	France	234.5	71.9	31.1	80.8	614.8	65.0	503.5	229.2	59.7	—	119.1	2009.6
1955	Germany	289.5	130.6	227.7	79.9	500.3	452.5	154.0	256.7	69.0	—	185.1	2345.3
	Britain	298.6	238.7	498.4	298.9	863.7	439.0	628.5	207.0	64.9	—	220.6	3758.3
	France	239.9	122.7	75.7	95.1	564.3	109.3	522.0	259.6	61.9	—	137.8	2188.3

Source: OEEC, Statistical Bulletins, *Foreign Trade*, series IV (Paris, quarterly). The commodity groups in this table correspond to the following numbers in the Standard International Trade Classification:

Commodity group	S.I.T.C. number
Oils & greases	22, 411, 412
Rubber	23
Wood & timber	24, excl. 242 05 & 243 01
Pulp & paper	25
Textile materials	26
Ores & metals	28
Crude petroleum	312
Skins & hides	222
Other	27, 29

TABLE V-H. *West German, British, and French Imports of Semifinished Materials, 1950–1955*
(in millions of current dollars)

Year	Country	(1) Oils & greases	(2) Rubber	(3) Wood & timber	(4) Paper materials	(5) Textile materials	(6) Ores & metals	(7) Skins & hides	(8) Chemicals	(9) Other	(10) Total
1950	Germany	12.5	0.1	6.0	11.9	92.5	94.2	24.9	46.2	105.0	393.3
	Britain	6.4	—	71.2	69.6	73.9	354.2	44.2	141.9	176.3	937.9
	France	6.2	0.8	6.7	8.5	30.5	114.2	9.2	83.1	39.7	298.9
1951	Germany	8.0	0.4	7.9	33.4	81.6	158.7	23.6	60.5	107.3	481.4
	Britain	9.3	0.3	128.3	207.2	158.2	548.6	73.8	261.2	244.5	1631.4
	France	9.2	1.3	11.2	34.0	42.9	180.9	14.2	127.0	50.7	471.4
1952	Germany	2.2	0.3	10.4	30.3	60.4	292.8	19.3	70.0	114.7	600.4
	Britain	6.0	0.5	92.9	111.7	110.4	891.6	83.1	171.1	129.0	1596.3
	France	5.2	1.4	13.5	29.1	15.8	255.2	28.6	116.0	42.2	507.0
1953	Germany	2.5	0.4	12.4	35.3	96.9	296.2	24.3	80.3	125.7	674.0
	Britain	5.0	0.7	67.0	90.5	33.0	609.0	58.1	163.0	175.7	1202.9
	France	5.9	1.7	13.3	13.5	15.6	166.9	10.6	107.5	38.2	373.2
1954	Germany	2.2	0.6	14.6	50.9	111.7	454.3	23.1	125.4	129.6	912.4
	Britain	8.0	1.4	109.3	140.9	62.1	569.9	57.4	226.9	160.7	1336.6
	France	7.0	2.1	15.5	18.0	12.9	226.0	11.2	115.5	37.5	445.7
1955	Germany	3.9	0.9	17.3	69.5	132.9	722.7	30.5	153.8	172.8	1304.3
	Britain	9.4	2.7	144.4	179.8	67.4	956.5	59.2	253.5	155.2	1828.1
	France	6.0	3.0	17.1	37.2	16.0	357.4	13.6	156.8	69.6	672.0

Source: OEEC, *Foreign Trade*. The commodity groups in this table correspond to the following numbers in the Standard International Trade Classification:

Commodity group	S.I.T.C. number
Oils & greases	413
Rubber	621
Wood & timber	63
Paper materials	641
Textile materials	651, 652 01
Ores & metals	671, 68
Skins & hides	611, 613
Chemicals	51, 52, 531, 532, 533, 551, 591, 599
Other	661, 662, 663, 664, 672, 699, 81

TABLE V-I. *West German, British, and French Imports of Industrial Materials, 1950–1955*
(in millions of current dollars)

Year	Country	(1) Oils & greases	(2) Rubber	(3) Wood & timber	(4) Pulp & paper	(5) Textile materials	(6) Ores & metals	(7) Crude petroleum	(8) Coal	(9) Skins & hides	(10) Chemicals	(11) Other	(12) Total
1950	Germany	222.9	56.8	49.5	43.8	516.0	187.9	40.8	41.6	80.9	46.2	179.9	1466.4
	Britain	354.6	144.3	284.0	201.4	1095.2	595.4	207.9	0.1	142.1	141.9	331.6	3498.5
	France	153.4	60.7	30.1	57.9	517.1	167.1	299.0	153.9	58.3	83.1	124.1	1704.7
1951	Germany	296.8	105.1	85.2	127.9	604.1	339.6	84.2	173.5	80.3	60.5	202.1	2159.3
	Britain	492.3	370.0	654.1	599.8	1651.0	883.9	445.7	24.8	198.4	261.2	492.7	6073.9
	France	305.6	162.3	62.0	185.7	817.9	268.0	457.0	280.3	84.4	127.0	168.7	2918.8
1952	Germany	228.7	80.0	140.6	94.6	485.9	569.6	98.1	207.6	77.6	70.0	235.7	2288.4
	Britain	457.4	155.2	436.0	389.9	1001.2	1302.7	664.1	86.3	140.8	171.1	337.2	5141.9
	France	194.7	111.5	78.4	134.8	568.9	373.4	557.3	323.9	75.6	116.0	146.8	2681.3
1953	Germany	248.9	70.3	126.4	82.1	540.0	571.3	107.0	207.6	82.7	80.3	246.9	2363.5
	Britain	349.5	131.3	467.0	280.2	1063.0	1004.6	610.1	98.8	142.0	163.9	347.5	4657.9
	France	211.5	77.8	47.4	78.9	588.7	259.6	482.0	229.9	74.5	107.5	133.1	2290.9
1954	Germany	273.2	76.2	176.1	116.8	593.7	755.8	130.1	119.7	78.5	125.4	282.7	2728.2
	Britain	328.1	134.7	510.0	383.5	1069.3	953.8	617.3	47.5	132.0	226.9	359.1	4762.2
	France	241.5	74.0	46.6	98.8	627.7	291.0	503.5	229.2	70.9	115.5	156.6	2455.3
1955	Germany	293.4	131.5	245.0	149.4	633.2	1175.2	154.0	256.7	99.5	153.8	357.9	3049.6
	Britain	308.0	241.4	642.8	478.7	931.1	1395.5	628.5	207.0	124.1	253.5	375.8	5586.4
	France	245.9	125.7	92.8	127.3	580.3	466.7	522.0	259.6	75.5	156.8	207.7	2860.3

Source: Sum of Tables V-G and V-H.

TABLE V-J. *Percent of Semimanufactures in Imports of Industrial Materials in West Germany, Great Britain, and France, 1950–1955* (based on current values)

Year	Country	(1) Oils & greases	(2) Rubber	(3) Wood & timber	(4) Pulp & paper	(5) Textile materials	(6) Ores & metals	(7) Crude petroleum	(8) Coal	(9) Skins & hides	(10) Other	(11) Total
1950	Germany	5.61	0.18	12.12	27.17	17.93	50.13	–	–	30.78	58.36	26.82
	Britain	1.80	0.00	25.07	34.56	6.75	59.50	–	–	31.10	53.17	26.80
	France	4.04	1.32	22.26	14.68	5.90	68.34	–	–	15.78	31.99	17.53
1951	Germany	2.70	0.38	9.27	26.11	13.51	46.73	–	–	29.39	53.09	22.29
	Britain	1.89	0.08	19.61	34.54	9.58	62.06	–	–	37.20	49.62	26.86
	France	3.01	0.80	18.06	18.31	5.25	67.50	–	–	16.82	30.05	16.15
1952	Germany	0.96	0.38	7.40	32.03	12.43	51.40	–	–	24.87	48.66	26.24
	Britain	1.31	0.32	21.31	28.65	11.03	68.44	–	–	59.02	38.26	31.04
	France	2.67	1.26	17.22	21.59	2.78	68.34	–	–	37.83	28.75	18.91
1953	Germany	1.00	0.57	9.81	43.00	17.94	51.85	–	–	29.38	50.91	28.52
	Britain	1.43	0.53	14.35	32.30	3.10	60.62	–	–	40.92	50.56	25.82
	France	2.79	2.19	28.06	17.11	2.64	64.29	–	–	14.23	28.70	16.29
1954	Germany	0.81	0.79	8.29	43.58	18.81	60.11	–	–	29.43	45.84	33.43
	Britain	2.44	1.04	21.43	36.74	5.81	59.75	–	–	43.48	44.75	28.06
	France	2.90	2.83	33.26	18.22	2.05	77.66	–	–	15.80	23.95	18.15
1955	Germany	1.33	0.68	7.06	46.52	20.99	61.50	–	–	30.65	48.28	35.74
	Britain	3.05	1.12	22.46	37.56	7.24	68.54	–	–	47.70	41.30	32.72
	France	2.44	2.39	18.43	25.29	2.76	76.58	–	–	18.01	33.65	23.49

Source: Computed from Tables V-G, V-H, and V-I.

TABLE V-K. *West German, British, and French Exports of Raw Materials, 1950–1955* (in millions of current dollars)

Year	Country	(1) Oils & greases	(2) Rubber	(3) Wood & timber	(4) Pulp & paper	(5) Textile materials	(6) Ores & metals	(7) Crude petroleum	(8) Coal	(9) Skins & hides	(10) Other	(11) Total
1950	Germany	2.4	0.4	9.6	6.9	33.3	34.5	–	317.1	0.2	31.5	435.9
	Britain	14.6	3.4	0.6	0.6	188.6	4.0	–	169.4	2.7	27.6	411.5
	France	14.3	0.9	50.4	1.5	130.3	39.1	0.2	85.5	9.8	47.8	379.9
1951	Germany	4.8	0.6	7.6	18.2	49.3	33.9	–	385.0	0.2	40.5	540.1
	Britain	12.1	4.1	0.8	0.9	236.8	4.3	–	95.6	4.3	31.3	390.2
	France	18.9	2.0	56.1	2.2	154.3	44.2	0.2	73.8	10.0	53.3	415.0
1952	Germany	3.1	0.9	3.0	7.6	27.5	31.1	–	438.9	0.3	37.4	549.8
	Britain	6.2	3.1	4.3	1.2	171.0	6.6	–	184.6	3.8	31.2	412.0
	France	23.6	1.0	34.8	3.5	123.2	51.3	0.4	73.8	9.3	55.0	375.9
1953	Germany	6.8	1.3	6.6	4.9	41.4	26.2	–	445.4	0.5	40.3	573.4
	Britain	13.6	2.6	1.1	2.1	204.5	4.8	–	198.3	4.0	30.6	461.6
	France	23.5	1.2	35.4	2.6	137.0	69.8	–	103.8	9.9	49.4	432.6
1954	Germany	9.1	1.2	10.1	8.0	47.8	33.7	–	481.2	2.1	47.6	640.8
	Britain	19.0	3.1	1.1	2.5	207.0	3.8	–	190.4	3.7	33.1	463.7
	France	15.4	0.8	50.8	2.6	150.5	80.9	–	109.1	11.7	55.2	477.0
1955	Germany	11.1	1.8	16.6	8.2	62.5	34.9	–	452.8	4.9	50.9	643.7
	Britain	22.2	3.9	1.4	3.1	225.4	4.8	3.4	178.9	5.2	36.6	484.9
	France	13.4	2.1	67.2	0.9	156.5	89.3	–	174.0	16.6	54.3	574.3

Source: OEEC, *Foreign Trade.*

TABLE V-L. *Raw-Material Content of French Semimanufactures, 1956*

SEEF classification	Sector	Direct plus indirect raw-material[a] content
084	Other nonferrous metals	.4153
114	Threads, yarns	.3787
120	Basic wood & sawmill products[b]	.2898
072	Blast furnaces, steel works	.2834
106	Rubber and asbestos products	.2729
092	Semifinished products in other nonferrous metals	.2362
101	Inorganic chemicals	.2151
058	Petroleum products	.2288
118	Worked skins & hides	.2011
083	Copper	.2000
124	Paper pulp[b]	.1953
115	Fabrics, tissues	.1878
091	Semifinished products in copper	.1602
121	Semifinished products in wood	.1532
102	Organic chemicals	.1372
093	Fabricated steel products	.1232
113	Synthetic and artificial textile raw materials	.1221
090	Semifinished products in aluminum	.1060
082	Aluminum	.0844
061	Glass	.0527

[a] The following were considered as raw-material-producing sectors: agriculture (010); chemical and diverse raw materials (011); scrap (071 and 081); iron ore (070); nonferrous metal ores (080); coal (030); crude petroleum (050); natural gas (051); construction materials (060); diverse minerals (100); rubber (105); wool (110); cotton (111); other natural fibers (112); unworked skins and hides (117); waste paper (123).

[b] Paper pulp and sawmill products, elsewhere considered raw materials, were treated here as semimanufactures in order to have more appropriate coefficients for imports of paper and wood semimanufactures.

Source: The coefficients were computed using the inverse of a preliminary version of the 1956 French input-output table prepared by the Service d'Etudes Economiques et Financières (SEEF). The numbers of the nomenclature are those of the published table for 1956. See Ministère des Finances, "Les Comptes de la nation," II: "Les Méthodes," *Statistiques et études financières*, 141:1509 supplement (Paris, September 1960).

2. COMPUTING THE FRENCH RATIO OF RAW-MATERIAL INPUTS TO INDUSTRIAL VALUE ADDED, ASSUMING IDENTICAL FRENCH AND GERMAN PRODUCTION STRUCTURES

The main problem in making this estimate is to decide which German sectors correspond to which French sectors. The German value-added data are more aggregative than the French; in addition, the French and German classification schemes are based on different principles. The aggregation procedure of the Service d'Etudes Economiques et Financières (SEEF) of the Ministry of Finances clearly follows the principle of an industrial hierarchy. The German classification scheme follows that of final usage and views commodities as producer, investor, or consumer goods. Column 3 of Table V-N shows that, under the French classification system, only certain kinds of goods have any appreciable inputs of raw materials. The essential task, therefore, is to identify that German value actually added in the immediate raw-material-using stage; misclassification of higher stages is not serious.

Table V-M shows the correspondence between the German and French nomenclatures for manufacturing sectors. Inspection of other French publications using the sector name *produits sidérurgiques* (sector 072) indicated that the title is at least as inclusive as the German *Eisenschaffende Industrie*,[5] and so the other German steel sectors were classified with the French sector 093 or, in the case of construction and railroad cars (German sector 310), with machinery (French sector 095). German value added by the precision-machinery and optical industry (German sector 370) was allocated equally to the two French machinery categories (sectors 094 and 095). The relative importance of each of the six nonferrous-metal industries in Germany was established with the aid of output data.[6] The same method was used to allocate the total value added by the various German chemical industries to the four sectors which the French table distinguishes.[7] Textiles, for which the French report two sectors but the Germans only one, posed another problem. Independent textile data did not seem to offer any way in which to break down the German total according to the two French components. Therefore, the only neutral assumption was chosen, namely that *fils et filés*

---

[5] See INSEE, *Annuaire statistique, 1958*, p. 55; and *Annuaire statistique, 1959*, pp. 137ff; Statistiques et Etudes Financières, 141:1510 (September 1960).

[6] *Statistisches Jahrbuch, 1958*, p. 192.

[7] The criteria for distinguishing between inorganic and organic chemicals were: relative consumption of sulphuric acid (OEEC, *The Chemical Industry in Europe* [Paris, 1957], p. 67); investments in petrochemicals (*ibid.*, p. 80); sales of plastics (*ibid.*, p. 187); output of paints, varnishes, soaps, and detergents (*ibid.*, pp. 100, 102, 177); and deliveries of synthetic and artificial textile materials to the textile sectors (OEEC, *The Textile Industry in Europe, 1954–1956* [Paris, 1957], pp. 109, 115).

TABLE V-M. *Correspondence between German and French Nomenclature for Manufacturing Sectors*

France		Germany	
Number	Sector	Number	Sector
052	Produits pétroliers raffinés	221	Mineralölverarbeitung
061	Verre	510	Feinkeramische Industrie,
		520	Glasindustrie
072	Produits sidérurgiques	270	Eisenschaffende Industrie
082	Aluminium,	281	N E-Metallhütten und Umschmelzwerke
083	Cuivre,		
084	Autres métaux non-ferreux		
090	Demi-produits en aluminium,	285	N E-Metallhalbzeugwerke
091	Demi-produits en cuivre,		
092	Demi-produits en autres métaux n.f.		
093	Produits de la première transformation de l'acier, fondérie, et travail des métaux	291	Eisen-, Stahl-, und Tempergiessereien,
		381	Ziehereien und Kaltwalzwerke,
		382	Stahlverformung (incl. Gesenkschmieden),
		383–9 + 398	Eisen-, Blech-, und Metallwarenindustrie
094	Machines et appareils mécaniques	310	Stahlbau (incl. Waggonbau),
		320	Maschinenbau,
		370	Feinmechanische und optische Industrie
095	Machines et appareils éléctriques	360	Elektrotechnische Industrie,
		370	Feinmechanische und optische Industrie
096	Automobiles et cycles	350	Automobilindustrie
097	Construction navale	340	Schiffbau
098	Construction aéronautique	330	Luftfahrzeugbau
099	Arméments et munitions		No German industry
101	Produits chimiques minéraux,	400, 225, 223	Chemische Industrie (incl. Chemiefasererzeugung)
102	Produits chimiques organiques,		
103	Produits de la parachimie		
104	Produits pharmaceutiques		
106	Ouvrages en caoutchouc et amiante	590	Kautschuk und Asbest verarbeitende Industrie
113	Matières premières textiles artificielles et synthétiques	400, 225, 223	Chemische Industrie (incl. Chemiefasererzeugung)
114	Fils et filés,	630	Textilindustrie
115	Ouvrages en filés		
116	Habillement	640	Bekleidungsindustrie
118	Cuirs et peaux ouvrés	610	Ledererzeugende Industrie
119	Articles en cuir	621	Lederverarbeitende Industrie,
		625	Schuhindustrie
121	Demi-produits et ouvrages en bois	540	Holzverarbeitende Industrie
122	Ameublement, litérie	550	(Holzschliff, Zellstoff)
125	Papier, carton	550	Papier,
		560	Papier und Pappe verarbeitende Industrie
126	Presse et édition	570	Druckerei-und Vervielfältigungsindustrie
127	Produits des industries diverses	391–6	Musikinstrumenten-, Turn-und Sportgeräteindustrie, Spiel-und Schmuckwarenindustrie

Source: French nomenclature—Ministère des Finances, "Les Comptes de la nation," p. 1510. German nomenclature—Statistisches Bundesamt, *Statistisches Jahrbuch für die Bundesrepublik Deutschland* (Wiesbaden, 1959), p. 194. For the English names of the sectors, see below, Table V-N.

TABLE V-N. *Computing French and German Raw-Material Requirements under Identical Industrial Structures*

SEEF number	Sector	(1) French value added (millions of new francs, 1956 prices)	(2) Direct raw-material input	(3) = (2)/(1) Raw material input ÷ value added	(4) German value added (millions of D.M., 1954 prices)	(5) = (3) × (4) Computed German requirements (millions of D.M., 1954 prices)
031	Manufactured gas	517	131	.2534	748.8	189.7
140	Electricity	2,133	366	.1716	2,185.2	602.7
141	Water works	60	1	.0167	52.8	0.9
052	Petroleum refinery products	5,710	2,110	.3695	1,041.0	384.6
061	Glass	614	29	.0472	1,233.0	58.2
072	Blast furnace products	2,725	2,149	.7886	3,648.0	2,876.8
082	Aluminum	141	194	1.3759	122.8	169.0
083	Copper	125	36	.2880	109.1	31.4
084	Other nonferrous metals	315	360	1.1143	340.1	379.0
090	Semifinished aluminum products	150	2	.0133	142.6	1.9
091	Semifinished copper products	345	2	.0058	410.7	2.4
092	Semifinished products in other nonferrous metals	91	1	.0110	94.7	1.0
093	Fabricated steel, foundry & forge products	4,534	88	.0194	5,320.0	103.2
094	Mechanical machinery & apparatus	6,627	55	.0083	8,754.5	72.7
095	Electrical machinery & apparatus	3,627	62	.0171	4,772.5	81.6
096	Automobiles, cycles	3,619	59	.0163	1,802.0	29.4
097	Shipbuilding	598	36	.0602	626.0	37.7
098	Aircraft	1,111	0	.0000	917.0	0
099	Armaments, munitions	248	17	.0685	0	0
101	Inorganic chemical manufactures	976	502	.5143	1,858.3	955.7

102	Organic chemical manufactures	1,293	206	.1593	2,131.7	339.6
103	Allied chemical manufactures	1,367	37	.0271	313.0	8.5
104	Drugs, cosmetics	538	32	.0595	1,189.4	70.8
106	Rubber & asbestos products	1,143	549	.4803	920.0	441.9
113	Artificial & synthetic textile materials	522	36	.0690	861.6	59.5
114	Threads, yarns	843	2,192	2.6002	888.4	2,310.0
115	Fabrics, tissues	3,970	89	.0224	4,183.6	93.7
116	Clothing	4,152	19	.0046	1,645.0	7.6
118	Worked skins & hides	349	520	1.4900	326.0	485.7
119	Leather goods	1,258	0	.0072	938.0	6.8
121	Semifinished and finished wood products	546	614	1.1245	686.9	772.4
122	Furniture	782	53	.0678	858.1	58.2
125	Paper, board	1,218	847	.6954	749.0	520.9
126	Printing, publishing	2,201	5	.0023	1,496.0	3.4
127	Musical instruments, toys, sporting goods, jewelry, misc. industries	1,748	247	.1413	492.0	69.5
130	Construction	12,607	3,344	.2652	8,622.0	2,286.6
	Totals	68,803	14,999	.2180	60,479.8	13,513.0

Source: France—The 1956 French input-output table, published in Ministère des Finances, "Les Comptes de la nation," p. 1510. Germany—Statistisches Bundesamt, *Statistisches Jahrbuch, 1959*, pp. 194–195; and other sources mentioned in the text.

The following sectors of the French input-output table were used in computing the raw-material content of the sectors listed in this table: Agricultural products (010) used by sector 103; raw materials for chemical industries (011); coal (030); crude petroleum (050); natural gas (051); construction material (060); iron ore (070); iron scrap (071); nonferrous metal ores (080); nonferrous metal scrap (081); diverse minerals (100); rubber (105); wool (110); cotton (111); other natural fibers (112); raw skins and hides (117); raw and sawed wood (120); waste paper (123); and pulp (124). The input of coal used to compute coal consumption by the electricity sector for column 5 was increased by a factor of 1,607 to reflect the greater German relative output of thermal electricity. See OEEC, *Industrial Statistics, 1900–1957*, pp. 78, 79.

(sector 114) bears the same relationship to *ouvrages en filés* (sector 115) in both countries. A similar adjustment was made for the woodworking sectors. The figure for value added in the German construction industry was reported as the contribution of construction to gross national product for 1954.[8] The same source provided figures for estimating that part of gross national product contributed by the electrical and gas industries (*Energiewirtschaft*).[9] The relative contribution of manufactured gas versus that of electricity was ascertained by means of data on the final output of each, in volume.[10] It was not possible to estimate German value added for the relatively unimportant sector, "water," and so it was assumed to have the same importance, relative to the rest of industry, in both countries.

[8] *Statistisches Jahrbuch, 1959*, p. 483, column 3.
[9] *Statistisches Jahrbuch, 1959*, pp. 194, 483.
[10] *Industrial Statistics*, pp. 62, 78.

INDEX

ture, 163–164; and factor intensity, 184; and price elasticities, 183–184; and protection, 123–126, 176–184
Factor space: and equalization region, 17–24, 47; defined, 11–12, 15–18; and trade patterns, 73–74, 84–86; and transformation function, 25–34, 128, 140
Factoral content: of commodities, 101, 252; of consumption, 102–103, 167, 170–171, 181, 252; of trade, 102–103, 140, 143, 167–171, 181–182, 252–253; and Leontief test, 103, 167–171; of Japanese trade, 195–196; of U. S. trade, 95, 168–169, 172–174
Faure, Edgar, 217, 218n
Foreign investment, 39, 246
France: factor endowments, 108–110, 266–270; prices, 205, 208, 224–225; production structure, 108–110, 238–241, 266–270, 285–290; wages, 223, 224

Gale, D., 138
Gainsborough, M., 7n
General Agreement on Tariffs and Trade, 194, 218–220, 247
Germany, production structure, 238–241, 285–290
Gilbert, M., 115n, 205, 229

Haberler, G., 50n
Harrod, R. F., 75n
Hecksher, E., 93
Hecksher-Ohlin trade theory: assumptions, 1–2; compared to classical trade theory, 1–2; empirical verification, 68–110, 166–169; and equalization region, 2, 68, 96–97; explanation of trade, 1, 96–97, 99–102, 164; and protection, 1–2, 53n, 164. See also Equalization region; Factor endowments; Factor space
Henderson, J. M., 257n
Homogeneity of production functions: defined, 134; and equalization region, 7–9, 13, 35–38; and intermediate goods, 48; and structural indeterminacy, 133
Humphrey, D., 191n

Ichimura, S., 195, 196n
Indeterminacy of the domestic production structure: assumptions, 133; in classical trade theory, 139; and determinacy of protection, 127, 148; explanation, 45–46, 127, 136–137, 139–140; and factoral content of trade, 143; and method of protection, 185–186; and protectionist policy, 127; and relative factor prices, 137–139; in a three-commodity example, 140–143
Industrial materials: availabilities, 234–238; defined, 231; imports, 232, 281–283. See also Raw materials
Input-output tables: industrial hierarchy, 183–185, 188–190; international comparison, 175, 189, 285–290; international-price comparisons, 91–94; and measurement of protection, 188–193
Intermediate goods: and factor-price equalization theorem, 10, 49, 53, 131n; and numerousness of commodities, 10–11, 48–49, 90–91; production processes, 48; and rank of matrix of factor intensities, 48–49, 53; and size of equalization region, 48–49, 66; and specialization boundaries, 49, 63

James, S. F., 10n
Japan: factor endowments, 195, 244; foreign trade, 195–196; relative prices 92–94, 199–201
Johnson, H. G., 75n
Jones, R. W., 75n, 105n

Komiya, R., 199, 200n, 201
Krause, L. B., 193–194
Kravis, I. B., 205, 229
Kreinin, M. E., 194
Kuznets, S., 65n

Labor: allocation in French economy, 108, 266–270; allocation in U. S. economy, 260–264; in classical trade theory, 28; in definition of factor intensity, 41, 50; education and training, 51–53; as factor of production, 4, 50; as specific factor, 50; French supply, 108; U. S. supply, 68, 108, 172,